THE JEROME KERN ENCYCLOPEDIA

Thomas S. Hischak

THE SCARECROW PRESS, INC.
Lanham • Toronto • Plymouth, UK
2013

Published by Scarecrow Press, Inc.
A wholly owned subsidiary of The Rowman & Littlefield Publishing Group, Inc.
4501 Forbes Boulevard, Suite 200, Lanham, Maryland 20706
www.rowman.com

10 Thornbury Road, Plymouth PL6 7PP, United Kingdom

British Library Cataloguing in Publication Information Available

Library of Congress Cataloging-in-Publication Data

Hischak, Thomas S.
  The Jerome Kern encyclopedia / Thomas S. Hischak.
    pages cm
  Includes bibliographical references and index.
  ISBN 978-0-8108-9167-8 (cloth : alk. paper) — ISBN 978-0-8108-9168-5 (ebook)
  1. Kern, Jerome, 1885-1945—Encyclopedias. 2. Musicals—Encyclopedias. I. Title.
  ML410.K385H57 2013
  782.1'4092—dc23   2013004605

∞™ The paper used in this publication meets the minimum requirements of
American National Standard for Information Sciences—Permanence of Paper
for Printed Library Materials, ANSI/NISO Z39.48-1992. Printed in the United States
of America.

In memory of
Gerald Bordman
(1932–2011)

TILL THE CLOUDS ROLL BY. As dreary as it was fictitious, this 1946 biopic of Kern's life only came alive when the songs were featured. One of the highlights was a young Angela Lansbury singing Kern's first song hit, "How'd You Like to Spoon with Me?," interpolated into the British import *The Earl and the Girl* (1905). Happily, Lansbury did her own singing, something Hollywood would not let her do again until *Bedknobs and Broomsticks* twenty-five years later. *MGM/Photofest ©MGM*

CONTENTS

PREFACE

Jerome Kern was the first real pioneer in the creation of a genuinely native musical theatre.

—Stanley Green

. . . the daddy of modern musical comedy music.

—Arthur Schwartz

. . . the Master.

—Alan Jay Lerner

On a Monday morning in November of 1945, a sixty-year-old man was browsing through some antiques shops in midtown Manhattan. While he was waiting for the traffic light to change so that he could cross the street, the gray-haired gentleman collapsed and fell to the pavement. Some bystanders gathered around the unconscious man and soon a policeman arrived on the scene. Since the man had no identification on him, he was brought to City Hospital on Welfare Island, the place where the poor and unidentified were brought. At the hospital, someone found in the patient's pocket an unsigned membership card for ASCAP, the union for songwriters. The ASCAP office was called, and someone located Oscar Hammerstein, a member who was on the board of the union. Hammerstein arrived at the hospital and was able to identify the unknown man, who had suffered a cerebral hemorrhage, as his friend and collaborator Jerome Kern. Within a week the celebrated composer of the American musical theatre and film was dead. The man who did so much to establish the American musical as a unique art form was rightly eulogized and mourned by everyone from President Harry Truman to every chorus girl on Broadway. Yet it was not until years later, with the gift of hindsight, that one could truly appreciate the impact Kern had on American music. Those who collaborated with him understood his genius, and the public loved his songs and his shows. But it was not until long after his death that theatre historians and musicologists were able to accurately pinpoint just how important Kern was in the long view. He created the sound of the American musical and then set such high standards for it that other remarkable composers and lyricists were able to build on Kern's work and bring the art form to heights that we will never see again.

Jerome Kern's career spanned from 1912 to 1946. He wrote the music for all kinds of musical plays and films ranging from silly musical comedies to profound musical dramas. He is considered the most versatile and influential of all American composers. Although only a handful of his stage works are revived today, Kern's songs are still very much with us, as are the films that continue to enthrall audiences. From the stage classic *Show Boat* to the Astaire-Rogers cinema favorite *Swing Time*, a Kern musical is a timeless work of art. There have been a handful of excellent Kern biographies over the years, but few of them take much time to describe and comment on each one of his many works. Also, Kern worked with some of the finest lyricists, librettists, directors, performers, and other artists of the first half of the twentieth century, and those collaborations have not been fully explored. I believe only an encyclopedia format can begin to cover the many aspects of this remarkable composer.

The Jerome Kern Encyclopedia includes entries on all of Kern's stage and screen musicals, over one hundred of his songs, and various subjects ranging from his working methods to his days in Hollywood. Also, all the major lyricists, librettists, performers, directors, and producers who worked with Kern have entries. Entries are cross-listed by appearing in **bold** in the text so the reader can quickly determine where more information lies. At the beginning of the book is a list of all entries by category and a brief biography of Jerome Kern that serves as an introduction to his work. At the back of the book are appendixes on his career, awards, a list of Kern interpolations, recordings of Kern songs, a bibliography, and an index. There is a lot of information here, and hopefully it is organized in a way that will be most useful to the reader. The goal is to provide the single most comprehensive work on Jerome Kern.

ACKNOWLEDGMENTS

I would like to acknowledge the work of Cathy Hischak in preparing the manuscript, Ron Mandelbaum at Photofest for his help in selecting and securing the photographs, and editor Stephen Ryan and the people at Scarecrow Press for the finished product.

LIST OF ENTRIES
BY CATEGORY

THEATRE PRODUCTIONS

The Beauty Prize (1923)
Blue Eyes (1928)
The Bunch and Judy (1922)
The Cabaret Girl (1922)
The Cat and the Fiddle (1931)
The City Chap (1925)
Cousin Lucy (1915)
Criss Cross (1926)
Dear Sir (1924)
Gentlemen Unafraid (1938)
The Girl from Utah (1914)
Good Morning, Dearie (1921)
Have a Heart (1917)
Head Over Heels (1918)
Hitchy-Koo (1920)
Jerome Kern Goes to Hollywood (1985)
La Belle Paree (1911)
Love o' Mike (1917)
Leave It to Jane (1917)
Lucky (1927)

Miss Information (1915)
Miss 1917 (1917)
Miss Springtime (1916)
Music in the Air (1932)
Never Gonna Dance (2003)
The Night Boat (1920)
90 in the Shade (1915)
Nobody Home (1915)
Oh, Boy! (1917)
Oh, I Say! (1913)
Oh, Lady! Lady!! (1918)
The Red Petticoat (1912)
Roberta (1933)
Rock-a-Bye Baby (1918)
Sally (1920)
She's a Good Fellow (1919)
Show Boat (1927)
Sitting Pretty (1924)
Stepping Stones (1923)
Sunny (1925)
Sweet Adeline (1929)

FILMS

LYRICISTS, LIBRETTISTS, AND ORCHESTRATORS

PERFORMERS

Robert Cummings
Dorothy Dickson
Jack Donahue
Irene Dunne
Deanna Durbin
Leon Errol
Tess Gardella
Ava Gardner
Kathryn Grayson
Louise Groody
George Grossmith, Jr.
Bettina and Natalie Hall
Rita Hayworth
Bob Hope
Allan Jones
Howard Keel
Gene Kelly
Dorothy Lamour
Jeanette MacDonald
Howard Marsh
Hattie McDaniel
Adolphe Menjou
Ann Miller
Marilyn Miller
Agnes Moorehead
Frank Morgan
Helen Morgan
Ramon Novarro
Edna May Oliver

Robert Paige
Lily Pons
Eva Puck and Sammy White
Lyda Roberti
Paul Robeson
Ginger Rogers
Julia Sanderson
Randolph Scott
Vivienne Segal
Oscar Shaw
Al Shean
Phil Silvers
Red Skelton
Walter Slezak
Queenie Smith
Fred Stone
Gloria Swanson
Tamara
Akim Tamiroff
Fay Templeton
Norma Terris
Ernest Truex
William Warfield
Clifton Webb
Helen Westley
Jack Whiting
Cornel Wilde
Charles Winninger

DIRECTORS AND PRODUCERS

Pandro S. Berman
F. Ray Comstock
Charles Dillingham
Arthur Freed

Charles Frohman
Max Gordon
George Grossmith, Jr.
Mervyn LeRoy

Rouben Mamoulian
Elisabeth Marbury
Otto Preminger
Edward Royce
William Seiter
Hassard Short

George Sidney
George Stevens
Charles Vidor
James Whale
Florenz Ziegfeld

MISCELLANEOUS

Awards
Ballads
Biographies
Cast Recordings and Soundtracks
Charm Songs
Choral Numbers
Collaborators
Comic Songs
Eulogy
Hollywood
"I Am" Songs
List Songs

London Stage
Love Songs
March Songs
Pastiche Songs
Personal Characteristics
Princess Theatre Musicals
Revivals and Remakes
Style of Songwriting
Tin Pan Alley
Torch Songs
Working Methods

SONGS

"Ah Still Suits Me"
"All in Fun"
"All the Things You Are"
"All Through the Day"
"Allegheny Al"
"And I Am All Alone"
"Any Moment Now"
"Babes in the Wood"
"Bill"
"Bojangles of Harlem"

"Bongo on the Congo"
"Bungalow in Quogue"
"Californ-i-ay"
"Can I Forget You?"
"Can't Help Lovin' Dat Man"
"Can't Help Singing"
"The Church Around the Corner"
"Cinderella Sue"
"Cleopatterer"
"Cotton Blossom"

BRIEF BIOGRAPHY OF JEROME KERN

Jerome David Kern was born in the midtown Manhattan section of New York City on January 28, 1885, the sixth son of Henry and Fannie Kern, German Jewish immigrants who fared well in the New World. Henry Kern was a successful businessman, at various times managing a street-sprinkling system, running a horse stable, and working in retail. Fannie was an accomplished pianist and gave the young Kern his first music lessons. When the boy was ten years old, his father was put in charge of a department store in Newark, New Jersey, so the family relocated there. Kern attended the local public high school where he began to write songs for school and community productions. One of his songs was published when he was only seventeen. He left high school early to study composition and music theory at the New York College of Music even as he took jobs at various music publishers as an office boy and song plugger. Kern went to Germany in 1902 to study music, but it has never been documented that he enrolled at any school or had private lessons with anyone. He first traveled to England in 1903 and was enamored of British musical comedy, which seemed to him more advanced than what he had seen in New York. Also, it was in England that he met Eva Leale, a publican's daughter, whom he married in 1910.

Kern's first job in the American musical theatre was as accompanist for vaudeville comedienne Marie Dressler at Hammerstein's Victoria Theatre. This led to rehearsal pianist jobs where he was able to study the process of creating musical comedy on Broadway. Having abandoned any ambitions of writing for the concert stage, Kern pursued his theatre songwriting career, and as early as 1904 his songs were being interpolated into New York shows. Many of these were London musicals that needed new tunes or more American-sounding numbers. Yet when he wrote the very British ditty "How'd You Like to Spoon with Me?" for the Broadway version of *The Earl and the Girl* (1905), the song caught on and Kern had his first success. Also during these early years, Kern traveled to London almost yearly where he wrote songs that were interpolated into British musicals. Although Kern was kept very busy (and well paid) for writing the odd song for dozens of London and Broadway shows, he longed to write a complete score. The revue *La Belle Paree* (1911) and *The Red Petticoat* (1912) provided him with his first opportunities and, although neither show ran very long, critics noticed the refreshingly new sound of Kern's music. Further renown came when Kern wrote "They Didn't Believe Me" for the London import *The Girl from Utah* (1914), and the innovative ballad changed the direction of American stage music.

It was with the "Princess Musical" *Very Good Eddie* (1915) that a complete Kern score found success in New York and the young composer's talents were fully realized. In such subsequent Princess shows as *Oh, Boy!* (1917) and *Oh, Lady! Lady!!* (1918), Kern and his collaborators, lyricist P. G. Wodehouse and librettist Guy Bolton, created a new kind of modern, intimate, sassy musical comedy that inspired a generation of later songwriters. Kern also found success writing full-scale Broadway musicals with a variety of collaborators in the 1920s, scoring such hits as *Sally* (1920), *Stepping Stones* (1923), and *Sunny* (1925). Kern pushed the musical form into a new arena when he and lyricist-librettist Oscar Hammerstein wrote the landmark work *Show Boat* (1927), the American theatre's first musical play. Throughout the 1920s and for the rest of his career, Kern often returned to London, writing original musicals as well as overseeing the West End versions of his New York successes. By the mid-1920s, Kern was the most respected, successful, and highly paid songwriter on Broadway, and he was equally popular in England.

When the Depression stifled production on Broadway, Kern went to Hollywood where he found mixed success. Some superior efforts, such as *High, Wide and Handsome* (1937), failed to find an audience, but others, such as *Swing Time* (1936), were very popular. But Kern's heart was in New York where he continued to compose such notable works as *Sweet*

Adeline (1929), *The Cat and the Fiddle* (1931), *Music in the Air* (1932), *Roberta* (1933), and *Very Warm for May* (1939). When this last musical, an uneven show with a superb score, flopped, Kern gave up on Broadway and went to Hollywood for good. He and Eva settled in California with their only child, Betty, and he found himself working with both new and old collaborators who had gone west before him. Such 1940s Kern movie musicals as *One Night in the Tropics* (1940), *You Were Never Lovelier* (1942), *Cover Girl* (1944), *Can't Help Singing* (1944), and *Centennial Summer* (1946) varied in their effectiveness, but all boasted superior scores. In 1945, Kern was coaxed back to Broadway by songwriters-producers Hammerstein and Richard Rodgers to write the score for the Ethel Merman vehicle *Annie Get Your Gun* with lyricist Dorothy Fields. But soon after arriving in New York, Kern died suddenly. He was sixty years old and still at the top of his composing powers, so the loss to the theatre community and the public was both a personal and professional one. At his death, Kern was considered the dean of American theatre composers. The new avenues for theatre music that he opened had by this time been explored by many talented composers, but still Kern was not considered out of date or a relic of the past. The very Hollywoodized film version of his life, *Till the Clouds Roll By* (1946), made before his death and released the next year, reminded everyone of the great legacy Kern left behind.

JEROME KERN
CHRONOLOGY

1885   January 18, Jerome David Kern born to Henry and Fannie Kern, New York City.

1895   Family moves to Newark, New Jersey.

1899   Kern starts attending Newark High School.

1902   Leaves high school to pursue a music career.
First song, "At the Casino," published.
Kern travels to Germany to study music.

1903   First of many trips to England.
Enrolls at New York College of Music.
Begins work as employee of song publisher T. B. Harms.
First Kern song heard on Broadway in *An English Daisy*.

1904   *Mr. Wix of Wickham*, with eleven songs by Kern, opens on Broadway; first critical recognition.

1905   Kern finds popular recognition for song "How'd You Like to Spoon with Me?" when the English import *The Earl and the Girl* opens at the Casino Theatre.

1907   Fannie Kern dies.

1908   Henry Kern dies.

1910   Kern marries Eva Leale.

1911   Kern's first full score heard in *La Belle Paree*, which opens at the Winter Garden Theatre but fails to run.

1914   Kern interpolates "They Didn't Believe Me" into the British import *The Girl from Utah* at the Knickerbocker Theatre; the song becomes a popular and critical sensation.

1915   *Nobody Home*, Kern's first Princess Musical, opens at the Princess Theatre.

Very Good Eddie, first Princess Musical hit, opens at the Princess Theatre.

1917   *Oh, Boy!*, first Princess Musical with lyricist P. G. Wodehouse, opens at the Princess Theatre.

Leave It to Jane opens at the Longacre Theatre.

1918   *Oh, Lady! Lady!!*, the last Kern Princess Musical, opens at the Princess Theatre.

London production of *Very Good Eddie* opens at the Palace Theatre.

1919   London production of *Oh, Boy!*, retitled *Oh, Joy!*, opens at the Kingsway Theatre.

1920   *The Night Boat* opens at the Liberty Theatre.

Sally opens at the New Amsterdam Theatre and proves to be Kern's biggest hit to date.

1921   *Good Morning, Dearie* opens at the Globe Theatre; the song "Ka-lu-a" becomes the subject of a sensational plagiarism suit.

London production of *Sally* opens at the Winter Garden Theatre.

1923   *Stepping Stones* opens at the Globe Theatre.

1924   *Sitting Pretty*, the last Kern musical with Princess Musical collaborators Wodehouse and Guy Bolton, opens at the Fulton Theatre.

Court decision on "Ka-lu-a" in favor of Kern.

1925   *Sunny*, Kern's first musical collaboration with lyricist-librettists Oscar Hammerstein and Otto Harbach, opens at the New Amsterdam Theatre.

1926   London production of *Sunny* opens at the Hippodrome Theatre.

1927   *Show Boat* opens at the Ziegfeld Theatre.

1928   London production of *Show Boat* opens at the Drury Lane Theatre.

1929   *Sweet Adeline* opens at Hammerstein's Theatre.

Film version of *Sally* released.

First screen version of *Show Boat* released.

1930   First film version of *Sunny* released.

1931   Kern's first original film musical, *Men of the Sky*, released with all the songs cut.

The Cat and the Fiddle opens at the Globe Theatre.

1932   *Music in the Air* opens at the Alvin Theatre.

London production of *The Cat and the Fiddle* opens at the Palace Theatre.

1933   *Roberta* opens at New Amsterdam Theatre.

London production of *Music in the Air* opens at the His Majesty's Theatre.

1934   *Three Sisters* opens at the Drury Lane Theatre, London.

Film version of *The Cat and the Fiddle* released.

Film version of *Music in the Air* released.

I Dream Too Much released.

1935   Film version of *Roberta* released; Kern's first collaboration with lyricist Dorothy Fields.

Film version of *Sweet Adeline* released.

1936   Second and most acclaimed film version of *Show Boat* released.

Swing Time released; "The Way You Look Tonight" wins the Academy Award.

1937   *High, Wide and Handsome* released.

1938   *Gentlemen Unafraid* opens in St. Louis, fails to continue on to New York.

Joy of Living released.

1939   *Very Warm for May*, Kern's last new work for Broadway, opens at the Alvin Theatre and fails to run; Kern and family move to California.

One Night in the Tropics released.

1941   *Lady, Be Good* released; "The Last Time I Saw Paris" wins the Academy Award.

Second film version of *Sunny* released.

1942   *You Were Never Lovelier* released.

1944   *Cover Girl* released.

Can't Help Singing released.

Broadway Rhythm, the much-altered film version of *Very Warm for May*, released.

1945   Kern returns to New York to work on *Annie Get Your Gun* for Rodgers and Hammerstein.

November 5, Kern suffers a stroke.

November 11, Kern dies of a cerebral hemorrhage at the age of sixty.

1946   *Centennial Summer* released.

Kern biopic *Till the Clouds Roll By* released.

1951   Third film version of *Show Boat* released.

1952   *Lovely to Look At*, the remake of *Roberta*, released.

ACADEMY AWARDS. See **Awards** and appendix D

"Ah Still Suits Me" is a charming character song that **Oscar Hammerstein** and Kern wrote for the 1936 screen version of *Show Boat*, one of three they added to their stage score for the film. Dockhand Joe (**Paul Robeson**) sang about his easygoing philosophy of life as he shelled peas in the galley of the *Cotton Blossom* while his sharp-tongued wife Queenie (**Hattie McDaniel**) made cutting comments about his eternal laziness. Hammerstein's penchant lyric is filled with laid-back honesty that keeps the scene from descending into racial stereotypes, and it helps that both performers are at their understated best. In some ways "Ah Still Suits Me" is a kind of antithesis of *Show Boat*'s most famous song, **"Ol' Man River,"** which views life with a weary resignation. Few stage revivals include "Ah Still Suits Me," but in the revue *Jerome Kern Goes to Hollywood*, David Kernan and Elisabeth Welch sang the duet in London in 1985 and Scott Holmes performed it with Welch on Broadway the next year. Some of the more complete studio recordings of the *Show Boat* score include it. Robeson recorded the number with Welch, and Bing Crosby, Tommy Dorsey's Orchestra (vocal by Sy Oliver), and Lee Wiley each performed it on disc as "I Still Suits Me."

"All in Fun" is a sassy, carefree song about not getting emotionally involved that reminds one of Kern's pre–World War I numbers yet it was written for his last Broadway show, *Very Warm for May* (1939). Summer stock actors Liz (Frances Mercer) and Johnny (**Jack Whiting**) sang the delectable number that was light and frolicsome, yet Kern put in some bittersweet chords and a few musical twists that hint at a more serious undertone. **Oscar Hammerstein**'s lyric is unusual for him, consisting of short verbal phrases that conclude with the realization that there is true love under all the kidding. "All in Fun" was among the many songs from *Very Warm for May* that were cut for the screen version titled *Broadway Rhythm* (1944), but notable recordings of the number were made by Tony Bennett, Danny Carroll, Margaret Whiting, June Ericson, Sandy Stewart, Jeri Southern, Barbara Carroll, the Mike Wofford Trio, and Andrea Marcovicci.

"All the Things You Are" is the much beloved and highly praised ballad that Kern and **Oscar Hammerstein** wrote for *Very Warm for May* (1939), the team's last Broadway musical together. Although it is usually performed as a heartfelt solo, in the stage musical it was introduced as a choral number in a summer stock show and was led by Hiram Sherman, Frances Mercer, Hollace Shaw, and Ralph Stuart; in the second act it was reprised by Ray Mayer as a solo. Although *Very Warm for May* was not a hit, the song soon caught on and over time it has become a standard. A poll of American composers in 1964 named "All the Things You Are" as their all-time favorite, and Richard Rodgers once publicly stated that of all the great songs that he did not write, this was the one he most wished he had written. Among the many outstanding qualities of the song is the perfect melding of words and music. Hammerstein's lyric is enthralling and very romantic, yet stops short of being mawkish. The gushing description of one being "the promised gift of springtime" rings true, and the way the title phrase sits on Kern's crescendo is masterful. The music is unusual and more difficult than most popular songs, written in A-flat, a key that is not very accessible to listeners. Then there are some odd but effective key changes and tempo variations that make the song distinctive but tricky. Kern himself stated that he wrote the music more to satisfy himself than to get on the pop charts, yet "All the Things You Are" remained on *Your Hit Parade* for eleven weeks and its sheet music and record sales have remained consistently healthy for over sixty years. Among the many who have recorded the ballad are such diverse artists as Gordon MacRae, Ella Fitzgerald, Frank Sinatra, Zoot Sims, Tommy Dorsey's Orchestra (vocal by Jack Leonard), Charlie Parker, Jessye Norman, Dick Haymes, Dave Brubeck, Artie Shaw (vocal by Helen Forrest), Sarah Vaughan, Kiri Te Kanawa, Helen Traubel, Laura Osnes, Barbara Cook, Art Pepper, Barbra Streisand, Lionel Hampton, Jack Jones, José Carreras, Mario Lanza, jazz pianist Beegie Adair, Andrea Marcovicci, Scott Hamilton, and Ann Hampton Callaway, as well as a 1992 choral version featuring Jeanne Lehman, George Dvorsky, Rebecca Luker, and Cris Groenendaal using Kern's original arrangements. *Very Warm for May* was not revived, but the song was heard again on stage when Liz Robertson, Elaine Delmar, and David Kernan sang it in the revue *Jerome Kern Goes to Hollywood*; Robertson and Delmar reprised the song with Scott Holmes in the Broadway version of the show the next year. Little of *Very Warm for May* remained when it was filmed as **Broadway Rhythm**, (1944) but "All the Things You Are" was kept and was sung by Ginny Simms. It was also sung on screen by Tony Martin in the Kern biopic *Till the Clouds Roll By* (1946) and Mario Lanza performed it in *Because You're Mine* (1952). The ballad was also heard on the soundtracks for *Tin Men* (1987), *New York Stories* (1989), *The Rookie* (1990), *Deconstructing Harry* (1997), *Anja & Viktor* (2001), *Mrs. Henderson Presents* (2005), and *The Music Never Stopped* (2011).

"All Through the Day" is the only song in the Kern film musical *Centennial Summer* (1946) in which **Oscar Hammerstein** provided the lyric, and it is arguably Kern's last superior ballad, completed only a few months before his death. Hammerstein's warm lyric concerns the way one daydreams throughout the sunlight hours, looking forward to the night when one will be with a beloved. Kern's music is appropriately nostalgic, for in the film it is used as a period piece sung by entertainer Richard Lewis, Esq. (Larry Stevens) during a demonstration of a magic lantern show at the Philadelphia Centennial Exposition of 1876. The color images of a pair of lovers in a bucolic setting were followed by the lyrics on the screen as the number turned into a sing-along. The Oscar-nominated ballad was recorded several times, most memorably by Frank Sinatra with Alex Stordahl's Orchestra; other discs were made by Doris Day, Kiri Te Kanawa, Perry Como with Andre Kostelanetz's Orchestra, Reid Shelton, Christina Lind, Margaret Whiting with Carl Kress's Orchestra, James Melton, Betty Madigan, and Helen Forrest with Dick Haymes.

"Allegheny Al" is a breezy song of low-down fun from the movie musical *High, Wide and Handsome* (1937) scored by Kern and **Oscar Hammerstein**. Frontier showgirls Molly (**Dorothy Lamour**) and Sally (**Irene Dunne**) let down their hair and gave the cornball number their best. Hammerstein's lyric is about the riverboat dandy of the title who has greased hair, a diamond stud, and a tendency to kiss the ladies so quickly that they don't know what's happened to them. Kern's music is flavored with an old-style minstrel number that is very catchy.

"And I Am All Alone" is a little-known ballad by Kern that admirers place among his very best. It was written with lyricist **P. G. Wodehouse** for their first full score together, *Have a Heart* (1917). Ruddy Schoonmaker (Thurston Hall) and his estranged wife Peggy (Eileen Van Biene) have eloped to an oceanside hotel on the eve of their divorce and rekindle an old flame in this lovely duet. The couple conjure up visions of blissful happiness that quickly dissolve, each of them realizing that they are left alone again. The harmonies in Kern's music are unusual and quite effective, and an unexpected pause before the final musical phrase gives the ballad a unique sense of dramatic songwriting. The ballad was recorded soon after *Have a Heart* opened by the tenor Henry Burr, who used the pseudonym Irving Gilette on the label. The Victor Light Opera later recorded "And I Am All Alone," and many decades later Andrea Marcovicci and Rebecca Luker each made a lovely recording of the song.

"Any Moment Now" is a rapturous ballad about the anticipation of ever-lasting love that **Deanna Durbin** sang as she surveyed a beautiful Western vista in the Kern movie musical *Can't Help Singing* (1944). **E. Y. Harburg** wrote the lighthearted lyric, and Kern's music, in the words of Gerald Bordman, starts "with sweet, simple phrases of the sort Kern had employed often in earlier days but quickly resorts to the darker, more advanced harmonies he preferred at the close of his career."

ASTAIRE, Adele [née Adele Austerlitz]. (1898–1981) Stage performer. Because she did not have a film career, the petite singer-dancer is not so well known as her brother **Fred Astaire**, but she was as big a star as he on Broadway where she played the leading role of Judy Jordan in Kern's *The Bunch and Judy* (1922). Astaire was born in Omaha, Nebraska, and as a teenager appeared with her younger brother in vaudeville before the two settled in New York and were on Broadway together by 1917 in *Over the Top*. The dancing-singing duo were featured in *The Passing Show* (1918), *Apple Blossoms* (1919), *The Love Letter* (1921), and *For Goodness' Sake* (1922) before becoming stars with the Gershwins' *Lady, Be Good* (1924). The team shone in *Funny Face* (1927), *Smiles* (1930), and *The Band Wagon* (1931), as well as in some London versions of their New York hits. Adele retired to marry the British Lord Cavendish and never performed again. She was as accomplished a dancer as Fred, possessed a pleasant soprano voice, and had an acute sense of comedy in both her acting and her singing. Biographies: *Footwork: The Story of Fred and Adele Astaire*, Roxane Orgill (2007); *The Astaires: Fred & Adele*, Kathleen Riley (2012).

ASTAIRE, Fred [né Frederick Austerlitz]. (1899–1987) Stage, film, and television performer. Arguably the most graceful, original, and sophisticated song-and-dance man in Hollywood musicals, he enjoyed a successful Broadway career prior to his remarkable film career, appearing in four Kern musicals: as the Manhattan dancer Gerald Lane in *The Bunch and Judy* (1922) on Broadway and the screen roles of bandleader Huckleberry Haines in *Roberta* (1935), the playboy Lucky Garnett in *Swing Time* (1936), and the American hoofer Robert Davis in Argentina in *You Were Never Lovelier* (1942). Astaire was born in Omaha, Nebraska, and was on the vaudeville stage with his elder sister **Adele Astaire** for some years before the team was on Broadway by 1917. After appearing in *The Passing Show* (1918), *Apple Blossoms* (1919), *The Love Letter* (1921), and *For Goodness' Sake* (1922), the team found fame in *Lady, Be Good* (1924), followed by the stage hits *Funny Face* (1927), *Smiles* (1930), and *The Band Wagon* (1931), and some London successes as well. Although the duo was at the peak of their popularity, Adele gave up show business to marry an English aristocrat and Fred's career was threatened. He was often seen as the less impressive of the twosome, playing earnest romantic roles while his sister got to play funny heroines. But Astaire proved just as appealing in *Gay Divorce* (1932), his only Broadway musical without Adele, and was whisked off to Hollywood, never to return to the legitimate stage again. He had a featured spot in his debut movie, *Dancing Lady* (1933), then caught the attention of moviegoers when he and **Ginger Rogers** were teamed as the secondary couple in *Flying Down to Rio* (1933), dancing "The Carioca" together and giving birth to Hollywood's most famous dancing couple. The twosome were reunited for nine more musicals, most of them major hits: *The Gay Divorcee* (1934), *Roberta, Top Hat* (1935), *Follow the Fleet* (1936), *Swing Time, Shall We Dance* (1937), *Carefree* (1938), *The Story of Vernon and Irene Castle* (1939), and *The Barkleys of Broadway* (1949). Although moviegoers and studio heads preferred Astaire with Rogers, he did find other dancing partners in *A Damsel in Distress* (1937), *Broadway Melody of 1940, You'll Never Get Rich* (1941), *You Were Never Lovelier, The Sky's the Limit* (1943), *Yolanda and the Thief* (1945), *Ziegfeld Follies* (1946),

Blue Skies (1946), and *Easter Parade* (1948). In the 1950s, many of Astaire's musicals did not do as well at the box office yet he still managed to shine in *Three Little Words* (1950), *Let's Dance* (1950), *Royal Wedding* (1951), *The Belle of New York* (1952), *The Band Wagon* (1953), *Daddy Long Legs* (1955), *Funny Face* (1957), and *Silk Stockings* (1957). He turned to dramatic roles with *On the Beach* (1959) and did many television specials in the 1960s and 1970s, returning to Hollywood for his last screen musical *Finian's Rainbow* (1968) and to narrate the documentaries *That's Entertainment* (1974) and *That's Entertainment Part 2* (1976). Astaire excelled in all manner of dance (tap, soft shoe, ballet, jazz, modern) while maintaining a distinctive persona of wit and romance that has never been equaled. He possessed a thin but appealing singing voice and was an expert interpreter of lyrics by **Ira Gershwin**, Irving Berlin, **Johnny Mercer**, Cole Porter, **Dorothy Fields**, and other top lyricists, allowing him to introduce more song standards than perhaps anyone else in Hollywood after Bing Crosby. Astaire was also actively involved with the dancing he performed, often helping to devise the choreography and finding inventive ways to use locations and inanimate objects in his limitless dancing imagination. Autobiography: *Steps in Time* (1959); biographies: *The Fred Astaire–Ginger Rogers Book,* Arlene Croce (1972); *Starring Fred Astaire,* Stanley Green (1977); *Fred Astaire: A Wonderful Life,* Bill Adler (1987); *Fred Astaire,* Sarah Giles (1988).

AWARDS won by Kern. It is surprising to learn that Kern received very few awards during his long career until one realizes that the major awards, particularly Broadway's Tony Awards, did not begin until after his death. Only Hollywood's Oscars, which began in 1929, coincided with Kern's productive years. He won the Best Song Oscar for **"The Way You Look Tonight"** (lyric by **Dorothy Fields**) in 1936 and **"The Last Time I Saw Paris"** (lyric by **Oscar Hammerstein**) in 1941. Kern revivals after 1974 have been nominated and won Tony Awards on occasion. Although Kern was praised and honored with dinners, radio broadcasts, and special concerts, he received few formal awards. Had he not died suddenly at the age of sixty, Kern most likely would have been awarded with special honors during his waning years. See appendix D for all nominations and awards for Kern musicals.

YOU WERE NEVER LOVELIER. Rita Hayworth and Fred Astaire had clicked together so well in *You'll Never Get Rich* (1941) that the next year they were reunited for this delectable musical set in Argentina. Also working well together were Kern and lyricist Johnny Mercer in their only musical collaboration. *Columbia Pictures/Photofest ©Columbia Pictures*

"Babes in the Wood" is a plaintive ballad that became the hit song by Kern and lyricist Schuyler Greene from *Very Good Eddie* (1915). Eddie Kettle (**Ernest Truex**) is on his honeymoon but gets separated from his bride. When he and Elsie Darling (Alice Dovey), who has also misplaced her spouse, find themselves comforting each other in an inn during a thunderstorm, they promise to be "twice as good" as the title babes in the wood. Kern's music is simple but alluring as its musical phrases leisurely climb the scale. The charming number became quite popular in its day with dance orchestras, but there have been few recordings, and surprisingly, the song has not been heard in any film. In the 1975 Broadway revival of *Very Good Eddie*, "Babes in the Wood" was sung by Charles Repole as Eddie Kettle and Virginia Seidel as Elsie Darling. **Irene Dunne** recorded the number in 1941, and decades later a distinctive duet recording was made by Hugh Panaro and Rebecca Luker.

BALLADS by Kern. The term "ballad" has many different meanings in music and literature, but in modern popular music it refers to any sentimental or romantic song, usually with the same melody for each stanza. Ballads have often been the big sellers, the songs that could move listeners without benefit of plot or character. Kern modernized the ballad form with his revolutionary song **"They Didn't Believe Me"** in 1914. Later jazz and swing had its influence on the form, and most ballads since World War II have a fox trot (4/4) base, but there are many exceptions to that generalization over the decades. Perhaps Kern's three most famous ballads are **"The Way You Look Tonight," "Smoke Gets in Your Eyes,"** and **"All the Things You Are."** Other outstanding examples include **"Yesterdays," "Look for the Silver Lining," "Why Do I Love You?," "I've Told Ev'ry Little Star," "Can I Forget You?," "Long Ago and Far Away," "Don't Ever Leave Me," "I Have the Room Above Her," "The Last Time I Saw Paris," "Lovely to Look At," "The Touch of Your Hand,"** and **"You're Devastating."**

BEAUTY PRIZE, THE. A musical comedy by **George Grossmith, Jr.**, **P. G. Wodehouse** (book and lyrics); Jerome Kern (music). [5 September 1923, Winter Garden Theatre, London, 214 performances] Produced and directed by George Grossmith, Jr., choreographed by Fred Leslie. After the success of Kern and Wodehouse's *The Cabaret Girl* (1922), producer Grossmith contracted the stars of that show and commissioned the songwriters to come up with a similarly frothy show to be titled *The First Prize*. The wealthy American Carol Stuart (**Dorothy Dickson**) pretends to be poor and loves the rich Englishman John Brooke (Jack Hobbs) who also is disguised as a penniless lad. When Carol's milliner Lovey Toots (Heather Thatcher) sends Carol's photograph into a newspaper beauty contest, Carol wins and learns that the prize is marriage to the oddball Odo Philpots (Leslie Henson). John and Carol both discover that the other is rich and feel so deceived that they part, though they still love each other. John's secretary Flutey Warboy (Grossmith) sends phony telegrams to each saying that they have lost all their money, the lovers are reunited, and Lovey marries Odo. Critics thought the plot for *The Beauty Prize* (as it was retitled) was contrived and felt the score was not as good as *The Cabaret Girl*, but audiences were attracted to the British stars and the show ran six months. The best number in *The Beauty Prize* was "A Cottage in Kent," which was a revised and very British version of Kern and Wodehouse's **"Bungalow in Quogue,"** which had been heard in New York in the operetta *The Riviera Girl* (1917). Other notable numbers included the wry duet "You Can't Make Love By Wireless," the warm ballad "Moon Love," the silly duet "Meet Me Down on Main Street" that was a comic nod to Sinclair Lewis' hit novel *Main Street*, and a song-ballet, "You'll Find Me Playing Mah-Jong," which satirized the recent and very popular game of tiles.

BENNETT, Robert Russell. (1894–1981) Orchestrator. The leading Broadway orchestrator of the twentieth century, he did the musical arrangements for over three hundred stage musicals, including many by Kern. Bennett was born in Kansas City, Missouri, to a musical family; his father was a trumpet player and violinist, his mother a pianist. Bennett knew how to play a variety of instruments by the time he was in his teens, then studied composition and began working as a copyist for a music publisher. His first Broadway assignment was orchestrating the score for *Daffy Dill* (1922). By the time he orchestrated *Rose-Marie* two years later, Bennett was the most sought-after talent in his field. He was also the most influential orchestrator in the American theatre, helping to create the Broadway orchestra sound that is so familiar to generations of theatregoers. A list of Bennett's Broadway credits is practically a record of the musical theatre in the 1920s through the 1960s. For Kern, he is credited with the orchestrations for the Broadway musicals *Hitchy-Koo* (1920), *Stepping Stones* (1923), *Dear Sir* (1924), *Sitting Pretty* (1924), *The City Chap* (1925), *Sunny* (1925), *Criss-Cross* (1926), *Lucky* (1927), *Show Boat* (1927), *Sweet Adeline* (1929), *The Cat and the Fiddle* (1931), *Roberta* (1933), and *Very Warm for May* (1939), as well as the London musical *Three Sisters* (1934). His Kern movie credits include *Show Boat* (1929 and 1936), *Swing Time* (1936), *High, Wide and Handsome* (1937), and *Joy of Living* (1938). Because orchestrators were often not listed in playbill programs or movie credits, there were many other shows that Bennett worked on that are uncredited. Bennett also wrote incidental music for plays, films, and television programs. He composed many musical works on his own, including operas, choral pieces, tone poems, and band selections. All in all, it is estimated that Bennett orchestrated more music than any other American. Kern and Bennett were healthy adversaries at times, the roles of composer and orchestrator sometimes being in conflict with each other. Yet Bennett had a strong respect for Kern and his musical abilities and the two worked well together for over twenty years.

BERMAN, Pandro S[amuel]. (1905–1996) Film producer. A proficient producer of musicals, dramas, and comedies, he presented most of the **Fred Astaire–Ginger Rogers** films, including Kern's *Roberta* (1935) and *Swing Time* (1936), as well as Kern's *I Dream Too Much* (1935) and *Lovely to Look At* (1952). Berman was born in Pittsburgh, the son of a film distributor, and began his career as an assistant director in the 1920s. By the arrival of sound he was producing features on his own, including the RKO musicals *Melody Cruise* (1933), *Hips Hips Hooray* (1934), *The Gay Divorcee* (1934), *Top Hat* (1935), *In Person* (1935), *Follow the Fleet* (1936), *That Girl From Paris* (1936), *Shall We Dance* (1937), *A Damsel in Distress* (1937), *Having Wonderful Time* (1938), and *Carefree* (1938). Berman moved to MGM in 1940 and produced many pictures over the next twenty-five years, including the musicals *Ziegfeld Girl* (1941), *Rio Rita* (1942), *Living in a Big*

Way (1947), and *Jailhouse Rock* (1957). He was an efficient and creative producer and knew how to cultivate up-and-coming stars, such as Katharine Hepburn, Lana Turner, Elizabeth Taylor, and Elvis Presley, in their early films.

"Bill" is one of the musical theatre's finest torch songs, a masterwork by Kern and lyricist **P. G. Wodehouse** that took awhile to be heard by the public. Originally written for the **Princess Theatre Musical *Oh, Lady! Lady!!*** (1918), it was sung by the betrothed Mollie (**Vivienne Segal**) to her mother to explain her affection for Willoughby Finch who was nicknamed Bill. The song was cut before opening for various reasons: it was too slow for its Act One position; Segal's voice didn't seem right for it; and Carl Randall, who played Bill, was so dashing and likable a man that the song didn't make much sense. Kern and Wodehouse held onto the number and gave it to **Marilyn Miller** to sing in *Sally* (1920), but again the song didn't work and was cut. "Bill" was finally heard on Broadway, with a slightly revised lyric by **Oscar Hammerstein**, in *Show Boat* (1927) in which **Helen Morgan**, as the dissipated Julie LaVerne, sang it in a Chicago nightclub as she perched on an upright piano and made both the song and herself famous. The number remained a trademark throughout her career. Kern's melody for "Bill" is leisurely and reflective, and the way Wodehouse's lyric sits on the notes gives the song its punch. The tone is not maudlin or morose, as torch songs often were, but rather self-aware with even a touch of self-mockery. Julie describes Bill's weaknesses with half a smile, then concludes with the famous pause before the phrase "I don't know" that leads into "because he's just my Bill." Wodehouse took the old model for the lament song and broke it, writing the first conversational torch song. Although "Bill" was listed in the opening-night program of *Show Boat* as having a lyric by Wodehouse, most credited the authorship to Hammerstein, who wrote the libretto and the other lyrics for the score and who only made minor changes to the original "Bill" lyric. Hammerstein took great pains on several occasions to point out that Wodehouse was the true lyricist and once even took out a newspaper ad to clarify the point. "Bill" was sung by Marie Burke as Julie in the 1928 London production of *Show Boat*. On screen it was sung by Morgan in the 1936 version and by **Ava Gardner** (vocal by Annette Warren) in the 1951 remake, and by Ann Blyth (dubbed by Gogi Grant) in *The Helen Morgan Story* (1957). In addition to the many stage revivals of *Show Boat*, the torch song was sung by Liz Robertson in the revue *Jerome Kern Goes to Hollywood*, which played in London in 1985 and on Broadway in 1986. "Bill" is one of Kern's most recorded songs with discs by such varied artists as Morgan, Burke, Carol Bruce, Shirley Bassey, Andrea Marcovicci, Morgana King, Oscar Peterson, Constance Towers, Lara Cazelet, Kiri Te Kanawa, Sally Burgess, Judy Garland, Dinah Washington, Lonette McKee, Gogi Grant, Anita Darian, Teresa Stratas, Kate Baldwin, Joan Morris with William Bolcom, and Cleo Laine.

BIOGRAPHIES of Jerome Kern. The five biographies of Kern written in English vary greatly in their approach. Some are diligently researched, others are less detailed but try to present Kern's personality in a theatrical way. Although the main facts about Kern's life are easily accessible and quite clear, details about his work—particularly during the first two decades of his career—are difficult to find and nearly impossible to verify. Even some facts about his early life pose problems. Kern crossed the Atlantic so often during those early working years that biographers have trouble knowing where he was and which shows he worked on while in London and which in New York. His wife's birthplace in England is still debated, as are certain myths about Kern's activities, most memorably his failure to board the fateful *SS Lusitania* in 1914. The most challenging task for a Kern biographer is to trace the songs themselves. Some were written for one show in New York and performed under a different title or lyric in London. Others were published with no clear link to any show although Kern always wrote for the stage (and later the screen) and not for Tin Pan Alley. Because Kern often reused a melody from one of his songs years later for a different song, tracing the origin of a Kern number is tricky. Only by comparing the sheet music itself can the puzzle begin to be solved. Few biographers are interested in such exacting work.

The first biography of Kern is David Ewen's *The World of Jerome Kern*, which was first published in 1960, fifteen years after the composer's death. Ewen interviewed **Oscar Hammerstein**, **Guy Bolton**, **Arthur Freed**, **Ira Gershwin**, **Otto Harbach**, **P. G. Wodehouse**, and others, as well as Kern's widow and daughter. Ewen is best at capturing the quixotic character of Kern, from his love for baseball and rare books to his dislike of grand opera and people who bite their nails. His writing is intelligent and fluid, and his biography perhaps best reveals the composer's personality. His description of the shows and songs is also admirable although there are errors here and there, mostly because later research by others found that some of Kern's colleagues' reminiscences were not always accurate. Ewen was one of the very first to write books about the American musical theatre, and his works are still invaluable even though he has been followed by so many others. In 1978 Michael Freedland's *Jerome Kern: A Biography* was published. Already the author of biographies of such stage and screen figures as **Fred Astaire**, Irving Berlin, Gregory Peck, Sophie Tucker, James Cagney, and Errol Flynn, Freedland offered a more theatrical tale filled with anecdotes and many direct quotations from conversations supposedly Kern had with others. Many of Kern's collaborators had died by 1978 so Freedland relies on interviews with Richard Rodgers, Leo Robin, Arthur Schwartz, Sammy Cahn, and other songwriters who did not work with the composer but knew him professionally and socially. He did get many stories from Kern's daughter, Betty Kern Miller, and uses them to create a chatty, accessible biography that pleases the casual rather than avid theatre- and moviegoer. Freedland's research is more anecdotal than professional. He states that nothing exists from Kern's work as a juvenile, yet other biographers uncovered plenty of information about his school efforts. This biography rarely describes either the shows or the songs so one gets no sense of what Kern's work is like beyond refreshing the memories of those already familiar with the songs.

By far the most detailed and most satisfying biography for the more discerning reader is Gerald Bordman's *Jerome Kern: His Life and Music*, published in 1980. True to its title, this biography spends a great deal of time discussing the many shows and even gives detailed descriptions of many of the songs, particularly regarding the music. Bordman spent ten years researching this large and meticulous work, interviewing not only surviving collaborators, performers, friends, and relatives, but also seeking out music arrangers and orchestrators for their memories and observations. Unlike previous biographers, Bordman also spent a good deal of time in England where a large amount on information existed in libraries and personal collections. The result is a biography that may be too detailed for the average reader but a treasure trove of fascinating material for those wishing to truly understand Kern the man and the composer. If there is any shortcoming in

Bordman's book, it is regarding the movies that Kern scored. Bordman is a theatre historian and it is obvious that he spends much less time on Kern's Hollywood career even though he interviewed many performers and directors there and still analyzes the movie songs with care.

Two shorter biographies also have their strengths. Andrew Lamb's *Jerome Kern in Edwardian London* was printed as a monograph with limited circulation in 1981. Lamb revised and expanded the booklet in 1985, and it was published in book form by the Institute for Studies in American Music. Concentrating on Kern's early London career, the work is meticulously researched, even uncovering sheet music and other information that Bordman missed. Lamb covers both biographical and professional aspects of Kern's England days. Because the show titles and several of the people are unfamiliar to American readers, he includes an appendix describing many of the latter in a concise manner. Lamb is also good at capturing the social era in which Kern found himself and relating the shows to what was going on in Great Britain at the time. Also short but very useful is Stephen Banfield's *Jerome Kern*, which was published in 2006 as part of the Yale Broadway Master Series. For those wishing to forego the overwhelming details of Bordman's biography, this is the best introduction to Kern. Banfield is very successful in presenting both the man and his work because of his concise writing and expert way of summarizing the important aspects of the subject. Obviously there is little room for music analysis in such a short book, but one comes away from this biography understanding the essence of Jerome Kern.

BLEDSOE, Jules. (1898–1943) Stage, concert, opera, and film performer. An African American singer with a resounding bass-baritone voice, his most famous credit is originating the role of Joe and introducing **"Ol' Man River"** in the original *Show Boat* (1927). He was born Julius C. Bledsoe in Waco, Texas, and studied music at Bishop College, Virginia Union College, and Columbia University. Bledsoe made his professional concert debut in 1924 and then was featured on Broadway in the drama *In Abraham's Bosom* (1926) and the operatic musical *Deep River* (1926). When **Florenz Ziegfeld** delayed the opening of *Show Boat* and **Paul Robeson** was no longer available to play Joe, Bledsoe was hired and found wide recognition with his sterling performance. He provided the singing voice for Joe (Stepin Fetchit) in the first screen version of *Show Boat* (1929), appeared in a few film shorts, and was the featured actor-singer in the movie *Drums of the Congo* (1942). Much of the rest of his career was on the concert and opera stage in the States and Europe where he, like Robeson, helped break down racial barriers for African American singers. Bledsoe was also an accomplished composer of spirituals and operatic vocal pieces.

BLORE, Eric. (1887–1959) Film and stage performer. A round, owlish character actor from England, he was a master at playing stuffy and fussy British butlers, hotel managers, clerks, waiters, and valets, as seen in the Kern musical films *I Dream Too Much* (1935), *Swing Time* (1936), and *Joy of Living* (1938). Blore was born in London and began his career as an insurance agent before going on the stage in comic roles in plays and musicals. He made his Broadway debut in 1923 and was seen in such musicals as *Andre Charlot's Revue* (1924), *Charlot Revue* (1925), *Just Fancy* (1927), *Here's Howe* (1928), *Here Goes the Bride* (1931), *Gay Divorce* (1932), and *Ziegfeld Follies* (1943). Blore had made some films in England before making his Hollywood debut in 1926, and with the coming of sound he was ideal as comic foils in talkies, making over eighty features during the next twenty-five years. His other musical credits, five **Fred Astaire-Ginger Rogers** movies among them, include *Flying Down to Rio* (1933), *The Gay Divorcee* (1934), *Folies Bergère de Paris* (1935), *Shall We Dance* (1937), *Swiss Miss* (1938), *Music in My Heart* (1940), *The Boys from Syracuse* (1940), *Road to Zanzibar* (1941), *The Sky's the Limit* (1943), *Happy Go Lucky* (1943), *Easy to Look At* (1945), *Romance on the High Seas* (1948), *Love Happy* (1949), and *Fancy Pants* (1950), as well as the voice of Mr. Toad in the animated film *The Adventures of Ichabod and Mr. Toad* (1949) and the TV cartoon *The Wind in the Willows* (1949). Autobiography: *Cock 'n Bull: The First Thirty Years* (1967).

BLUE EYES. A musical play by **Guy Bolton**, Graham John (book and lyrics), Jerome Kern (music). [27 April 1928, Piccadilly Theatre, London, 276 performances] Produced by Lee Ephraim, musical direction by Kennedy Russell, orchestrations by **Robert Russell Bennett**. A historical romance inspired by Bonnie Prince Charlie's attempt to take the throne, *Blue Eyes* was serious fare even though some comic characters and songs were added to help bring it to life. London stage actress Nancy Anne Bellamy (Evelyn Laye) disguises herself as a soldier to help her brother Jamie (George Vollaire) who is imprisoned by the Duke of Cumberland (Bertram Wallis) after the battle of Culloden. Her adventures include fighting a duel, being tried for high treason, falling in love with Sir George (Geoffrey Gwyther), and escaping to freedom and true love. The secondary couple of Jamie and Flora Campbell (Sylvia Cecil) was also very serious, so the comedy was provided by the low comedian Pilbeam (W. H. Berry) who disguised himself as a silly Scotsman, a flea circus owner, a French dancing teacher, and other delightful characters. Although the press applauded the beautiful sets and costumes (as well as the brand-new Piccadilly Theatre), the lovely Kern score was mostly ignored. Kern's attempt to sound Scottish was deemed unsuccessful, made all the more obvious when traditional Gaelic airs were played in one scene. Yet Kern wrote some entrancing songs for *Blue Eyes*, such as the lovers' "Back to the Heather," the anachronistic comic number "Vodeodo," the sweeping "Charlie Is the Darling of My Heart," and the lilting title duet. The most famous song to come out of *Blue Eyes* was cut before opening: "Do I Do Wrong?" Years later Kern would use the melody for **"You're Devastating"** in *Roberta* (1933). Despite mixed notices, *Blue Eyes* ran a successful eight months. Musicologists looking at Kern's score find it a very flowing arioso, and more in the operetta mode than that of musical comedy. Coming soon after *Show Boat* (1927), the show made it clear that Kern was moving in a new direction. As was more common in London than in New York, Evelyn Laye and other members of the original cast made a recording of highlights of the score in 1928.

"Bojangles of Harlem" is the swinging tribute to African American tap dancer Bill Robinson that Kern wrote with lyricist **Dorothy Fields** for the movie *Swing Time* (1936). **Fred Astaire**, in blackface makeup, danced the number at the Silver Sandal nightclub in New York while a chorus of chorines sang of Bojangles's dancing genius. The number climaxed with Astaire dancing with three huge silhouettes of himself. While the blackfaced minstrel aspect of the number is offensive to some viewers today, it is not filled with the gross caricature and exaggerated gestures that often make such numbers so difficult to watch. The music, a rhythm number with a distinct march tempo, is unusual for Kern who disliked swing. Legend has it that Astaire had to tap out the rhythm for Kern as he wrote the song in his hotel room. Although "Bojangles of Harlem" is primarily a dance piece, it was successfully recorded by Astaire, Bob Howard, the Tempo Kings, Bobby Short, Malcolm McNeill, and Barbara Cook. In the revue *Jerome Kern Goes to Hollywood*, David Kernan, Liz Robertson, and Elaine Delmar sang it in London in 1985, and Scott Holmes performed it with Delmar and Robertson on Broadway the next year.

BOLES, John. (1895–1969) Stage and film performer. A handsome, if somewhat stiff, leading man who starred in silents, he saw his career soar when sound came in and he was a favorite in early film operettas, such as Kern's *Music in the Air* (1934) in which he played the Brussels playboy Bruno Mahler. Boles was born in Greenville, Texas, the son of a banker, and studied at the University of Texas for a medical career. During World War I, he worked in espionage activities in Europe, then studied voice in New York and Paris before making his Broadway debut as a replacement in the musical *Little Jesse James* (1923). After featured roles in *Mercenary Mary* (1925) and *Kitty's Kisses* (1926), Boles went to Hollywood where his dashing aristocratic looks made him a popular romantic figure in silents. He got to use his voice training when talkies arrived and he sang the leading role of the Red Shadow in *The Desert Song* (1929), the first film made from a Broadway show. Boles's other musical credits include *Rio Rita* (1929), *Song of the West* (1930), *Careless Lady* (1932), *My Lips Betray* (1933), *Bottoms Up* (1934), *Redheads on Parade* (1935), *Curly Top* (1935), *The Littlest Rebel* (1935), *Rose of the Rancho* (1936), *Romance in the Dark* (1938), and *Thousands Cheer* (1943), as well as specialty spots in *King of Jazz* (1930) and *Stand Up and Cheer* (1934). He returned to Broadway to play the art museum curator Whitelaw Savory in *One Touch of Venus* (1943), but by the 1950s he retired from show business.

BOLTON, Guy [Reginald]. (1884–1979) Stage and film writer. A prolific author of over fifty stage musicals in New York and London, he was instrumental in developing the new musical comedy model in the 1910s when he worked with Kern on the **Princess Theatre Musicals**. Bolton was born in Broxbourne, England, to American parents and studied in New York and Paris to be an architect before turning to the theatre in 1912 when his first play opened in London. Although he would occasionally write dramas and comedies for Broadway and the West End, much of his career was occupied with musical librettos. His first on Broadway was Kern's *90 in the Shade* (1915), and that same year he and Kern wrote the first Princess Theatre musical, *Nobody Home*. After writing the libretto for the hit *Very Good Eddie* (1915), Bolton and Kern were joined by British lyricist **P. G. Wodehouse** and the famous trio penned the groundbreaking shows *Oh, Boy!* (1917), *Leave It to Jane* (1917), and *Oh, Lady! Lady!!* (1918). Also with Kern, Bolton scripted *Miss Springtime* (1916), *Have a Heart* (1917), *Miss 1917* (1917), *Sally* (1920), and *Sitting Pretty* (1924). Working with a variety of collaborators, Bolton wrote the books for such musicals as *The Riviera Girl* (1917), *The Rose of China* (1919), *Tangerine* (1920), *Lady, Be Good!* (1924), *Tip-Toes* (1925), *The Ramblers* (1926), *Oh, Kay!* (1926), *Rio Rita* (1927), *The Five O'Clock Girl* (1927), *Rosalie* (1928), *Simple Simon* (1930), and *Anything Goes* (1934). He spent much of the 1930s in London where he wrote a dozen West End musicals (most with Wodehouse), then returned to Broadway for *Walk with Music* (1940), *Hold on to Your Hats* (1940), *Jackpot* (1944), *Follow the Girls* (1944), *Ankles Aweigh* (1955), and *Anya* (1965). Many of Bolton's stage works were filmed, and he also contributed to the movie musicals *The Love Parade* (1929), *Delicious* (1931), *Careless Lady* (1932), *Ziegfeld Follies* (1946), *Easter Parade* (1948), and *Words and Music* (1948), as well as the Kern musical bio *Till the Clouds Roll By* (1946). Although most of Bolton's work was lighthearted musical comedy with few pretensions to musical drama, he was an expert craftsman and an important innovator for musical comedy structure. Autobiography: *Bring on the Girls! The Improbable Story of Our Life in Musical Comedy*, with Wodehouse (1953).

"Bongo on the Congo" is a delectable comic trio from Kern's Broadway musical *Sitting Pretty* (1924) that stopped the show each night with so many encores that, as one critic wrote, it "threatened to ruin the audience." At a swank country home in New Jersey, Horace Peabody (Dwight Frye) and his jewel thief uncle Jo (Frank McIntyre) sing to Judson Waters (Eugene Revere) about life among the natives in Africa where the girls wear little more than a freckle and a man with only twenty-four wives is considered a bachelor. **P. G. Wodehouse** wrote the risible lyric and Kern's music avoided a bongo beat and used a merry march in the refrain. "Bongo on the Congo" was written for the Kern musical *Pat* (1924), which was not produced but the songwriters recognized that the comic piece would be an audience favorite and worked it into *Sitting Pretty*. Music historian and conductor John McGlinn recorded the facetious number with Jason Graae, Paul V. Ames, and Merwin Goldsmith in 1989.

BRIAN, Donald. (1877–1948) Stage performer. With his dimpled good looks, wavy hair, and light but lyrical singing voice, he became a favorite matinee idol on Broadway in the early decades of the twentieth century, but his most important musical credit was introducing Kern's first major song, **"They Didn't Believe Me,"** with **Julia Sanderson** in *The Girl from Utah* (1914). Brian was born in St. John's, Newfoundland, where he sang in a chorus as a child. After an education in Boston, he got roles in stock operetta companies and reached New York in 1899. Brian had featured roles in *The Supper Club* (1901), *The Belle of Broadway* (1902), *Little Johnny Jones* (1904), and *Forty-Five Minutes from Broadway* (1906) but did not achieve fame until he played Prince Danilo in the first American production of *The Merry Widow* (1907). Brian's other Broadway musicals include *The Dollar Princess* (1909), *The Siren* (1911), *The Marriage Market* (1913), *Her Regiment* (1917), *Buddies* (1919), and *The Chocolate Soldier* (1921). His stage career concluded with two Kern works: as a replacement for the character of wealthy Bruno Mahler in *Music in the Air* (1933) and as the fatherly William Graham in *Very Warm for May* (1939).

BROADWAY RHYTHM. See *Very Warm for May*.

BROWN, Joe E[vans]. (1892–1973) Film, stage, and television performer. A wide-mouth, physical comedian who looks like a cartoon character, he gave one of his best performances as Cap'n Andy Hawks in the 1951 screen version of Kern's *Show Boat*. Brown was born in Holgate, Ohio, and left home at the age of nine to be a circus acrobat. After playing semi-pro baseball he went into vaudeville and burlesque before making his Broadway debut in 1918. Brown was cast in farcical supporting roles in comedies and such musicals as *Jim Jam Jems* (1920), *Greenwich Village Follies* (1921), *Betty Lee* (1924), *Captain Jinks* (1925), and *Twinkle Twinkle* (1926). By

1928 he was in silent movies and with the advent of sound, starred in some low-budget comedies that relied on his physical agility for laughs. Brown was also featured in the film musicals *On with the Show* (1929), *Song of the West* (1930), *Hold Everything* (1930), *Top Speed* (1930), *The Lottery Bride* (1930), *Maybe It's Love* (1930), *Bright Lights* (1935), *Sons o' Guns* (1936), *Joan of the Ozarks* (1942), *Chatterbox* (1943), *Pin-Up Girl* (1944), and *Hollywood Canteen* (1944). He returned to the stage, appearing on Broadway in the musical *Courtin' Time* (1951), and did radio and nightclubs before returning to Hollywood for his two best roles: Cap'n Andy in *Show Boat* and millionaire Osgood Fielding III in *Some Like It Hot* (1959). Brown was also busy on television in the 1950s and 1960s. Autobiography: *Laughter Is a Wonderful Thing* (1959); biography: *Joe E. Brown: Film Comedian and Baseball Buffoon*, Wes D. Gehring and Conrad Lane (2006).

THE BUNCH AND JUDY. A musical entertainment by Hugh Ford (book), **Anne Caldwell** (book and lyrics), Jerome Kern (music). [28 November 1922, Globe Theatre, 63 performances] Produced by **Charles Dillingham**, directed by Fred G. Latham, choreographed by **Edward Royce** (uncredited), musical direction by Victor Baravalle, orchestrations by Stephen Jones. An odd mixture of musical comedy, operetta, and revue, *The Bunch and Judy* was pretty much a grab bag with some delectable things in it. The musical comedy star Judy Jordan (**Adele Astaire**) forsakes Broadway to marry the Scottish Lord Kinlock (Philip Tonge) but finds that all the gentry in Scotland snub her because of her American background. When Judy's old theatre pals are touring in Great Britain, she leaves Kinlock and returns home with them and marries her former leading man Gerald Lane (**Fred Astaire**). Much of the first act was taken up with the operetta *Love Will Find a Way* that Judy performs in before quitting the stage. The second act included a long cabaret scene in which specialty acts were included, such as the Six Brown Brothers who did amazing things with saxophones. With rising stars Adele and Fred Astaire leading the cast and a Kern score, the run of only eight weeks was disappointing. Critics placed the blame on the hackneyed book, and while the songs were pleasant, they were unexceptional. The most applauded number was "How Do You Do, Katinka?" but much of that was credited to the Astaires' dancing. Other notable songs include the polka "Hot Dog," the mock blues "Have You Forgotten Me?

(Blues)," and the flowing "Morning Glory." *The Bunch and Judy* failed to make money either in New York or during the subsequent road tour. As for the Astaires, they would not find wide recognition until the Gershwins' *Lady, Be Good!* (1924). Ironically, *The Bunch and Judy* would prove to be somewhat prophetic. Adele Astaire later did become a big stage star, she did marry a British lord, and was unhappily married to him, though she never returned to the stage as Judy did.

"Bungalow in Quogue" is a playful duet about lovers settling down and living in a rural cottage, written by Kern and lyricist **P. G. Wodehouse** and interpolated into the operetta import *The Riviera Girl* (1917). The duet ditty, Kern and Wodehouse's only number in the Emmerich Kalman–composed score, was sung by Harry Morton and Juliette Day as a young married couple who jokingly talk about the rustic life they will lead on Long Island. Wodehouse, who often lived at Quogue when he was working in the States, uses the names of several Long Island towns in his witty lyric about comparing mosquito bites and reading the almanac in the evening. Kern's music uses many repeated notes, but he varies the tempo in such a way that the song springs to life. "Bungalow in Quogue" was the hit of the show, and it was recorded by Rachel Grant and Billy Murray in 1918 and sold plenty of sheet music. Often listed as "Let's Build a Little Bungalow in Quogue," the number was sung by **Dorothy Dickson** and Leslie Henson in the London musical *The Beauty Prize* (1923) but was retitled "A Cottage in Kent" and the lyric was revised to include English rural names. The song was heard on Broadway again when Virginia Seidel and Nicholas Wyman performed it in the 1975 Broadway revival of *Very Good Eddie*. There is also a delectable recording of the duet by Joan Morris and William Bolcom.

BUTTERWORTH, Charles [Edward]. (1896–1946) Stage and film performer. A comic character actor, he polished his shy, awkward stage persona into a series of routines that delighted audiences on Broadway and then in Hollywood. On stage he played the shy Rupert Day in Kern's *Sweet Adeline* (1929), and on screen he was the reticent Charles in Kern's *The Cat and the Fiddle* (1934). Butterworth was born in South Bend, Indiana, and received a law degree from Notre Dame but went into journalism before pursuing an acting career. After many years touring in vaudeville and perfecting his act, he was featured in Broadway revues, such as *Americana* (1926), *Allez-Oop!* (1927), *Flying Colors* (1932), and *Count Me In* (1942), where he delivered comic monologues. Butterworth also played comic supporting roles in *Good Boy* (1928) and *Sweet Adeline* before going to Hollywood where he played meek and indecisive characters in over thirty movies, including the musicals *Love Me Tonight* (1932), *The Cat and the Fiddle*, *Hollywood Party* (1934), *The Night Is Young* (1935), *Swing High, Swing Low* (1937), *The Boys from Syracuse* (1940), and *This Is the Army* (1943). He was still in great demand when he died prematurely in a car crash at the age of forty-eight.

THE CABARET GIRL. A musical comedy by **George Grossmith, Jr.**, **P. G. Wodehouse** (book and lyrics); **Anne Caldwell** (lyrics); Jerome Kern (music). [19 September 1922, Winter Garden Theatre, London, 361 performances] Produced by George Grossmith, Jr., J. A. E. Malone; directed by George Grossmith, Jr.; musical directions by John Ansell. Hoping to present a Cinderella musical like the recent hit *Sally*, producers Grossmith and Malone hired Sally's composer Kern to write a show featuring London star **Dorothy Dickson** (who had played Sally in the West End). The plot they concocted was far from original. James Paradene (Geoffrey Gwyther) is in love with cabaret chorine Marilynn Morgan (Dickson), but he must have the approval of his trustees Lord and Lady Hastings who do not think highly of chorus girls or cabarets. When Marilynn refuses to give up the stage for Jim, he works a plan in which word gets to the Hastings that he and Marilynn are already married and living in the country. The ruse almost works but the truth gets out, and not until Marilynn is a last-minute replacement in the cabaret at London's Hotel Metropole and wins over the audience (and the Hastings) is there a happy ending. The comedy was supplied by the song publishers Gripps (Grossmith) and Gravvins (Norman Griffin) who stopped the show each night with the comic duet "Mr. Gravvins–Mr. Gripps," which recalled the popular "Mr. Gallagher and Mr. Shean" from Broadway. Other highlights in the score include the contagious "Dancing Time," the ballad "Journey's End," and two numbers for Dickson: the flowing **"Ka-lu-a"** (which had been heard earlier on Broadway in 1921's *Good Morning, Dearie*) and the rousing "Shimmy with Me." *The Cabaret Girl* was welcomed by the press and the public and ran eleven months, encouraging more Cinderella musicals on both sides of the Atlantic. In 1922 an orchestral recording of some of the score was made, and in 1937 Dorothy Dickson recorded some of the songs from the show.

CALDWELL, Anne [Payson]. (1867–1936) Stage lyricist and writer. A performer-turned-writer in the developing American musical theatre, she was one of the earliest women pioneers in the field and worked with Kern on eight Broadway shows. Caldwell was born in Boston and began her career as a singer in operetta, vaudeville, and burlesque, appearing on Broadway in musicals in the 1890s. At the turn of the century she gave up performing and turned to writing lyrics and librettos for musicals, beginning her New York career with the scripts for *Top o' the World* (1907) and *The Lady of the Slipper* (1912). Caldwell had a major hit with *Chin-Chin* (1914) before she partnered with Kern for the first time on ***She's a Good Fellow*** (1919). Sometimes writing book and lyrics, she also collaborated on the Kern shows ***The Night Boat*** (1920), ***Hitchy-Koo*** (1920), ***Good Morning, Dearie*** (1921), ***The Bunch and Judy*** (1922), ***Stepping Stones*** (1923), ***The City Chap*** (1925), and ***Criss-Cross*** (1926). With others she wrote scores for *Pom-Pom* (1916), *Jack o' Lantern* (1917), *The Canary* (1918), *The Lady in Red* (1919), *The Sweetheart Shop* (1920), *Tip Top* (1920), *Peg o' My Dreams* (1924), *The Magnolia Lady* (1924), *Oh, Please!* (1926), *Yours Truly* (1927), *Take the Air* (1927), and *Three Cheers* (1928). Caldwell was a practical craftsman and gifted lyricist who was much respected in the rough-and-tumble days when the American musical was still being defined. Her shows are not revived, but some of her songs live on, such as "I Know That You Know," "Left All Alone Blues," **"Ka-lu-a,"** and "Wait Till the Cows Come Home."

"Californ-i-ay" is the robust ode to the territory where "the hills have more splendor and the girls have more gender," as sung by Caroline Frost **(Deanna Durbin)**, Johnny Lawlor **(Robert Paige)**, and the other wagon train arrivals in Kern's movie operetta ***Can't Help Singing*** (1944). The waltzing lyric by **E. Y. Harburg** and Kern's rigorous music were obviously inspired by the popular title song *Oklahoma!* on Broadway the year before, yet Harburg's lyric is more tongue-in-cheek, filled with such hyperbolic claims as the ocean there is wetter than elsewhere and it rains champagne. Kern's music is also distinctive, effectively employing sections of the verse in the refrain. In the revue ***Jerome Kern Goes to Hollywood***, David Kernan, Liz Robertson, and Elaine Delmar sang the song in London in 1985, and Scott Holmes performed it with Delmar and Robertson on Broadway the next year. Marni Nixon is among the few who have recorded "Californ-i-ay."

"Can I Forget You?" is a popular ballad that Kern and lyricist **Oscar Hammerstein** wrote for the pioneer movie musical *High, Wide and Handsome* (1937). The lovely farewell song was sung by Sally Watterson (**Irene Dunne**) to Peter Cortlandt (**Randolph Scott**) when they parted. Hammerstein's lyric is lush and romantic without being cloying, and Kern's music manages to sound true to the period but remains contemporary by avoiding a too-predictable melodic line. Among those who recorded "Can I Forget You?" are Guy Lombardo, Andy Williams, Bing Crosby, Arthur Tracey, Richard Tauber, Henry Allen, Jeri Southern, Marni Nixon, David Whitfield, Elisabeth Welch, Al Haig, Sylvia McNair, Kelly Harland, the Light Blues, Sandy Stewart, Malcolm McNeill, and Andrea Marcovicci. David Kernan, Liz Robertson, and Elaine Delmar sang it in the London revue *Jerome Kern Goes to Hollywood* (1985), and Scott Holmes performed it with Delmar and Robertson when the show transferred to Broadway the next year.

"Can't Help Lovin' Dat Man" is a unique torch song in that it is spirited and rhythmic yet still has a touch of pathos. Kern and lyricist **Oscar Hammerstein** wrote the song for the original Broadway production of *Show Boat* (1927) and it immediately caught on and has remained a standard ever since. Kern's contagious music is bluesy yet joyous and Hammerstein's famous lyric, with its memorable phrase "fish gotta swim, birds gotta fly," manages to be earnest and flippant at the same time. The riverboat actress Julie LaVerne (**Helen Morgan**) recalls a "colored" folk song from her youth and sings it with Magnolia (**Norma Terris**), Queenie (**Tess Gardella**), Joe (**Jules Bledsoe**), and Windy (Allan Campbell). Unknown to the others, Julie is a mulatto, so the song's ethnic heritage is more than appropriate. Also, the lyric fits with the character and situation, for Julie is in love with her troublesome husband Steve, but she can't say why. Later in *Show Boat,* Magnolia sings the song plaintively as her audition for a music hall job in Chicago. When the manager tells her the number is too sad, she does a lively, jazzed-up version of the song. "Can't Help Lovin' Dat Man" was heard in all three film versions of *Show Boat.* Helen Morgan sang it as part of the prologue to the 1927 film, and **Irene Dunne**, **Hattie McDaniel**, **Paul Robeson**, and the chorus sang it in the 1936 screen version. In the 1946 Kern biopic *Till the Clouds Roll By,* the song was sung by Lena Horne, and in the 1951 remake of *Show Boat,* it was performed by **Kathryn Grayson** and **Ava Gardner**

SHOW BOAT. The plays that were performed on the *Cotton Blossom* were non-musical melodramas, as witnessed by this photograph from the original 1927 Broadway production, showing both the riverboat stage and audience. The seated figure down left is Cap'n Andy (Charles Winninger) who seems to be all fiddled out. *Photofest*

(dubbed by Annette Warren) as Magnolia and Julie. Ann Blyth (dubbed by Gogi Grant) sang "Can't Help Lovin' Dat Man" in the film *The Helen Morgan Story* (1957). Morgan recorded the song twice and sang it throughout her too-short career. The many later recordings include those by Horne, Gardella, Marie Burke (who introduced the number to England in the 1928 London production), Barbara Cook, Margaret Whiting, jazz pianist Beegie Adair, Ella Fitzgerald, Frances Langford with Tony Martin, Barbra Streisand, Cleo Laine, Trudy Richards, Constance Towers, Carol Bruce, Teresa Stratas, Kiri Te Kanawa, Trudy Richards, Oscar Peterson, Lonette McKee, and Anita Darian with Louise Parker. Liz Robertson and Elaine Delmar performed "Can't Help Lovin' Dat Man" in the London revue *Jerome Kern Goes to Hollywood* (1985) as well as in the 1986 Broadway version. Morgan's recording was used in the film *Alice Sweet Alice* (1976), and the song was also heard in the movies *The Adventures of Priscilla, Queen of the Desert* (1994), *Meet Joe Black* (1998), and *Boat Trip* (2002).

CAN'T HELP SINGING. A movie musical by Lewis Foster, Frank Ryan (screenplay); **E. Y. Harburg** (lyrics); Jerome Kern (music). [Universal 1944] Produced by Felix Jackson; directed by Frank Ryan; musical direction by Hans J. Salter, Edgar Fairchild; orchestrations by Frank Skinner.

Plot: In Washington, DC, in 1847, Caroline, the daughter of East Coast senator Martin Frost, ignores her father's threats and sets off across country

---

CAST OF *CAN'T HELP SINGING*

Character	Performer
Caroline Frost	**Deanna Durbin**
Johnny Lawlor	**Robert Paige**
Prince Stroganovsky	**Akim Tamiroff**
Lt. Robert Latham	David Bruce
Sen. Martin Frost	Ray Collins
Koppa	Leonid Kinsey
Aunt Cissy Frost	Clara Blandick
Sad Sam	Andrew Tombes
Jake Carstairs	Thomas Gomez
Jeannie McLean	June Vincent

---

to wed an army officer. But on the wagon train heading to Sonora, California, she falls in love with the outdoorsman Johnny Lawlor, and after a few contrived complications Caroline wins Lawlor and her father's approval. The humor was supplied by a pair of European fortune hunters, Prince Gregory and Koppa, who are bumbling across the prairie.

With more than a passing nod to *Oklahoma!*, which opened on Broadway the year before, this frontier musical captured the enthusiasm for land (there was even a rousing song celebrating "Californ-i-ay") and the pioneer spirit of the Rodgers and Hammerstein musical, yet the movie has a charm of its own. Foster and Ryan penned the screenplay, which was loosely based on the novel *Girl of the Overland Trail* by Samuel and Curtis Warshawsky. It was far from a gripping or even original tale, but the cast was amiable, the songs pleasing, and the movie boasted magnificent Technicolor photography and stunning outdoor locations. In their only collaboration, Harburg and Kern came up with a varied and tuneful score, from the gentle "Any Moment Now" to the rowdy "Californ-i-ay." The gushing "More and More," the rousing "Swing Your Sweetheart," and the exhilarating title number were also quite accomplished. While *Can't Help Singing* was viewed as simply a Durbin vehicle, it is perhaps her best and afforded her what many consider her finest performance.

CAN'T HELP SINGING SONGS

"Can't Help Singing"
"Elbow Room"
"Any Moment Now"
"Swing Your Sweetheart"
"More and More"
"Californ-i-ay"

Recording: A soundtrack recording of *Can't Help Singing* was released in 1945, but it did not contain all the songs. It was later re-released on an album with the movie soundtrack for *DuBarry Was a Lady*.

"Can't Help Singing" is the lilting title number from the 1944 pioneer movie musical scored by Kern and lyricist **E. Y. Harburg**. Senator Frost's daughter Caroline (**Deanna Durbin**) sang the expansive number about how the coming of spring makes her want to sing as she drove a carriage through the countryside near Washington, DC. The number was reprised later in the film by Durbin and gambler Johnny Lawlor (**Robert Paige**) out West as each sat in wooden outdoor bathtubs separated by a wall, their voices joining in a

CAN'T HELP SINGING. The sixteen-year-old Deanna Durbin had charmed an entire orchestra in *One Hundred Men and a Girl* (1937). It seems the twenty-three-year-old soprano has to settle for only seven male admirers when she played the senator's rebellious daughter in *Can't Help Singing* (1944) in which she gives, arguably, her finest screen performance. *Universal Pictures/Photofest ©Universal Pictures*

silly, sensual manner. Kern's music is a no-holds-barred waltz, and blending with Harburg's soaring lyric, the song is, as musicologist Alec Wilder describes, "cheery, direct, uncomplex and spring-like." Recordings of "Can't Help Singing" were made by Ambrose and His Orchestra, Miss Ann Watt, Sylvia McNair, Christina Lind, Abbey Lincoln, Rebecca Luker, and Katrina Murphy.

CAST RECORDINGS and SOUNDTRACKS of Kern musicals. Of Kern's thirty-seven Broadway productions, only the last—*Very Warm for May* (1939)—and the 1932 revival of *Show Boat* received anything close to an original cast recording. This is not as odd as it sounds when one remembers that the Broadway cast album, as we think of it today, did not come about until *Oklahoma!* (1943). The invention of the phonograph in 1877 coincides with the developing American musical theatre, for it was at that time that musicals started to boast original scores with possible hit songs. Yet the earliest recordings of songs from Broadway on cylinders and 78-rpm discs rarely used the stage performers. It was felt that recording artists were better suited for these records, and often the house band for the recording company played their own orchestrated version of the song. When a performer of renown did get to record his or her hit song, rarely did it resemble the manner in which it was done in the theatre. In Great Britain, on the other hand, recording companies felt differently, and in 1900 the complete score for the musical *Florodora* was recorded on 78s. On several occasions the British would record the West End versions of American musicals, and the earliest and most accurate recordings of Kern's *Show Boat*, *Sally*, *Sunny*, and *The Cat and the Fiddle* were made this way. The first American to try and preserve stage scores accurately on records was Jack Kapp, who took selections from *Blackbirds of 1928* and the 1932 revival of *Show Boat* and recorded them with the original artists on the Brunswick label in 1932. Kapp was also responsible for putting all of the songs and some narration from *The Cradle Will Rock* (1938) on six 78s. The first complete cast recording of a full-scale Broadway musical was Kapp's 78s of *Oklahoma!* on the Decca label. The cast recording of *Very Warm for May* was compiled some years after the show closed, using bits of dialogue and songs that had been recorded during the run.

Recordings of movie musicals, or soundtrack recordings, have a different history. Because the score for a film musical is done before the movie is shot, there is no need to go back into the recording studio and make a record. A recording company could just pick and choose which musical selections to release as a single or an album without the overhead expense of recording anything. This did not mean that complete soundtrack recordings were readily available. Too often only the highlights were put on record and released when the movie came out as a way of promoting the film. Other times a single song from a movie musical might be released as a single and find success. Most of the Kern movie musicals have some kind of recording, though very few are close to complete. One must go to the video or DVD version of a Kern film to hear all of the songs that were heard in the movie. See appendix C for a listing of all known recordings of Kern shows.

THE CAT AND THE FIDDLE. A contemporary operetta by **Otto Harbach** (book and lyrics), Jerome Kern (music). [15 October 1931, Globe Theatre, 395 performances] Produced by **Max Gordon**, directed by José Ruben, choreographed by Albertina Rasch, musical direction by Victor Baravalle, orchestrations by **Robert Russell Bennett,** Jerome Kern.

Plot: At the Music Conservatoire in Brussels, the Rumanian composer Victor Florescu writes serious music while his sweetheart, the American composer Shirley Sheridan, writes jazz. Producer Clement Daudet plans to present Victor's opera *The Passionate Pilgrim* but insists on interpolating some of Shirley's tunes to liven it up. Victor, who is tempted by the jealous diva Odette, is furious until he learns that he and Shirley can harmonize nicely onstage and off. A comic subplot concerning Shirley's dancing

CASTS FOR *THE CAT AND THE FIDDLE*

Character	1931 Broadway	1932 London	1934 film
Victor Florescu	Georges Metaxa	Francis Lederer	**Ramon Novarro**
Shirley Sheridan	**Bettina Hall**	Peggy Wood	**Jeanette MacDonald**
Odette/Alice	Odette Myrtil	Alice Delysia	**Vivienne Segal**
Pompineau	George Meader	Henri Leoni	
Clement/Jules Daudet	José Ruben	Austin Trevor	**Frank Morgan**
Prof. Bertier			Jean Hersholt
Charles			**Charles Butterworth**

brother Alexander and his wife Angie filled out the story, which was held together by the street singer Pompineau.

Although Kern and Harbach were aiming for a new kind of operetta, the plot was conventionally old-fashioned. The melodic score, on the other hand, was a refreshingly effective blend of the old and the new. The two hit songs were the farewell ballad "Try to Forget" and lush serenade "The Night Was Made for Love," but also impressive were the wry "She Didn't Say 'Yes' (She Didn't Say 'No')," the flowing "I Watch the Love Parade," and the sweeping duet "One Moment Alone." All in all, theatre historians consider this score to be Kern's most ambitious yet as he moved further away from musical comedy. *The Cat and the Fiddle* opened in the depths of the Depression and producer Gordon cut salaries and made other efforts to allow the show to run nearly a year, followed by a road tour. A London production starring Peggy Wood and Francis Lederer managed to run 226 performances. The musical has very rarely been revived, probably because of its book rather than its glorious score.

THE CAT AND THE FIDDLE SONGS

"The Night Was Made for Love"
"I Watch the Love Parade"
"The Breeze Kissed Your Hair"
"Try to Forget"
"Poor Pierrot"
"She Didn't Say 'Yes'"
"A New Love Is Old"
"One Moment Alone"
"Hah! Cha! Cha!"

Film Version: The Cat and the Fiddle. A movie musical by Bella and Sam Spewack (screenplay), Otto Harbach (lyrics), Jerome Kern (music). [1934, MGM] Produced by Bernard Hyman, directed by William K. Howard, choreographed by Albertina Rasch, musical direction by Herbert Stothart, orchestrations by Charles Maxwell (uncredited). *The Cat and the Fiddle* came to the screen with all of its Broadway score intact, a rare feat even for the best of stage musicals. Yet the screenwriters made many changes in the plot, such as resetting the tale mostly in Paris and coming up with a satirical ending in which the prima donna Odette (Vivienne Segal) walks out of the show and Shirley has to go on in her place even though she had previously not even been involved in the production. That opening night performance was shot in the new three-color Technicolor and enthralled audiences. While the songs remained, they were reassigned to different characters and situations, such as "The Night Was Made for Love" being the hit song that Shirley (Jeanette MacDonald) wrote and the reason for her and Victor (Ramon Novarro) to separate until the happy ending. It was MacDonald's first MGM film and her popularity grew because of the movie. Despite its many alterations, *The Cat and the Fiddle* on screen was faithful to Kern and his music, making it one of the better film adaptations of his work.

Recordings: Peggy Wood and members of the original London cast recorded four of the songs in 1932. That same year a medley of numbers from *The Cat and the Fiddle* was made by the Savoy Hotel Orpheans featuring Jessie Matthews, Raymond Newell, Binnie Hale, and Jack Plant. A medley of songs from the Broadway production was made by the Victor Light Opera Company in 1938, and another medley was recorded by the Leo Reisman Orchestra with vocalists Frank Munn and Frances Maddux. The film soundtrack with MacDonald is not very complete. Two London studio recordings are much more satisfying: a 1953 album with Patricia Neway and Stephen Douglass, and a 1958 recording with Doreen Hume and Denis Quilley.

CATLETT, Walter. (1889–1960) Stage and film performer. A favorite character actor who specialized in blustering, scatterbrained types, he was featured in a dozen Broadway musicals, including four by Kern, and in many movies, including some musicals. Catlett was born in San Francisco, educated at St. Ignatius College, started acting in 1906, and gained plenty of vaudeville and touring experience before he made his Broadway debut in the musical *The Prince of Pilsen* (1910). Catlett was soon featured in New York and London musicals, most memorably as the unscrupulous theatrical agent Otis Hooper in Kern's **Sally** (1920) and the cigar-chomping lawyer J. Watterson Watkins introducing the title song in *Lady, Be Good* (1924). His other Broadway musicals include *So Long, Letty* (1916), *Ziegfeld Follies* (1917), *Follow the Girl* (1918), *Little Simplicity* (1918), *Here's Howe* (1928), and *Treasure Girl* (1928), as well as Kern's **Dear Sir** (1924) and **Lucky** (1927). Catlett made his screen debut in 1924 and over the next thirty years played dozens of colorful character roles, including those in the musicals *Every Night at Eight* (1935), *On the Avenue* (1937), *Every Day's a Holiday* (1938), *Going Places* (1939), *My Gal Sal* (1942), *Yankee Doodle Dandy* (1942), *Up in Arms* (1944), *Look for the Silver Lining* (1949), *The Inspector General*

(1949), *Dancing in the Dark* (1950), and *Here Comes the Groom* (1951). Perhaps his most recognized role was never seen: the voice of the cunning fox J. Worthington Foulfellow in the animated classic *Pinocchio* (1940).

CENTENNIAL SUMMER. A movie musical by Michael Kanin (screenplay); Leo Robin, **Oscar Hammerstein**, **E. Y. Harburg** (lyrics); Jerome Kern (music). [1946, 20th Century-Fox] Produced and directed by **Otto Preminger**, choreographed by Dorothy Fox, musical direction by Alfred Newman, orchestrations by Conrad Salinger, Herbert Spencer, Maurice De Packh.

Plot: The Philadelphia Rogers family is caught up in the excitement of the 1876 Centennial Exposition, especially daughters Edith and Julia, who both fall for the Frenchman Philippe Lascalles when he comes to manage the French pavilion. Mr. Rogers is a railroad worker who has invented a special clock that no one seems to be interested in. Caught up in the mild complications is Mrs. Rogers's sister Zenia Lascalles from Paris who tries to help promote Mr. Rogers but only makes trouble in the Rogerses' marriage. The sweet Julia wins Phillippe away from the conniving Edith, Rogers's clock is finally a success, and Edith returns to her faithful beau Ben Phelps, Philadelphia's first obstetrician.

Without question an attempt by 20th Century-Fox to come up with their own *Meet Me in St. Louis* (1944), the period musical rarely measured up to the earlier film, but it boasted Jerome Kern's last score and the music was resplen-

CAST FOR *CENTENNIAL SUMMER*

Character	Performer
Julia Rogers	**Jeanne Crain**
Phillippe Lascalles	**Cornel Wilde**
Edith Rogers	Linda Darnell
Jesse Rogers	Walter Brennan
Mrs. Rogers	Dorothy Gish
Ben Phelps	William Eythe
Zenia Lascalles	Constance Bennett
Susanna Rogers	Barbara Whiting
Richard Lewis, Esq.	Larry Stevens
Specialty	Avon Long

dent as the story and characters were mediocre. Musical highlights include the soulful ballad "All Through the Day," the rustic "Cinderella Sue," the cheerful "Up With the Lark," and the torchy "In Love in Vain." Instead of the St. Louis World's Fair of 1904, scriptwriter Michael Kanin, adapting Albert E. Idell's novel, offered a different exposition, but the similarities between the two movies were hard to ignore. The cast is merely competent (hardly any of the principals do their own singing), but the musical is beautifully filmed in Technicolor. *Centennial Summer* has its moments, such as the lantern-slide presentation of "All Through the Day" and Avon Long's rendition of "Cinderella Sue," that make it worth viewing, but the movie is hardly a fit tribute to its composer in his last Hollywood effort.

Recording: The film soundtrack is very complete, even including some of the short numbers in the score and even the cut ballad "Two Hearts Are Better Than One." Avon Long's rendition of "Cinderella Sue" is outstanding.

CENTENNIAL SUMMER SONGS

"The Right Romance"
"Up with the Lark"
"All Through the Day"
"In Love in Vain"
"Cinderella Sue"
"Railroad Song"
"Two Hearts Are Better Than One"
  (cut from final print)

CHAMPION, Gower [Carlyle]. (1920–1980) Stage and film choreographer, performer, director. The oft-awarded dancer-turned-director-choreographer was known for his staging that was as bright and stylish as it was witty, but in Hollywood he is most remembered as a performer, as in the Kern musicals *Till the Clouds Roll By* (1946), the 1951 movie remake of *Show Boat*, and *Lovely to Look At* (1952). Champion was born in Geneva, Illinois, the son of an ad executive, and when his parents divorced he was raised in Los Angeles by his mother, a successful dressmaker in Hollywood. He quit high school to form a dance act, then, after serving in the Coast Guard, he teamed up with Marjorie Belcher and they became famous as **Marge** and Gower **Champion**, one of the country's favorite dance duos in nightclubs, on television, and in movies. Champion danced in a few Broadway musicals, such as *The Streets of Paris* (1939), *The Lady Comes Across* (1942), and *Count Me In* (1942), then went to Hollywood where he was featured solo in *Till the Clouds Roll By* and with Marge in *Mr. Music* (1950), *Show Boat*, *Everything I Have Is Yours* (1952), *Lovely to Look At*, *Give a Girl a Break* (1953), *Jupiter's Darling* (1955), and *Three for the Show* (1955). The couple also starred in the TV musicals *A Bouquet for Millie* (1953) and *What Day Is It?* (1956). He returned to the New York stage in 1948 to direct and choreograph the revue *Small Wonder*, followed by the popular Broadway revue *Lend an Ear* (1948), as well as the TV musical *Cindy's Fella* (1959). The quintessential Champion style was first witnessed in his staging of the surprise hit *Bye Bye Birdie* (1960), finding clever and amusing ways to illustrate the effects of rock and roll on America. Yet he also shone with his delicate and atmospheric production of the French tale *Carnival* the next year. Giant hits such as *Hello, Dolly!* (1964), *I Do! I Do!* (1966), and *42nd Street* (1980) made Champion the most sought-after director-choreographer on Broadway for two decades, yet his genius for creating imaginative and vibrant musicals was also noticeable in less successful ventures, such as *The Happy Time* (1968) and *Mack and Mabel* (1974). His other Broadway musicals include *Make a Wish* (1951), *Sugar* (1972), *Irene* (1973), *Rockabye Hamlet* (1976), and *A Broadway Musical* (1978), as well as a handful of non-musicals. Champion's premature death was announced to a shocked cast and audience at the end of the opening-night performance of *42nd Street*. He was perhaps the last in the line of Busby Berkeley-like artists who instinctively knew how to provide dazzling entertainment values in all that he touched. Biographies: *Gower Champion: Dance and American Musical Theatre*, David Payne-Carter (1999); *Before the Parade Passes By*, John Anthony Gilvey (2005).

CHAMPION, Marge [née Marjorie Celeste Belcher]. (b. 1919) Film and television performer and choreographer. A beaming dancer-singer in Hollywood musicals, she is most remembered for her performances with her then-husband **Gower Champion**, as in the Kern movies ***Show Boat*** (1951) and ***Lovely to Look At*** (1952). A native of Los Angeles, her father was Ernest Belcher, a dance coach for the movies, and he saw that his daughter took dance lessons as a child. As an adult she worked as a model and was used to create the initial drawings and movements for the heroine of Walt Disney's *Snow White and the Seven Dwarfs* (1937) and the Blue Fairy in *Pinocchio* (1940). Champion did dance specialties in three movie musicals under the name Marjorie Bell: *The Story of Vernon and Irene Castle* (1939), Kern's bio-musical *Till the Clouds Roll By* (1944), and *Mr. Music* (1950). She married hoofer Gower Champion in 1947, and the two worked together in night-clubs and on screen in such musicals as *Show Boat, Everything I Have Is Yours* (1952), *Lovely to Look At, Give a Girl a Break* (1953), *Jupiter's Darling* (1955), and *Three for the Show* (1955), as well as the television musicals *A Bouquet for Millie* (1953) and *What Day Is It?* (1956). Gower Champion had started choreographing in the late 1940s and she assisted her husband in staging the dances for the Broadway musicals *Lend an Ear* (1948), *Make a Wish* (1951), and *Hello, Dolly!* (1964). In the 1960s she acted in non-musical films and television shows, and also choreographed some television specials, including the TV musical *Queen of the Stardust Ballroom* (1975). Champion was a dance teacher for many years and choreographed some non-musical films and the Broadway play-with-music *Stepping Out* (1987). She made a belated Broadway singing-dancing debut as the veteran hoofer Emily Whitman in the 2001 revival of *Follies*.

CHARM SONGS by Kern. A musical number that is less about character development than it is about utilizing the character's warmth and/or comic entertainment value has been termed a charm song. Although charm songs are often expendable to the plot, they have sometimes been audience favorites. Kern's song hit **"How'd You Like to Spoon with Me?"** might be termed a charm song. Because Kern wrote before the predominance of the integrated musical, which eschewed unnecessary songs, his shows often included at least one charm song. Some examples are **"D'Ye Love Me?,"** **"You Couldn't Be Cuter," "Cinderella Sue," "Bungalow in Quogue," "The Church Around the Corner,"** "Let's Say Good Night Till It's Morning," **"Napoleon,"** and **"My Houseboat on the Harlem."**

CHORAL NUMBERS by Kern. A chorus or choral number is one that emphasizes the group over the individual though many songs are sung by principals accompanied by a chorus. A strong and frequently used chorus was essential in operetta, but even as Kern moved the American musical away from European operetta, he still utilized choral numbers in his shows. One of his most complex choral pieces is **"Cotton Blossom,"** a concerted number that Kern and lyricist **Oscar Hammerstein** devised for the opening of *Show Boat* (1927). Most musicals before *Oklahoma!* (1943) opened with a choral number and Kern's shows were no exception. Even when the size of the chorus was reduced greatly for the **Princess Theatre Musicals**, the show still opened with a choral piece. Similarly, most acts in a musical concluded with a chorus number. Many of Kern's films have a chorus singing over the opening credits, as was standard for the 1930s and 1940s. Among Kern's many notable choral numbers for stage and screen are **"Californi-ay," "Sunny," "Cover Girl," "A Girl Is on Your Mind," "Bojangles of Harlem," "There's a Hill Beyond a Hill," "Leave It to Jane," "The Enchanted Train,"** and **"Once in a Blue Moon."**

"The Church Around the Corner" is a waltzing romantic song that Kern wrote with lyricist **P. G. Wodehouse** for the 1916 unproduced musical *The Little Thing*, which later became the Broadway hit *Sally* (1920). In that hit show, the sly manicurist Rosalind Rafferty (Mary Hay) and the theatrical agent Otis Hooper (**Walter Catlett**) sang the nimble ditty about the frugal wedding and humble lifestyle they will have together. Kern's music is lively, using only quarter notes except for the last note of each musical sequence. Wodehouse's lyric is saucy and playful, the comic couple planning to wed in the out-of-the-way church where you don't need to have a lot of money to begin life together. The church referenced in the lyric is an actual Episcopalian house of worship in the Madison Square neighborhood of Manhattan. When the popular nineteenth-century actor Joseph Jefferson was making funeral arrangements for a fellow thespian, a minister at one church refused to bury an actor and recommended Jefferson try "the little church around the corner." Ever since then the miniature gothic structure has been a favorite of actors and theatre folk. Wodehouse was very familiar with the church, having been married there in 1914. There are memorials inside to many theatre artists, including Jefferson and Wodehouse. "The Church Around the Corner" was sung by **George Grossmith, Jr.**, as Otis and Heather Thatcher as Rosalind in the 1921 London production of *Sally*. The song was not used in the 1929 film version but was heard in the 1948 Broadway revival where it was sung by Jack Goode as Otis and Kay Buckley as Rosie. The number has been listed in no less than four different ways over the years, from "Little Church Around the Corner" to "Church 'Round the Corner."

"Cinderella Sue" is a forgotten gem from Kern's film ***Centennial Summer*** (1946) that compares favorably with the composer's finest character songs. The African American singer-dancer Avon Long and a group of children sang the pseudo-Negro folk song for patrons in a Philadelphia saloon and then went into a bouncy dance. **E. Y. Harburg**'s narrative lyric, about a shantytown Cinderella with a "Dixie nose" and "patches on her gown," is wily and yet endearing. Kern's toe-tapping music and harmonica accompaniment recalls the ethnic songs he wrote for ***Show Boat*** (1927). George Reinholt made a recording of the number in the early 1970s.

THE CITY CHAP. A musical comedy of country life by James Montgomery (book), **Anne Caldwell** (lyrics), Jerome Kern (music). [26 October 1925, Liberty Theatre, 72 performances] Produced by **Charles Dillingham**, directed by R. H. Burnside, choreographed by David Bennett, musical direction by Victor Baravalle, orchestrations by **Robert Russell Bennett**. Winchell Smith's 1909 comedy *The Fortune Hunter* was the hit of its season and established John Barrymore as a Broadway star, so a musical version of the play seemed to producer Dillingham to be a good idea. The plot was very similar: penniless Nat Duncan (Skeets Gallagher) hears that there are plenty of rich girls in small towns so he moves to Radford, gets a job at Graham's Drug Store, and woos Josie Lockwood (Ina Williams), the daughter of the richest man in town. When Nat is falsely accused of embezzling money from the store, he clears his name but loses Josie. But that is all right because by this time he has fallen in love with coworker Betty Graham (Phyllis Cleveland). The story still worked but was offset by the fact that the three most impressive performers in the cast played minor characters: George Raft, who did a spectacular dance routine, sultry Betty Compton, and soprano **Irene Dunne** who was still spelling her name Dunn. Most disappointing of all was Kern's score, which offered little of interest. In fact, only three of the songs were published, in those days a sign of little faith in the score. *The City Chap* had a forced run of nine weeks then disappeared, leaving little of value.

"Cleopatterer" is a comic ditty from ***Leave It to Jane*** (1917), the early collegiate musical with a score by Kern and lyricist **P. G. Wodehouse**. The sultry waitress Flora Wiggins (Georgia O'Ramey) sang the number while she did a whirling Egyptian dance that stopped the show each night. Kern's music is pseudo-exotic with a vamp-like flavor, and Wodehouse's lyric, which details the ways the legendary Cleopatra used her sexual and political talents to mesmerize men, is filled with arch rhymes and a sly sense of humor. "Cleopatterer" is considered one of Wodehouse's finest comic lyrics and foreshadows the wit and playfulness of the later lyricists Lorenz Hart, **Ira Gershwin**, and Cole Porter, all of whom stated that Wodehouse was their inspiration. While no film version of *Leave It to Jane* was made, this song and the title number were featured in the Kern biopic *Till the Clouds Roll By* (1946) where "Cleopatterer" was sung by June Allyson as Jane, not Flora. The lyric is still sassy but Allyson's interpretation is far from sexy or funny. Comic actress Dorothy Greener was hilarious as Flora when she sang it in the long-running 1959 Off-Broadway revival of *Leave It to Jane*. It was also performed by Faith Prince with panache in the 1985 Goodspeed Opera House revival. A distinctive recording was made by singer Joan Morris with pianist William Bolcom.

COLLABORATORS of Kern. Over a period of forty years, Kern collaborated with dozens of American and British lyricists and book writers for Broadway, the West End, and Hollywood. In term of lyrics, his three most important collaborators were **P. G. Wodehouse**, **Oscar Hammerstein**, and **Dorothy Fields**. The Kern-Wodehouse songs were heard on stage, the Kern-Fields numbers on the screen, and the songs with Hammerstein on both. **Otto Harbach** (who also wrote lyrics) and **Guy Bolton** were Kern's most prodigious librettists. His most frequent orchestrators were **Frank Saddler** and **Robert Russell Bennett**. Yet so many other outstanding artists worked with Kern that the breadth of his career can only be understood by looking at the variety of creative men and women with whom he collaborated. From early writers such as **Harry B. Smith** and **Anne Caldwell** to much younger artists like **Howard Dietz** and **Johnny Mercer**, Kern collaborated with more people than perhaps any other composer in the American theatre. Kern once stated that Hammerstein was his favorite lyricist and librettist partner, and the two worked together on many projects. Some of this was a matter of talent, but much of it was Hammerstein's personality and how the two had very similar ideas about what the musical form could do.

MAJOR COLLABORATORS OF JEROME KERN

Collaborator	Stage works	Original film scores
Guy Bolton (librettist)	14	
Anne Caldwell (lyricist, librettist)	8	
Howard Dietz (lyricist)	1	
Dorothy Fields (lyricist)		4
Ira Gershwin (lyricist)		1
Oscar Hammerstein (lyricist, librettist)	7	1
Otto Harbach (lyricist, librettist)	3	
Johnny Mercer (lyricist)		1
Herbert Reynolds (lyricist)	6	
Harry B. Smith (lyricist, librettist)	4	
P. G. Wodehouse (lyricist, librettist)	8	

COMIC SONGS by Kern. Any number intended more for getting laughs than for plot or character can be termed a comic song, though in the later integrated musicals comedy was often used to reveal character. Since much of Kern's career was writing light musical comedies, he wrote dozens of songs that might be classified as comic. While it is possible to compose music that has a light or silly air to it, it is the lyricist who must make a comic number work. Kern's collaborators served him well in coming up with such comic delights as **"Life Upon the Wicked Stage," "Napoleon," "She Didn't Say 'Yes,'" "Bongo on the Congo," "Cleopatterer,"** "Greenwich Village," **"The Lorelei," "A Mormon Life," "Thirteen Collar,"** and **"Tulip Time in Sing Sing."**

COMSTOCK, F. Ray. (1880–1949) Stage producer. Although he presented dozens of plays and musicals on Broadway between 1907 and 1927, he is most remembered for producing the **Princess Theatre Musicals** and bringing recognition to Kern. Comstock began his career as an usher in his native Buffalo then moved to New York where he became assistant treasurer at the Criterion Theatre. His first Broadway production was *Fascinating Flora* (1907), then he mounted *Bandana Land* (1908), one of the earliest "Negro" musicals. Comstock became manager of the Princess Theatre when it was built to house experimental dramas, and when these failed he and **Elisabeth Marbury** initiated a policy of intimate musical comedies that soon became known as the Princess Theatre Musicals. These included the Kern shows *Nobody Home* (1915), *Very Good Eddie* (1915), *Oh, Boy!* (1917), and *Oh, Lady! Lady!!* (1918), as well as Kern's *Leave It to Jane* (1917) and *Sitting Pretty* (1924), which were technically not Princess shows because they played at other theatres. Among his successful non-musical plays were *Adam and Eva* (1919), *Polly Preferred* (1923), and many classic revivals of Ibsen and Chekhov. Comstock also imported a number of major foreign attractions, often in association with Morris Gest, including *Chu Chin Chow* (1917), *Aphrodite* (1919), *Mecca* (1920), *Chauve-Souris* (1922), and *The Miracle* (1924), as well as the Moscow Art Theatre and Eleonora Duse.

"Cotton Blossom" is the title of the complex opening chorus number in Kern's *Show Boat* (1927), which is really three different songs. The landmark musical opens with the African American stevedores singing about working on the Mississippi River. They are echoed by the black "gals" who sing about cooking. When the riverboat *Cotton Blossom* pulls into the dock, the white chorus enters and the "town beaux" flirt and sing with the "mincing misses." The black and white choruses sing together, while remaining separate, about Captain Andy's show boat. Andy (**Charles Winninger**) then enters and is greeted by the misses and beaux before he launches into his "ballyhoo" song about how great this year's show is. The boat's comic couple Frank (**Sammy White**) and Ellie (**Eva Puck**) then give the crowd a taste of the entertainment to come by going into a dance. The number also introduces other members of the company and concludes with the chorus praising the *Cotton Blossom* and looking forward to that evening's performance. Kern's music is rousing yet textured. The difference in tone from the black chorus to the white one is subtle but effective. The melody of **"Ol' Man River"** is hinted at in the music, the title musical phrase "Cotton Blossom" being the same notes as the title "Ol' Man River" played in reverse. The lyric by **Oscar Hammerstein** is similarly segregated. The African Americans sing in short terse phrases while the white chorus has frilly, fanciful rhymes. "Cotton Blossom" contains the most controversial lyric Hammerstein ever wrote. Using the vernacular of the period, the stevedores refer to themselves as "niggers" who toil on the river until the Judgement

Day. Later productions and most recordings have substituted "darkies" and "colored folk" for the racially derogatory expression.

COUSIN LUCY. A musical comedy by Charles Klein (book), Schuyler Green (lyrics), Jerome Kern (music). [27 August 1915, George M. Cohan Theatre, 43 performances] Produced by A. H. Woods, directed by Robert Milton, choreographed by David Bennett, musical direction by August Kleinecke, orchestrations by **Frank Saddler**. More a comedy with songs than a full-fledged musical evening, the show was a vehicle for female impersonator Julian Eltinge who played Jerry Jackson, disguised as Cousin Lucy in order to infiltrate Madame Lucette's Dressmaking Establishment. Three of Kern's four songs are worth noting: the blues-like "Society," the ballad "Those 'Come Hither' Eyes," and the waltz "Two Heads Are Better Than One," all sung by Eltinge in drag. Fans of the celebrated cross-dresser, at the peak of his popularity, kept *Cousin Lucy* on the boards for five weeks.

COVER GIRL. A movie musical by Virginia Van Upp (screenplay), **Ira Gershwin** (lyrics), Jerome Kern (music). [1944, Columbia] Produced by Arthur Schwartz; directed by **Charles Vidor**; choreographed by Val Raset, Seymour Felix, Stanley Donen; musical direction by Morris Stoloff; orchestrations by Carmen Dragon, Gil Grau, Paul Weston.

Plot: Dancer Rusty Parker works in a Brooklyn nightclub run by Danny McGuire, but she dreams of moving into the big time. Danny is in love with her and, with his sidekick Genius, does what he can to promote Rusty's career. When she wins a contest to be the cover girl for a popular magazine, Rusty becomes famous, neglects her old friends, and nearly marries the Broadway producer Noel Wheaton before coming to her senses and returning to her Brooklyn buddies. In one section of the movie, the magazine publisher John Coudair recalls Rusty's grandmother, Maribelle Hicks, whom he idolized, and in some flashbacks their aborted relationship is revealed.

Intended as another showcase for Rita Hayworth, the musical was dominated by the up-and-coming Gene Kelly, proving to be a better actor and more versatile dancer than previously seen. Yet *Cover Girl* is filled with memorable songs, exciting performances, and innovative dancing. The film boasts two memorable production numbers. While the chorus sang the title number, Hayworth ran down a seemingly endless ramp, her hair and dress

CAST FOR *COVER GIRL*

Character	Performer
Rusty Parker/Mirabelle Hicks	**Rita Hayworth**
Danny McGuire	**Gene Kelly**
Genius	**Phil Silvers**
Noel Wheaton	Lee Bowman
Maurine	Leslie Brooks
Cornelia "Stonewall" Jackson	Eve Arden
John Coudair	Otto Kruger

blowing seductively, a scene ripe for parody over the years. More impressive was Kelly's *pas de deux* with his alter ego as he scampered down a lonely Brooklyn street. (Kelly and Stanley Donen devised the complicated number themselves.) The Kern-Gershwin score also included the haunting ballad "Long Ago and Far Away," the peppy "Make Way for Tomorrow," and the period pastiche number "Sure Thing." *Cover Girl* foreshadowed the bold and creative work Kelly and Donen would do in the 1950s, but the movie stands on its own as a unique delight.

COVER GIRL SONGS

"The Show Must Go On"
"Who's Complaining"
"Sure Thing"
"Make Way for Tomorrow"
"Put Me to the Test"
"Long Ago and Far Away"
"Poor John" (not by Kern)
"Cover Girl"

Recording: The film soundtrack is not complete but has the highlights of the score. It was re-released on CD with the movie soundtrack for *Good News* and on another compilation CD with Kern's *You Were Never Lovelier*.

"Cover Girl" is the lush paean to magazine model Rusty Parker (**Rita Hayworth**) and the title song of the 1944 movie musical scored by Kern and lyricist **Ira Gershwin**. The production number, with a male chorus singing and dancing with Hayworth as she ran down a long winding ramp on stage in a Broadway show, is the stuff of parody, but the song itself is rather intriguing with Kern's music smoothly rising and falling in an effective manner. The number is sometimes listed as "That Girl on the Cover."

CRAIN, Jeanne. (1925–2003) Screen performer. An attractive girl-next-door movie star who appeared in several musicals (though she had to be dubbed), one of her best roles was Philadelphian Julia Rogers in Kern's *Centennial Summer* (1946). She was born in Barstow, California, the daughter of a high school English teacher, and studied acting at the University of California at Los Angeles. After winning a beauty contest at the age of sixteen, she turned to modeling with great success. Hollywood signed her in 1943 and she made her film debut in a bit part in the musical *The Gang's All Here*. Two years later she enchanted moviegoers with her fresh, engaging performance as farm girl Margy Frake in *State Fair* where she introduced "It Might as Well Be Spring" using Louanne Hogan's singing voice. Crain's subsequent musicals included *Centennial Summer*, *You Were Meant for Me* (1948), *Gentlemen Marry Brunettes* (1955), and *The Joker Is Wild* (1957). She was equally popular in light comedies and melodramas, such as *Apartment for Peggy* (1948), *A Letter to Three Wives* (1949), *Pinky* (1949), *Cheaper by the Dozen* (1950), and *O. Henry's Full House* (1952). Crain's popularity waned in the 1960s, though she made occasional screen appearances into the 1970s.

CRISS CROSS. A musical comedy by **Otto Harbach**, **Anne Caldwell** (book and lyrics); Jerome Kern (music). [12 October 1926, Globe Theatre, 210 performances] Produced by **Charles Dillingham**; directed by R. H. Burnside; choreographed by David Bennett, Mary Read; musical direction by Victor Baravalle; orchestrations by Maurice De Packh, **Robert Russell Bennett**. Created as a vehicle for the beloved comic **Fred Stone**, who had starred in a handful of musicals early in the century, *Criss Cross* recalled those early extravaganzas with a ridiculous plot and a series of exotic locales as the action moved across Europe and Asia. When the evil Ilphrahim Benani (Oscar Ragland) tries to rob Dolly Day (Dorothy Stone) of her birthright and the fortune connected with it, the aviator Christopher Cross (Fred Stone) assists her sweetheart Captain Carleton (Roy Hoyer) in rescuing Dorothy and her money. The chase took the cast from France to Algiers as palaces, deserts, gardens, and bazaars were re-created on stage. There was even a prologue set in a fantasyland with bits of the Cinderella story to start the evening off. The scenery and costumes were lavish (some critics thought garish) and the songs by Kern, Caldwell, and Harbach pleased, but fifty-three-year-old Fred Stone remained the show's chief attraction as he performed acrobatics, did a harem dance, played half of a camel, and flew in on a trapeze to rescue Dolly. The beguiling "You Will—Won't You?" was the only song to enjoy any popularity, but also notable were the evocative "In Araby with You" and the delightful trio "Rose of Delight." Stone's many fans allowed *Criss Cross* to run a profitable six months before setting out on a successful road tour.

CUMMINGS, [Charles Clarence] **Robert** [Orville]. (1908–1990) Film, stage, and television performer. A handsome, youthful-looking leading man who excelled at light comedy, he enjoyed a long and impressive career in different media, including the Kern film ***One Night in the Tropics*** (1940) in which he played the playboy Steve Harper. Cummings was born in Joplin, Missouri, and educated at Carnegie Tech and the American Academy of Dramatic Arts. The enterprising young actor went to Broadway posing as a British thespian named Blade Stanhope Conway and was quickly cast in plays. When he decided to try Hollywood in 1935, Cummings called himself Bruce Hutchins and told studio agents he was a rich Texan. Again he was immediately cast as appealing if bumbling juveniles. Among his sixty films are fifteen musicals in which he usually played Ivy League types. His musical credits include *Millions in the Air* (1935), *Three Cheers for Love* (1936), *College Swing* (1938), *Three Smart Girls Grow Up* (1939), *Spring Parade* (1940), *One Night in the Tropics*, *Moon Over Miami* (1941), *The Petty Girl* (1950), *Lucky Me* (1954), and *Beach Party* (1963). Yet he found greater fame on television as Bob Cummings where he had his own sitcom in the 1950s and another in the 1960s, still playing hapless young men. He continued doing films through the 1960s and appeared on dozens of other television programs through the 1970s.

DEAR SIR. A musical comedy by Edgar Selwyn (book), **Howard Dietz** (lyrics), Jerome Kern (music). [23 September 1924, Times Square Theatre, 15 performances] Produced by Philip Goodman, directed by David Burton, choreographed by David Bennett, musical direction by Gus Salzer, orchestrations by Allan Foster. Remembered less as a Kern musical than as the show that introduced lyricist Howard Dietz to Broadway, *Dear Sir* had a trite book and a lightweight score. Playboy Laddie Munn (**Oscar Shaw**) has been publicly humiliated by socialite Dorothy Fair (Genevieve Tobin) so at a charity ball auction he wins her services as a maid for one week, hoping to get even with her. But, with the help of the vaudevillian Andrew Bloxom (**Walter Catlett**) disguised as a millionaire, Laddie and Dorothy fall in love. Despite the top-notch cast, *Dear Sir* refused to catch fire and closed in two weeks. It was Kern who suggested newcomer Dietz as lyricist, having read his light verse in the newspapers. Comic songs such as **"A Mormon Life"** and **"My Houseboat on the Harlem"** had delicious lyrics, and the critics felt Dietz was a promising talent. Musicologists looking back at Kern's music notice some surprising innovation in numbers such as "Weeping Willow Tree" and "I Want to Be There." Although Kern and Dietz worked well together on the show, the two never collaborated again; most of Dietz's subsequent career would be with composer Arthur Schwartz.

"Dearly Beloved" is the alluring song about a marriage ceremony that Argentine Maria Acuña (**Rita Hayworth** dubbed by Nan Wynn) and American Robert Davis (**Fred Astaire**) sang and danced to, played by Xavier Cugat's Orchestra at a wedding reception in the Kern movie musical *You Were Never Lovelier* (1942). Kern's music, which some have pointed out bears a resemblance to the duet "Or son contenta" in Puccini's *Madama Butterfly*, is a favorite for study by musicologists because of its ingenious chromatics; the song is written in the key of C but the main theme is in alternating G and F chords. **Johnny Mercer** wrote the slick lyric asking for wedded bliss, and the song was nominated for an Oscar. "Dearly Beloved" remained on the *Your Hit Parade* for seventeen weeks and has been frequently recorded, including discs by Dinah Shore, Alvino Rey (vocal by Bill Schallen), Ted Fio Rito (vocal by Jimmy Baxter), Dorothy Kirsten, Nancy Wilson, Reid Shelton, Helen Merrill, Rebecca Kilgore, Jack Dieval Trio, Paul Weston Orchestra, Helen Steber, David Allen, Glenn Miller Orchestra (vocal by Skip Nelson), Sonny Rollins, Audubon Quartet, Derek Smith Trio, and Danielle Carson. Liz Robertson sang it in the revue *Jerome Kern Goes to Hollywood*, which played in London in 1985 and on Broadway in 1986, a duet version by Jonathan Dokuchitz and Darcie Roberts was featured in the Broadway Mercer revue *Dream* (1997), and it was sung by Noah Racey with Roxane Barlow, Sally Mae Dunn, and Jennifer Frankel in the Broadway musical *Never Gonna Dance* (2003).

DICKSON, Dorothy. (1893–1995) Stage performer. A leading lady favorite on the London stage, she started her career in New York where she danced in Kern's *Oh, Boy!* (1917) then was featured on Broadway in Kern's *Rock-a-Bye Baby* (1918) before going to England where she played the leading roles in Kern's *Sally* (1921), *The Cabaret Girl* (1922), and *The Beauty Prize* (1923). Dickson was born in Kansas City, Missouri, and began her professional career as the ballroom dancing partner for her then husband Carl Hyson. The two were featured in *Oh, Boy!* and *Ziegfeld Follies* (1917). Dickson soon developed into a funny ingenue who found some fame in New York but was more successful in London. After becoming a West End star as Sally, she triumphed there in such musicals as *The Cabaret Girl, The Beauty Prize, Patricia* (1924), *Charlot's Revue* (1925), *Tip-Toes* (1926), *Peggy-Ann* (1927), *The Wonder Bar* (1930), *Casanova* (1932), and *Careless Rapture* (1936). Dickson also appeared in variety and in some non-musical plays, most memorably *Peter Pan*.

DIETZ, Howard. (1896–1983) Stage and film lyricist and writer. The incisive lyricist with two very different careers—as a leading songwriter, usually paired with composer Arthur Schwartz, and as an executive at MGM where he was in charge of publicity for over thirty years—he began his Broadway career as lyricist for Kern's *Dear Sir* (1924). Dietz was born in New York and studied journalism at Columbia University where he got involved with campus theatricals. While he wrote advertising slogans for companies, he penned lyrics as well and had a few songs interpolated into Broadway shows. Dietz came to Kern's attention through his witty pieces in the newspaper and the composer asked him to collaborate on *Dear Sir* (1924); the show was not a hit but it brought attention to Dietz and launched his career. He found wider success when he teamed up with Schwartz to score the innovative revue *The Little Show* (1929). The twosome also provided songs for the inventive revues *The Second Little Show* (1930), *The Band Wagon* (1931), *Flying Colors* (1932), *At Home Abroad* (1935), and *Inside U.S.A.* (1948). They had less success with their book musicals *Revenge with Music* (1934), *Between the Devil* (1937), *The Gay Life* (1961), and *Jennie* (1963), though some exceptional songs came from the scores. With composer Vernon Duke, Dietz provided the scores for the short-run musicals *Jackpot* (1944) and *Sadie Thompson* (1944). For many of these musicals Dietz also wrote the libretto or sketches. His advertising career at MGM ran parallel to his Broadway writing and on occasion he wrote for the movies, such as the screenplay for the musical *Hollywood Party* (1934) and the score for *Under Your Spell* (1936) with Schwartz. The songs from the Dietz-Schwartz stage revues were used in the Hollywood musicals *Dancing in the Dark* (1949) and *The Band Wagon* (1953), the team writing the new song "That's Entertainment" for the latter. The twosome also collaborated on the score for the TV musical *A Bell for Adano* (1956). Dietz's lyrics are known for their wit, intoxicating sense of mystery and romance, and ability to lead to dancing. He was married to costume designer Lucinda Ballard (1906–1993). Autobiography: *Dancing in the Dark* (1974).

DILLINGHAM, Charles [Bancroft]. (1868–1934) Stage producer. The prolific and tasteful presenter of some two hundred Broadway productions from the turn of the twentieth century into the 1930s, he produced over sixty musical shows, including ten by Kern. Dillingham was born in Hartford, Connecticut, the son of a minister, and worked as a journalist on various newspapers before turning to writing theatre reviews for the *New York Evening Sun*. After working as a press agent for producer **Charles Frohman** and a manager for actress Julia Marlowe, he took up producing on his own and presented new comedies and dramas, British imports, adaptations of foreign works, and all kinds of musicals. Dillingham's first Kern musical was

Miss Information (1915), followed by *Miss 1917* (1917), *She's a Good Fellow* (1919), *The Night Boat* (1920), *Good Morning, Dearie* (1920), *The Bunch and Judy* (1922), *Stepping Stones* (1923), *The City Chap* (1925), *Sunny* (1925), *Criss Cross* (1926), and *Lucky* (1927). Among his many other notable musical offerings are *Babette* (1903), *Mlle. Modiste* (1905), *The Red Mill* (1906), *The Tattooed Man* (1907), *The Lady of the Slipper* (1912), *Chin-Chin* (1914), *Watch Your Step* (1914), *Stop! Look! Listen!* (1915), *The Century Girl* (1916), *Jack O' Lantern* (1917), *Apple Blossoms* (1919), *Tip Top* (1920), *China Rose* (1925), *Oh, Please!* (1926), *Sidewalks of New York* (1927), *She's My Baby* (1928), *Ripples* (1930), and *New Faces* (1934). Dillingham also produced musical extravaganzas at the mammoth Hippodrome Theatre. He was wiped out in the stock market crash of 1929 and died a few years later.

DONAHUE, Jack. (1892–1930) Stage performer and writer. A rubber-limbed dancer who lit up a number of musicals, including Kern's *Sunny* (1925), he was on the brink of major stardom when he died at the age of thirty-eight. Donahue was born in Charlestown, Massachusetts, and was only eleven years old when he joined a medicine show. He danced in vaudeville and burlesque before making his Broadway debut in the chorus of *The Woman Haters* (1912), followed by the musicals *Angel Face* (1919), *Ziegfeld Follies* (1920), *Molly Darling* (1922), and *Be Yourself* (1924). Donahue was the romantic partner for **Marilyn Miller** in both *Sunny* and *Rosalie* (1928), then was starred in *Sons o' Guns* (1929). He wrote the libretto for the last show, as well as for *Princess Charming* (1930) that opened after his death. Autobiography: *Letters of a Hoofer to His Ma* (1911).

"Don't Ever Leave Me" is a romantic duet from *Sweet Adeline* (1929), the "gay nineties" operetta scored by Kern and lyricist **Oscar Hammerstein**. Addie Schmidt (**Helen Morgan**), a Broadway star with humble beginnings, sings this plea with society notable James Day (Robert Chisholm). Both Kern's music and Hammerstein's lyric are in the traditional operetta mode, which was going out of fashion but was appropriate for this nostalgic musical. **Irene Dunne** sang the ballad as a solo in the 1935 film version of *Sweet Adeline*, and in 1992 Judy Kaye and Davis Gaines made a memorable recording of the duet version. Other discs were made by Morgan, Barbara

Cook, Carmen McRae, Judy Garland, Peggy King, Philip Chaffin, Lew Stone, Margaret Whiting, Kelly Harland, Dorothy Kirsten, Sylvia Sims, Joan Morris and William Bolcom, Peggy Lee with George Shearing, Stanley Black, Andrea Marcovicci, Polly Bergen, and Joely Fisher.

DUNNE, Irene [Marie]. (1898–1990) Stage and screen performer. An aristocratic beauty with a flowing soprano voice, she might be considered the quintessential Kern actress-singer having appeared in more of his works than any other performer. Dunne was born in Louisville, Kentucky, the daughter of a steamship inspector and a musician, and raised and educated in rural Indiana. After studying at the Indianapolis Conservatory, she went to the Chicago Musical College to train as an opera singer. When she failed to get accepted by the Metropolitan Opera in New York in 1920, she turned to musical theatre and got a job as the title heroine in the national touring company of *Irene*. Dunne made her Broadway debut in 1922 and was featured in a half-dozen forgettable musicals, including Kern's ***The City Chap*** (1925), before getting cast as Magnolia in the 1929 tour of Kern's ***Show Boat***. She was so effective in the role that she got to reprise her performance in the 1936 screen version of the musical. Dunne never returned to Broadway but was seen in over forty movies, ranging from operettas to screwball farces to melodramas. Her Kern screen roles are the saloon singer Addie Schmidt in ***Sweet Adeline*** (1935), Princess Stephanie in ***Roberta*** (1935), the pioneer gal Sally Cortlandt in ***High, Wide and Handsome*** (1937), and the stage star Maggie Garret in ***Joy of Living*** (1938). Dunne was also a bankable movie star in non-musicals, praised for her fine performances in *Cimarron* (1931), *The Age of Innocence* (1934), *Theodora Goes Wild* (1936), *The Awful Truth* (1937), *Love Affair* (1939), *Anna and the King of Siam* (1946), *Life with Father* (1947), *I Remember Mama* (1948), *The Mudlark* (1950), and other films. Dunne retired in 1952 and concentrated on political causes, diplomacy (she was a UN delegate), charities, and business. Biography: *Irene Dunne: First Lady of Hollywood*, Wes D. Gehring (2003).

DURBIN, Deanna [née Edna Mae Durbin]. (1921–2013) Film performer. A classically trained singer who excelled at playing wholesome youths with a bubbly personality, she was one of the top box office attractions for a time and a leader in record sales. Arguably her best screen role was the defiant senator's daughter Caroline Frost in Kern's *Can't Help Singing* (1944). Durbin was born in Winnipeg, Canada, and raised in California where she showed a talent for singing at a young age. By the time she was fourteen she was starring in such screen musicals as *Three Smart Girls* (1935), *One Hundred Men and a Girl* (1937), *Mad About Music* (1938), *That Certain Age* (1938), *Three Smart Girls Grow Up* (1939), *First Love* (1939), *It's a Date* (1940), *Spring Parade* (1940), *Nice Girl!* (1941), and *It Started with Eve* (1941). As Durbin matured and her roles approached adulthood, she remained popular and starred in the musicals *The Amazing Mrs. Holliday* (1943), *Hers to Hold* (1943), *His Butler's Sister* (1943), *Can't Help Singing*, *Lady on a Train* (1945), *Because of Him* (1946), *I'll Be Yours* (1947), *Something in the Wind* (1947), *Up in Central Park* (1948), and *For the Love of Mary* (1948). At the age of twenty-seven, Durbin left films and retired to France where for decades she has refused film offers and requests for interviews. Biography: *Deanna Durbin: Fairy Tale*, W. E. Mills (1996).

"D'Ye Love Me?" is one of the hits to come out of Kern's Broadway musical *Sunny* (1925) where it was sung by the circus bareback rider Sunny Peters (**Marilyn Miller**) and the chorus. Kern's gentle, lullaby-like music is so pliable in its construction that the song was reprised later in the show as a waltz and then at another time as a fox trot. **Jack Donahue** did a dance routine to the song that stopped the show each evening. The lyric by **Oscar Hammerstein** and **Otto Harbach** uses slang in a playful manner, giving the song a jazz-age flair. Miller reprised "D'Ye Love Me?" in the 1930 screen version of *Sunny* and it was sung by Anna Neagle in the 1941 remake. Judy Garland recorded and filmed a version of the song for the Kern biopic *Till the Clouds Roll By* (1946) but it was cut from the final print. The number was originally listed as "Do You Love Me" in the Broadway program but used the slangy title when it was published and has been known as "D'Ye Love Me?" ever since. A distinctive recording of the song was made by Margaret Whiting.

"The Enchanted Train" is an inviting song by Kern and lyricist **P. G. Wodehouse** that is a tribute to, of all trains, the Long Island Railroad. The charming number was sung by sweethearts May Tolliver (Gertrude Bryan) and Bill Pennington (Rudolf Cameron) in *Sitting Pretty* (1924), the couple seeing the train as highly romantic because it was the commuter line that brought him home from work to their bungalow on Long Island. Kern's music is like a tingling lullaby, and Wodehouse's lyric is earnest and adoring. The song was listed as "The Magic Train" in the Broadway playbill but was later published and better known as "The Enchanted Train." Paige O'Hara and Davis Gaines made a pleasing recording of the duet in 1989 and there are also recordings by Hal Cazalet and songwriter Sheldon Harnick.

ERROL, Leon [né Leonce Errol Simms]. (1881–1951) Stage and film performer, director. An agile, sour-faced, and balding comic who was featured in Broadway musicals and revues and then enjoyed a successful film career, he became a Broadway star as the exiled grand duke "Connie" in Kern's *Sally* (1920). A native of Sydney, Australia, Errol was pursuing a medical degree at the local university when he went on the vaudeville stage to earn money for tuition. He was such a hit that he gave up medicine and soon was performing in circuses, Shakespeare plays, and comic operas. While touring in the States, he was hired by producer **Florenz Ziegfeld** to appear in the 1910 edition of the *Ziegfeld Follies*. Errol's rubber-legged drunk routine and other comic bits were so well received that he was featured in six later editions of the *Follies*, as well as in the revues *Hitchy-Koo* (1917 and 1918) and *Ziegfeld Midnight Frolic* (1921). Errol also shone in book musicals, as in *Sally, A Winsome Widow* (1912), *The Century Girl* (1916), *Louie the 14th* (1925), *Yours Truly* (1927), and *Fioretta* (1929), some of which he also cowrote. Errol was also a respected director and staged sections of the *Follies* revues as well as the musicals *Words and Music* (1917) and *The Blue Kitten* (1922). He made his film debut as a specialty act in *Paramount on*

Parade (1930), followed by many comedy shorts, then two dozen musicals in which he usually played harassed and henpecked husbands, including *We're Not Dressing* (1934), *Coronado* (1935), *Melody Lane* (1941), *Strictly in the Groove* (1943), *Higher and Higher* (1943), *Babes on Swing Street* (1944), *Riverboat Rhythm* (1946), and *Footlight Varieties* (1951).

EULOGY for Kern. **Oscar Hammerstein** delivered the following eulogy at the funeral services for Jerome Kern on November 12, 1945.

"I have promised myself not to play upon your emotions—or on mine. We, in this chapel, are Jerry's 'family.' We all know him very well. Each of us knows what the other has lost. I think he would have liked me to say a few words about him. I think he would not have liked me to offer feeble bromides of consolation—butterfly wings of trite condolence to beat against the solid wall of our grief. He would have known our grief was real, and must be faced. On the other hand, I think Jerry would have liked me to remind you that today's mourning and last week's vigil will soon recede from our memories, in favor of the bright recollections of him that belong to us.

"At the moment, Jerry is playing 'out of character.' The masque of tragedy was never intended for him. His death yesterday and this reluctant epilogue will soon be refocused into their properly remote place in the picture. This episode will soon seem to us to be nothing more than a fantastic and dream-like intrusion on the gay reality that was Jerry's life.

"His gayety is what we will remember most—the times he has made us laugh; the even greater fun of making him laugh. It's a strange adjective to apply to a man, but you'll understand what I mean: Jerry was 'cute.' He was alert and alive. He 'bounced.' He stimulated everyone. He annoyed some, never bored anyone at any time. There was a sharp eye to everything he thought or said.

"We all know in our hearts that these few minutes we devote to him now are small drops in the ocean of our affections. Our real tribute will be paid over many years of remembering, of telling good stories about him, and thinking about him when we are by ourselves.

"We, in this chapel, will cherish our special knowledge of this world figure. We will remember a jaunty, happy man whose sixty years were crowded with success and fun and love. We thank whatever God we believe in that we shared some part of the good, bright life Jerry led on this earth."

"Every Little While" is a neglected Kern ballad that was the victim of film audience's loss of interest in musicals in the very early 1930s. Lyricist **Otto Harbach** and Kern wrote the poignant love duet for the movie *Men of the Sky* (1931), a musical melodrama about flying aces, where it was sung by American pilot Jack Ames (**Jack Whiting**) and French lass Madeleine (Irene Delroy). But musicals had become box office poison by 1931 so the studio cut all the songs and released the film as a drama. Not until years later was the song published and praised for its gently flowing melody that climaxes with a series of cascading triplets. "Every Little While" was recorded by Blythe Walker in 1990 and by George Dvorsky and Jeanne Lehman in 1993.

FIELDS, Dorothy. (1904–1974) Stage and film lyricist and writer. An astute, highly gifted songwriter who did some of her finest work with Kern, she had one of the longest Broadway careers in the history of the American musical, from 1928 to 1973. Fields was born in Allenhurst, New Jersey, the daughter of the celebrated stage comic and producer Lew Fields, and as a boarding school student she wrote light verse. In the late 1920s she teamed up with composer Jimmy McHugh, and some of their songs were introduced at the Cotton Club in Harlem in 1927. The next year they scored the popular Broadway revue *Blackbirds of 1928*, which introduced "I Can't Give You Anything but Love" and other memorable songs. The team provided the score for *Hello, Daddy* (1928) and *International Revue* (1930), then they went to Hollywood where they scored the musicals *Love in the Rough* (1930), *Cuban Love Song* (1931), *Hooray for Love* (1935), and *Every Night at Eight* (1935). Fields worked with Kern for the first time when they wrote some additional songs for the 1935 screen version of **Roberta** and they would re-team for **I Dream Too Much** (1935), **Swing Time** (1936), **Joy of Living** (1938), and **One Night in the Tropics** (1940). She returned to Broadway to coauthor with her brother Herbert Fields the librettos for the musical hits *Let's Face It!* (1941), *Something for the Boys* (1943), *Mexican Hayride* (1944), and *Annie Get Your Gun* (1946). Fields collaborated with composer Arthur Schwartz on the Broadway musicals *Stars in Your Eyes* (1939), *A Tree Grows in Brooklyn* (1951), and *By the Beautiful Sea* (1954), with Sigmund Romberg on *Up in Central Park* (1945), with Morton Gould on *Arms and the Girl* (1950), and with Albert Hague on *Redhead* (1959). In Hollywood she worked with various composers on the scores for *In Person* (1935), *The King Steps Out* (1936), *Mr. Imperium* (1951), *Excuse My Dust* (1951), *Texas Carnival* (1951), and *The Farmer Takes a Wife* (1953), as well as the TV musical *Junior Miss* (1953). Just when most thought Fields was going to retire, she teamed up with the much-younger Cy Coleman and wrote vivacious scores for the Broadway musicals *Sweet Charity* (1966) and

Seesaw (1973). Among her many song standards are "On the Sunny Side of the Street," "Exactly Like You," " Hey Big Spender," **"Never Gonna Dance,"** **"A Fine Romance,"** and **"The Way You Look Tonight,"** the first song by a female songwriter to win the Oscar for Best Song. Fields was a practical craftsman when writing stage librettos and a prodigious talent with lyric writing, equally at home with character songs, romantic ballads, and jazz-flavored dance numbers. Few have made the crossover from one medium to another and from one decade to another so effortlessly. Her other brother was writer Joseph Fields. Biography: *On the Sunny Side of the Street*, Deborah Grace Winer (1997).

"A Fine Romance" is the marvelous comic-romantic duet from Kern's movie musical *Swing Time* (1936) and a unique number because of its integration into the plot. Lyricist **Dorothy Fields** subtitled the duet "a sarcastic love song" and it afforded **Fred Astaire** and **Ginger Rogers** perhaps their finest non-dancing musical number. The song was actually cut up with bits of dialogue, making it a true musical scene, as gambler Lucky Garnett (Astaire) and dance instructor Penny Carrol (Rogers) walked through a snowy woodland setting and sang about the strange (or lack of) romance they were experiencing. Kern's delectable music abandons his usual operetta melody line and opts instead for a brief grouping of notes with longer intervals. According to musicologist Alec Wilder, the music "keeps piling up, tossing in pleasantries and surprises, and has a wonderful quality of uninterrupted movement." Fields's lyric (which was, atypical for Kern, written before the music was composed) is among her finest as she explores funny but apt metaphors, such as chilly as leftover mashed potatoes or difficult to steer as the *Ile de France*. Even the title is ambiguous; critic Philip Furia suggests it is taken from the expression "a fine kettle of fish" and thereby is meant to be sarcastic from the start. Astaire's solo recording reached number one on the charts, and Bing Crosby and Dixie Lee made a successful duet recording that was very popular. The dozens of other discs over the years include those by Guy Lombardo and his Royal Canadians, Billie Holiday, Christina Lind, jazz pianist Beegie Adair, Kiri Te Kanawa, jazz violinist Joe Venuti, Frederica von Stade, Oscar Peterson, Ann Hampton Callaway, and duet versions by Ella Fitzgerald and Louis Armstrong, Johnny Mercer and Martha Stilton, Mel Tormé and Janet Waldo, and Roger Rees and Jane

Carr. Michael Feinstein's 1988 solo disc utilized a restored lost verse for Astaire that was not used in the film. Virginia O'Brien gave a droll rendition of "A Fine Romance" in the Kern biopic *Till the Clouds Roll By* (1945) and the number was heard on the soundtrack of the films *Another Woman* (1988), *The Adventures of Priscilla, Queen of the Desert* (1994), and *Around the Bend* (2004). David Kernan and Elaine Delmar sang it in the London revue *Jerome Kern Goes to Hollywood* (1985) and Scott Holmes performed it with Delmar on Broadway the next year, and it was sung by two couples, Noah Racey with Nancy Lemenager and Peter Geraty with Karen Ziemba, in the Broadway version of *Swing Time* titled *Never Gonna Dance* (2003).

"The Folks Who Live on the Hill" (1937) is a domestic ballad of married devotion that Kern and **Oscar Hammerstein** wrote for the pioneer film musical *High, Wide and Handsome* (1937). **Irene Dunne**, as the nineteenth-century Pennsylvania woman Sally, sang the tender number about growing old together to her new husband Peter (**Randolph Scott**) as they sat on their hill and dreamed of the future. Kern's music is appropriately simple and wistful, and Hammerstein's lyric is filled with the kind of rural charm he would develop further six years later in *Oklahoma!* (1943). Although written for the mid-1880s setting of the film, the ballad echoed the sentiments of many Americans slowly coming out of the Depression and the song was very popular. Bing Crosby, Maxine Sullivan, Guy Lombardo and his Royal Canadians, Stan Getz, Mel Tormé, Jo Stafford, Sammy Davis, Jr., Arthur Prysock, and Ozzie Nelson (vocal by Harriet Hilliard) were among those who made early discs of the song, and more recent recordings by Peggy Lee, Mel Tormé, Judy Kaye with David Green, Bette Midler, Kiri Te Kanawa, Diana Krall, Thomas Hampson, Jimmy Scott, Sylvia McNair, Andrea Marcovicci, Johnny Mathis, and Tony Bennett have shown that the song has lost none of its power. Scott Holmes sang the ballad in the Broadway revue *Jerome Kern Goes to Hollywood* (1986) and the number was heard in the movies *Children* (1976) and *Random Hearts* (1999).

FREED, Arthur [né Arthur Grossman]. (1894–1973) Film producer, lyricist. Arguably the most influential producer of Hollywood musicals, he presented the Kern musicals *Till the Clouds Roll By* (1946) and *Show Boat* (1951). A native of Charleston, South Carolina, he began his career as a song plugger for a music publisher then performed in vaudeville before enlisting in the service during World War I. After the armistice, Freed returned to vaudeville where he started writing song lyrics for his act and for others. His first hit song, "I Cried for You," came out in 1923, but Freed changed careers again and went to Hollywood where he directed silent films. With the coming of sound, MGM hired him to write lyrics for original songs to be featured in the talkies. With composer Nacio Herb Brown, he wrote the scores for early film musicals such as *The Broadway Melody* (1929), *Hollywood Revue of 1929* (1929), *Good News!* (1930), *Going Hollywood* (1933), *Broadway Melody of 1936* (1935), and *Broadway Melody of 1938* (1937). After serving as coproducer for the classic *The Wizard of Oz* (1939), Freed abandoned lyric writing for producing. He established the celebrated "Freed Unit" at MGM and for the next twenty years presented some of the greatest of all Hollywood musicals, including *Babes in Arms* (1939), *For Me and My Gal* (1942), *Cabin in the Sky* (1943), *Meet Me in St. Louis* (1945), *The Harvey Girls* (1946), *Good News!* (1947), *Easter Parade* (1948), *On the Town* (1949), *Annie Get Your Gun* (1950), *An American in Paris* (1951), *Singin' in the Rain* (1952), *The Band Wagon* (1953), and *Gigi* (1958). Biography: *The Movies' Greatest Musicals: Produced in Hollywood U.S.A. by the Freed Unit*, Hugh Fordin (1984).

FROHMAN, Charles. (1860–1915) Stage producer and manager. A much-admired and respected presenter of theatre on both sides of the Atlantic, the enterprising producer offered Broadway thirty musicals during his career, as well as another thirteen in London, and can be said to have discovered Kern. Frohman was born in Sandusky, Ohio, the son of a traveling peddler, and went to New York at the age of twelve to work for various newspapers. By 1877 he was helping to book touring theatre productions, and with his brothers Daniel and Gustave, eventually managed the prestigious Madison Square Theatre in Manhattan. Frohman began producing in 1888 and over the next three decades presented new American plays, vehicles for stars, foreign-language works adapted for Broadway, British hits, and musicals, including *His Excellency* (1895), *The Girl from Up There* (1901), *Three Little Maids* (1903), *The Rich Mr. Hoggenheimer* (1906), *The Hoyden* (1907), *The Dollar Princess* (1909), *The Arcadians* (1910), *The Girl from Montmartre* (1912), *The Marriage Market* (1913), *The Laughing Husband*

(1914), and *The Girl from Utah* (1914). It was in this last musical that Frohman hired Kern to write some new songs for the Broadway version of the London show. Kern's **"They Didn't Believe Me"** was the hit of the musical and brought Kern recognition. Frohman used Kern songs in a handful of his shows but died before ever commissioning the composer to write a full score for him. He managed theatres in New York and London and was famous for creating and nurturing stars such as Ethel Barrymore, Maude Adams, and John Drew, and for the high quality and good taste of his productions. Frohman was at the height of his career when he drowned during the sinking of the *Lusitania*. Biography: *Charles Frohman: Manager and Man*, Isaac F. Marcosson and Daniel Frohman (1916/2009).

"Gallivantin' Aroun'" is a pastiche of a "coon song" that was added to the 1936 movie version of Kern's *Show Boat*. Originally the banjo-strumming number was to be sung by Magnolia to a group of young ladies about how to make a beau jealous by acting wild. In the final print, the number was sung by Magnolia (**Irene Dunne**) in blackface as a performance on the *Cotton Blossom* stage. Filmed, but cut and now lost, was a reprise of the song delivered by Magnolia's grown daughter Kim (Sunnie O'Dea) as a jazz number. Kern's music is vibrant and accurately folksy. The lyric by **Oscar Hammerstein**, written in Negro dialect, is about the free-spirited Liza Matilda Hill who parties all night in Louisville, making her boyfriend angry until she admits that loving him is more fun than "gallivantin' aroun'."

GARDELLA, Tess. (1897?–1950) Stage performer. A white character actress and singer who often appeared on stage in blackface under the name Aunt Jemima, she created the role of the no-nonsense cook Queenie in the original production of Kern's *Show Boat* (1927) and reprised her performance in the prologue of the 1929 screen version and in the 1932 Broadway revival. Gardella was born in Wilkes-Barre, Pennsylvania, and started singing on stage at a young age. She created the character of the bossy African American Aunt Jemima who wore a bandana, sang, and did comic monologues in vaudeville. Gardella's characterization was so well established that producer George White hired her to do her act on Broadway in *George White's Scandals* (1921). Her characterization was so believable that she was hired to play Queenie in *Show Boat*, the only blackface performer in the large cast. Gardella made a handful of movie shorts in the 1930s as Aunt Jemima but also appeared as a white character in some others, most memorably the film *A Swing Opera* (1939) in which she played the Gypsy Queen.

GARDNER, Ava [Lavinia]. (1922–1990) Film performer. One of Hollywood's most glamorous movie stars of the 1940s and 1950s, she appeared in several musicals even though her singing had to be dubbed, as when she played the tragic Julie LaVerne in *Show Boat* (1951). Gardner was born in rural North Carolina, the daughter of a tobacco farmer and the youngest of seven siblings, and was strikingly beautiful by the time she was a teenager. When her brother-in-law put a picture of her in his New York photography studio, Gardner was spotted by an MGM agent who put her under contract even though she had no acting experience. Gardner appeared in bit parts for seventeen years before she was featured in *The Killers* (1946) and quickly became popular. Of her more than seventy movies, eight were musicals, and her finest performance in them was as the mulatto Julie in *Show Boat*. Autobiography: *Ava: My Story* (1992); biographies: *Ava Gardner*, John Daniell (1984); *Ava Gardner: Love Is Nothing*, Lee Server (2007); *Ava Gardner: Touches of Venus*, Gilbert L. Gigliotti (2010).

GENTLEMEN UNAFRAID. A musical play by **Oscar Hammerstein, Otto Harbach** (book and lyrics); Jerome Kern (music). [3 June 1938, Municipal Opera, St. Louis, 8 performances] Produced by the "Muny" Opera, directed by Zeke Colvan, choreographed by Theodor Adolphus and Al White, Jr., musical direction by George Hirst, orchestrations by **Robert Russell Bennett**. An ambitious musical with a historical and expansive musical sweep, *Gentlemen Unafraid* was one of Kern's last stage projects. When the Civil War breaks out, some of the cadets at West Point Academy find themselves torn between two loyalties: the U.S. Army and their Southern homeland. Cadet Bob Vance (Ronald Graham) from Virginia has a further dilemma: although he wants to remain loyal to the Union, his sweetheart back home, Linda Mason (Hope Manning), urges him to return and fight for the Confederacy. After much thought, Bob decides to remain in the North, and only after the war is over does he learn that Linda was faithful to him and the two are finally reunited. The score was equally ambitious, with such expert numbers as the spiritual "De Land o' Good Times," the catchy period piece "What Kind of Soldier Are You?," the stirring "Abe Lincoln Has Just One Country," the torchy "Mister Man," and the lovely ballad **"Your Dream."** Although several Broadway producers were interested in the property, none would commit to such an expensive and serious musical. So Kern and his collaborators mounted *Gentlemen Unafraid* in St. Louis at the huge outdoor Municipal Opera. The story was indeed serious, but many found it well written and moving. There was even higher praise for the score. Several New York producers traveled to see the one-week engagement, and worthy as they found the musical, it was deemed too risky for the current Broadway climate. Sadly, *Gentlemen Unafraid* never made it to New York and was never recorded. The song "Your Dream (Is the Same as My Dream)" was later heard in the Kern movie musical *One Night in the Tropics* (1940) and the patriotic "Abe Lincoln Has Just One Country" was used during World War II by the Treasury Department to promote defense bonds and stamps. *Gentlemen Unafraid* was one of Hammerstein's greatest disappointments and for many years after he and Harbach rewrote and polished the script, hoping to see it performed on Broadway someday. In 1942 a production, now titled *Hayfoot, Strawfoot,* was presented by Syracuse University and a few others colleges followed suit during the war years, but the musical remains a neglected masterwork by three of the American theatre's most accomplished songwriters.

GERSHWIN, Ira [né Israel Gershwin]. (1896–1983) Stage and film lyricist. Too often overshadowed by his composer brother George Gershwin, the meticulous, gifted songwriter was one of the finest American lyricists and contributed to many innovative or landmark musicals, both on stage and in Hollywood where he collaborated with Kern on *Cover Girl* (1944). Gershwin was born in Brooklyn and started writing light verse and lyrics while a student at Columbia University. Since his brother was gaining notoriety as a popular composer, Ira wrote under the penman Arthur Francis so as not to ride on his fame. His first Broadway score was for *Two Little Girls in Blue* (1921) with composer Vincent Youmans, then he teamed up with his brother for *Lady, Be Good!* (1924), the first of a series of jazz-influenced scores they wrote for Broadway. The brothers' subsequent shows together were *Tell Me More!* (1925), *Tip-Toes* (1925), *Oh, Kay!* (1926), *Funny Face* (1927), *Rosalie* (1928), *Treasure Girl* (1928), *Show Girl* (1929), *Strike Up the Band* (1930), *Girl Crazy* (1930), *Of Thee I Sing* (1931), *Pardon My English* (1933), and *Let 'Em Eat Cake* (1933). Ira Gershwin collaborated with other composers on the London musical *That's a Good Girl* (1928) and the Broadway revue *Life Begins at 8:40* (1934), then the brothers teamed with lyricist DuBose Heyward to write the American folk opera *Porgy and Bess* (1935). The brothers went to Hollywood during the Depression to score films together, but Ira returned to Broadway to write songs for *Ziegfeld Follies* (1936) with composer Vernon Duke. The Gershwins wrote the scores for the Hollywood musicals *Shall We Dance* (1937), *Damsel in Distress* (1937), and *The Goldwyn Follies* (1938) before George's untimely death. It took time for Ira Gershwin to recover from the loss of his brother and primary collaborator, but by 1941 he was back on Broadway with the innovative *Lady in the Dark* (1941) with music by Kurt Weill. The two re-teamed for the short-lived *The Firebrand of Florence* (1945), then Gershwin suffered a second flop with *Park Avenue* (1946) with composer Arthur Schwartz. The two failures ended his stage career, but Gershwin remained active in Hollywood for another decade. He wrote lyrics from some of his brother's "trunk" music for *The Shocking Miss Pilgrim* (1947), then collaborated with various composers on *The Barkleys of Broadway* (1949), *Give a Girl a Break* (1953), *A Star Is Born* (1954), and *The Country Girl* (1954). Perhaps the most inventive of his Hollywood projects was *Cover Girl* for which he and Kern provided a superb score. Gershwin retired in 1954, though musicals using his old songs surfaced on the screen, as with *Funny Face* (1957), *Kiss Me, Stupid* (1964), and *When the Boys Meet the Girls* (1965), and on Broadway with *My One and Only* (1983), *Crazy for You* (1992), and *Nice Work If You Can Get It* (2012). Among Ira Gershwin's many talents were his unique use of slang in lyric writing, an ingenious turn of phrase in his romantic songs, and a satirical wit that was accurate and delightful. Although he did not write an autobiography, his ideas about songwriting and his past shows are revealed in his book *Lyrics on Several Occasions* (1959). Biographies: *The Gershwin Years*, Edward Jablonski, Lawrence Stewart (1973); *Fascinating Rhythm: The Collaboration of George and Ira Gershwin*, Deena Ruth Rosenberg (1998).

THE GIRL FROM UTAH. A musical comedy by James T. Tanner (book); Percy Greenbank, Adrian Ross, etc. (lyrics); Paul Rubens, Sydney Jones, Jerome Kern (music). [24 August 1914, Knickerbocker Theatre, 120 performances] Produced by **Charles Frohman**, directed by J. A. E. Malone, musical direction by Gustave Salzer. A British import of minor importance, the musical contained five songs by the young Kern, the most yet heard in one Broadway score. The libretto was about the American girl Una Trance (**Julia Sanderson**) who runs away from her Mormon husband in Salt Lake

City and goes to England where she falls in love with Sandy Blair (**Donald Brian**), the dashing leading man at the Gaiety Theatre. The British score by Rubens, Jones, Greenbank, and Adrian Ross was considered weak by American producer Frohman, so he hired the unknown Kern to write a handful of new songs for the Broadway production. One of them was **"They Didn't Believe Me,"** one of the most influential songs in the history of the American theatre. The ballad introduced a modern 4/4 time that broke away from the waltz tempo and created the pattern for musical comedy songs for the next fifty years. Kern's other contributions to *The Girl from Utah* were the slightly swinging "Same Sort of Girl," the plaintive ballad "You Never Can Tell," the stomping "Why Don't They Dance the Polka?," and the romantic "Land of Let's Pretend" that opened and closed the show. Although the critical reaction to *The Girl from Utah* was not enthusiastic, audiences enjoyed the show and it ran for nearly four months. Much of the credit can be attributed to Kern's interpolations. Sanderson made early recordings of "They Didn't Believe Me" and "Same Sort of Girl," and there were medley recordings of highlights of the score made by the Chappell Light Opera Company in 1913 and the Victor Light Opera Company in 1938.

"A Girl Is on Your Mind" is a captivating choral number from Kern's Broadway musical *Sweet Adeline* (1929) that makes for a thrilling musical sequence utilizing the male characters in the show—Jim (Robert Chisholm), Thornton (Jim Thornton), Tom (Max Hoffman, Jr.), and Sid (John D. Seymour)—and the male chorus. In a turn-of-the-century New York City tavern, the men gather to forget that special girl who cannot be forgotten. They question each other's strange behavior and offer each other consoling drinks, but they always come to the same realization: some girl is always on your mind. At one point in the nearly seven-minute sequence, tavern singer Addie (**Helen Morgan**) appears and sings a similar lament from the feminine point of view. Kern's music is stirring and blues-flavored while the lyric by **Oscar Hammerstein** is succinct and never exaggerated, resulting in a remarkable musical sequence. *Sweet Adeline* had a disappointing run on Broadway due to the stock market crash a month after it opened, so the song did not catch on. An abridged version of the song was titled "Pretty Jenny Lee" and was sung by a barbershop quartet in the 1935 movie version of the musical, but the enticing number was rarely recorded and seemed to fade from memory.

Conductor John McGlinn's 1992 recording with reconstructed orchestrations, using the alternate title "Some Girl Is on Our Mind," brought the song newfound recognition. The recording featured Cris Groenendaal, Brent Barrett, George Dvorsky, Davis Gaines, and Judy Kaye.

GOOD MORNING, DEARIE*. A musical comedy by **Anne Caldwell** (book and lyrics), Jerome Kern (music). [1 November 1921, Globe Theatre, 347 performances] Produced by **Charles Dillingham**, directed by **Edward Royce**, musical direction by Victor Baravalle, orchestrations by Stephen Jones. A better-than-average story and a pleasing score made *Good Morning, Dearie* one of the best book musicals of its season. High society lad Billy Van Cortlandt (**Oscar Shaw**) is betrothed to the well-connected Ruby Manners (Peggy Kurton), but he has fallen hopelessly in love with Rose-Marie (**Louise Groody**), a couturiere's assistant who is promised to the crook Chesty Costello (Harlan Dixon). When Chesty gets out of prison, he plots to steal the jewels belonging to Mrs. Greyson Parks (Roberta Beatty) during a crowded house party. Billy and Rose-Marie catch Chesty in the act and agree to not turn him in to the police if he will give up Rose-Marie. Chesty agrees, Ruby weds Billy's cousin George (John Price Jones), and Billy and Rose-Marie anticipate a honeymoon at Niagara Falls. The cast was filled with talent and the songs were mostly expert, the pseudo-Hawaiian **"Ka-lu-a"** becoming the most popular. The two-part harmony number "Blue Danube Blues," the sprightly "Didn't You Believe?," and the charming title song were also applauded by the press and the public. *Good Morning, Dearie* received glowing notices and ran for over ten months.

GORDON, Max [né Mechel Salpeter]. (1892–1978) Stage producer. The flamboyant Broadway producer who had the temperament of an actor, he produced some of the most distinctive musicals of the 1930s, including Kern's ***The Cat and the Fiddle*** (1931), ***Roberta*** (1933), and ***Very Warm for May*** (1939). The native New Yorker started in show business as a press agent then became a talent agent in vaudeville before joining up with Sam H. Harris to produce plays and musicals. Later he would go solo and become one of the most successful producers of his era. Most of Gordon's musical credits were in the 1930s when revues flourished, and his offerings in that genre were among the best: *Three's a Crowd* (1930), *The Band Wagon*

(1931), *Flying Colors* (1932), and *Sing Out the News* (1938). His book musicals were *The Cat and the Fiddle*, *Roberta*, *The Great Waltz* (1934), *Jubilee* (1935), *Very Warm for May*, *The Firebrand of Florence* (1945), *Hollywood Pinafore* (1945), and *Park Avenue* (1946). In the 1940s he concentrated on comedies, such as *My Sister Eileen* (1940) and *Born Yesterday* (1945). Autobiography: *Max Gordon Presents* (1963).

GRAYSON, Kathryn [neé Zelma Kathryn Elizabeth Hedrick]. (1922–2010) Film singer, actress. An attractive coloratura in 1940s and 1950s movie musicals, she gave perhaps her finest performance as Magnolia in the 1951 screen version of Kern's ***Show Boat***. Born in Winston-Salem, North Carolina, she began her career singing on the radio. Hollywood signed her in 1941 and the next year she was playing the title heroine in *Rio Rita*. Grayson was featured in the Kern bio-musical ***Till the Clouds Roll By*** (1946) and played Stephanie in ***Lovely to Look At*** (1952). Her other screen musicals include *Anchors Aweigh* (1945), *It Happened in Brooklyn* (1947), *The Toast of New Orleans* (1950), *Kiss Me, Kate* (1953), *The Desert Song* (1953), *So This Is Love* (1953), and *The Vagabond King* (1956). Grayson left films in the 1950s and concentrated on stage, concert, and nightclub appearances, though she played some television roles through the 1980s. She was married to singer-actor Johnny Johnston (1915–1996).

GROODY, Louise. (1897–1961) Stage performer. A spirited singer-dancer in stage musicals in the 1920s, she was known for her dimpled good looks and exuberant dancing, as witnessed in the Kern musicals ***Toot-Toot!*** (1918), ***The Night Boat*** (1920), and ***Good Morning, Dearie*** (1921). Groody was born in Waco, Texas, and educated in San Antonio before heading to New York where she became a cabaret dancer. Her act became so popular that producers featured her in several musicals before she got her two best roles: the unconventional Nanette in *No, No, Nanette* (1925) and the determined saloon gal Loulou in *Hit the Deck!* (1927). After appearing in a few non-musicals on Broadway, Groody turned to vaudeville for the rest of her career.

GROSSMITH, George, Jr. (1874–1935) Stage producer, performer, writer, director, lyricist, manager. One of the most versatile and successful

figures of the London musical stage in the first decades of the twentieth century, he worked with Kern in different capacities on five West End shows.
He was born in London, the son of the famous D'Oyly Carte performer
George Grossmith who originated several Gilbert and Sullivan roles. The
younger Grossmith made his stage debut at the age of eighteen in one of his
father's productions, and soon he developed the character of the London
top-hatted, monocled dandy Bertie who was featured in several musicals.
He often wrote his own scripts and lyrics, later moving into management
so that by 1914 he was also producing his shows. Grossmith first worked
with Kern as producer, writer, and performer in *Theodore & Co.* (1916). He
produced *Oh, Joy!* (1919), the London version of Broadway's **Oh, Boy!**,
then was featured as the sly lawyer Otis Hooper in the West End production
of **Sally** (1921). Grossmith also wrote, produced, and appeared in Kern's
The Cabaret Girl (1922) and **The Beauty Prize** (1923). Among his many
other London musicals were *The Shop Girl* (1894), *A Night Out* (1920), *Tell
Me More* (1925), *No, No, Nanette* (1925), *Kid Boots* (1926), and *Princess
Charming* (1930). Some of Grossmith's shows transferred to Broadway,
where he appeared in two of them. He acted in several non-musicals, managed theatres in London, most notably the Gaiety Theatre, Winter Garden,
and Royal Drury Lane, and even produced and acted in films for a time.
Grossmith might be termed the "George M. Cohan of the London stage" for
his remarkably eclectic career. Autobiography: *GG* (1933).

HALL, Bettina (1906–1997) and **Natalie HALL** (1904–1994). Stage performers. Two sisters popular in Broadway musicals in the 1930s, each played leading ladies in different Kern musicals. Bettina was a pretty, clear-voiced musical comedy singer-actress who also had credits in operetta and opera. She was born in North Easton, Massachusetts, and by the age of twenty was singing professionally in Gilbert and Sullivan operettas, appearing on Broadway in *Iolanthe* (1927), *The Mikado* (1927), and *The Pirates of Penzance* (1927). She sang major opera roles for the American Opera Company then returned to Broadway for a series of musicals, including *The Little Show* (1929) and *Meet My Sister* (1930). Hall was most remembered for playing the American composer Shirley Sheridan in Kern's ***The Cat and the Fiddle*** (1931) and the at-sea heroine Hope Harcourt in *Anything Goes* (1934). Her other musicals include *The Only Girl* (1934) and *Susanna, Don't You Cry* (1939). Her sister Natalie Hall was born in Providence, Rhode Island, and also appeared in opera before making her Broadway debut in 1930. Her most notable role was the temperamental diva Frieda Hatzfeld in Kern's ***Music in the Air*** (1932). Her other New York musicals include *Through the Years* (1932) and *Music Hath Charms* (1934). The Hall sisters performed in only one Broadway show together, *Three Little Girls* (1929). Both sisters wed wealthy men and retired from the stage at a young age.

HAMMERSTEIN, Oscar [né Greeley Clendenning], **II.** (1895–1960) Stage, film, and television lyricist, playwright. Arguably the American musical theatre's premiere lyricist and librettist, some of his finest works were in collaboration with Kern. Hammerstein was born in New York City into a famous theatrical family; his grandfather was the colorful theatre and opera impresario Oscar Hammerstein I and his uncle Arthur Hammerstein was a prosperous Broadway producer. He was educated at Columbia University to become a lawyer, but his involvement in the campus theatre productions convinced him to follow in the family profession. Hammerstein began as a stage manager for his uncle's productions, then took up writing non-musical plays but with no success. He wrote his first lyrics and libretto for the short-lived *Always You* (1920) and followed it with a forty-year career writing all forms of musicals, from operettas to musical comedy to the musical play, which he pretty much invented with **Show Boat**. Hammerstein usually wrote both the book and the lyrics for his shows, sometimes collaborating with more experienced writers such as **Otto Harbach** during the first half of his career. He also collaborated with many of the major composers of the American theatre. With Herbert Stothart he wrote *Tickle Me* (1920), *Jimmie* (1920), and *Daffy Dill* (1922). He collaborated with Rudolf Friml on *Rose-Marie* (1924) and *The Wild Rose* (1926); with George Gershwin on *Song of the Flame* (1925); with Vincent Youmans on *Wildflower* (1923), *Mary Jane McKane* (1923), and *Rainbow* (1928); and with Sigmund Romberg on *The Desert Song* (1926), *The New Moon* (1928), *East Wind* (1931), *May Wine* (1935), and *Sunny River* (1941). One of the most fruitful of Hammerstein's collaborations was with Kern, resulting in **Sunny** (1925), *Show Boat* (1927), **Sweet Adeline** (1929), **Music in the Air** (1932), and **Very Warm for May** (1939), as well as the London musical **Three Sisters** (1934) and the ambitious **Gentlemen Unafraid** (1938), which never made it to Broadway. Hammerstein's most famous partnership was with composer Richard Rodgers, the two first working together on Broadway with the landmark *Oklahoma!* (1943), followed by *Carousel* (1945), *Allegro* (1947), *South Pacific* (1949), *The King and I* (1951), *Me and Juliet* (1953), *Pipe Dream* (1955), *Flower Drum Song* (1958), and *The Sound of Music* (1959). The duo also scored the film musical *State Fair* (1945); the television musical *Cinderella* (1957); produced plays and musicals on Broadway, most memorably *Annie Get Your Gun* (1946); and supervised the film versions of their stage hits. Hammerstein even had a surprise hit with *Carmen Jones* (1943), an American version of the opera *Carmen*. He saw most of his early works filmed by Hollywood, but his original movie musicals were rarely successes at the box office. With Romberg he wrote original scores for *Viennese Nights* (1930), *Children of Dreams* (1931), and *The Night Is Young* (1935), and with Kern he scored **High, Wide and Handsome** (1937). Hammerstein also contributed to other screen musicals, including *Give Us This Night* (1936), *Swing High, Swing Low* (1937), *The Great Waltz* (1938), *The Lady Objects* (1938), and *The Story of Vernon and Irene Castle* (1939). Hammerstein directed his stage musicals on occasion, though often he was uncredited, as in the case of *Show Boat* and *The King and I*. The contribution Hammerstein made to the American musical cannot be overestimated. He brought an integrity to the stage libretto, raised the level of truthfulness in operetta books, created the serious musical play, introduced the integrated musical, and left a model for musical play construction that has served artists ever since. Biographies: *Getting to Know Him: A Biography of Oscar Hammerstein II*, Hugh Fordin (1977); *The Hammersteins*, Oscar Andrew Hammerstein (2010).

HARBACH, Otto [né Otto Abels Hauerbach]. (1873–1963) Stage lyricist, librettist. One of the first musical theatre craftsmen to aim for better books and lyrics on Broadway, he collaborated with Kern on his two most successful shows of the 1930s: *The Cat and the Fiddle* (1931) and *Roberta* (1932). Harbach was born in Salt Lake City, Utah, to Danish immigrant parents and worked his way through Knox College, teaching English and public speaking after graduation at Whitman College in the state of Washington. In 1901 he moved to New York City to take graduate courses at Columbia University, but soon his money ran out and he took a series of jobs, mostly writing for small newspapers. When Harbach discovered Broadway and musical comedy, he shifted his attention to writing lyrics and librettos and had some success with his first collaborator, composer Karl Hoschna. Their most memorable musical was *Madame Sherry* (1910), which produced the song standard "Every Little Movement (Has a Meaning All Its Own)." Hoschna died young so Harbach turned to other composers and cowriters. Between 1908 and 1936, he wrote over forty musicals (in 1925 he had five shows running on Broadway) with composers Rudolf Friml, Kern, Louis Hirsch, Herbert Stothart, Vincent Youmans, George Gershwin, Sigmund Romberg, and others. Harbach first worked with the young **Oscar Hammerstein** in 1920, teaching him the craft of lyric writing, urging him toward librettos that were more integrated with the songs, and approaching musical theatre writing as a serious art form. Many of the lessons Hammerstein learned lasted him throughout his career, and he was never shy about crediting Harbach. Among the musicals Harbach and Hammerstein worked on together were *Tickle Me* (1920), *Jimmie* (1920), *Wildflower* (1923), *Rose-Marie* (1924), *Song of the Flame* (1925), *The Wild Rose* (1926), *The Desert Song* (1926), *Golden Dawn* (1927), and *Good Boy* (1928), as well as Kern's *Sunny* (1925). Harbach's most notable musicals without Hammerstein include *Mary* (1920) and *No, No, Nanette* (1925), as well as Kern's ***Criss-Cross*** (1926), ***Lucky*** (1927), *The Cat and the Fiddle*, and *Roberta*. Many of his musicals were filmed, and he also contributed to a handful of screen scores. Ironically, Harbach never achieved his goal of a fully integrated musical play, but his pupil Hammerstein did with ***Show Boat*** (1927), *Oklahoma!* (1943), and other musical classics. Biography: *Otto Harbach*, Dewayne Rocky Aloysius (2012).

HARBURG, E. Y. (Yip) [né Isidore Hochberg]. (1896–1981) Stage, film, and television lyricist and writer. A sly Broadway songwriter and librettist who used fantasy and satire to write about weighty issues, he was better known for his tamer and more accessible Hollywood efforts such as Kern's ***Can't Help Singing*** (1944). Harburg (called Yip by his family and friends) was born in New York City and educated at City College of New York, where he wrote light verse and submitted it to local newspapers, then worked for his father's electronics business. When the stock market crash wiped out the family business, Harburg was free to pursue his dreams of writing lyrics, and soon some of his songs written with composer Jay Gorney and others were sung in the Broadway revues *Earl Carroll's Sketchbook* (1929), *Earl Carroll's Vanities* (1930), *Ballyhoo of 1932*, *Americana* (1932), *Walk a Little Faster* (1932), *Ziegfeld Follies* (1934), and *Life Begins at 8:40* (1934). His song "Brother, Can You Spare a Dime?," written with Gorney, was one of the famous songs to come from these shows, and none had more impact on Americans during the Depression than the musical cry of desperation heard in his lyrics. Harburg's first Broadway book musical was the satiric *Hooray for What!* (1937) written with Harold Arlen, the composer he had collaborated with on the movie musicals *The Singing Kid* (1936) and *Gold Diggers of 1937* (1936). When the two men scored the film classic *The Wizard of Oz* (1939) they entered the top ranks of American songwriters. Harburg and Arlen went on to score the Hollywood musicals *At the Circus* (1939), new songs for *Cabin in the Sky* (1943), *Meet the People* (1944), and the animated *Gay Purr-ee* (1962). On Broadway the team wrote the Civil War–era musical *Bloomer Girl* (1944) and the sardonic *Jamaica* (1957). Harbach collaborated with Kern on the film musical *Can't Help Singing* (1944), with Burton Lane on the movie *Ship Ahoy* (1942) and the Broadway musicals *Hold on to Your Hats* (1940) and *Finian's Rainbow* (1947), and with Sammy Fain on the oddball stage musical *Flahooley* (1951). His other musical credits are the Hollywood films *The Sap from Syracuse* (1930), *Moonlight and Pretzels* (1933), *Cairo* (1942), and *California* (1946); the Broadway musicals *The Happiest Girl in the World* (1961) and *Darling of the Day* (1968), and the TV musical *The Great Man's Whiskers* (1973). Harburg contributed to the scripts of several of his stage works, covering such topics as feminism, slavery, big business, prejudice, the atom bomb, and war. Yet all of his musicals can be categorized as comedies, for he thought it was through humor that the theatre could tackle the most fearsome topics. His lyrics are considered among the wittiest in the American musical and yet he wrote such simple, heartfelt classic songs like "Look to the Rainbow," "April in Paris," "What a Wonderful World," and "Over the Rainbow." Biographies: *Who Put the Rainbow in The Wizard of Oz? Yip Harburg, Lyricist*, Harold Myerson and Ernest Harburg [his son] (1993); *Yip Harburg: Legendary Lyricist and Human Rights Activist*, Harriet Hyman Alonso (2012).

HAVE A HEART. A musical comedy by **Guy Bolton**, **P. G. Wodehouse** (book and lyrics); Jerome Kern (music). [11 January 1917, Liberty Theatre, 76 performances] Produced by Henry B. Savage, directed by **Edward Royce**, musical direction by Gus Salzer, orchestrations by **Frank Saddler**. Although it was created by Bolton, P. G. Wodehouse, and Kern, *Have a Heart* was not a **Princess Theatre Musical**, but it had the spirit of the famous series. The daffy "up-to-the-minute" plot concerned the estranged married couple Ruddy (Thurston Hall) and Peggy Schoonmaker (Eileen Van Biene). They still love each other, but he is involved with the predatory Dolly Barbizon (Louise Dresser) and she is being wooed by the deceiving confidence man Capt. Charles Owen (Roy Gordon) who is passing forged currency. On the eve of their divorce, Ruddy and Peggy run off together and hide out in the Ocean View Hotel in Rhode Island. Dolly, Owen, and others track them down, and through the quick thinking of the elevator boy Henry (Billy B. Van), the forger is exposed. The breezy story and charming cast were aided by a superb score that was contemporary and tuneful. The heartfelt **"And I Am All Alone,"** the risible **"Napoleon,"** the catchy ballad **"You Said Something,"** the saucy "Honeymoon Inn," and the sprightly title song were among the highlights of the show. Although it received appreciative notices, *Have a Heart* never caught on with the public and was forced to close after ten weeks. It was Wodehouse's first full score heard on Broadway, and his lyrics were a vivid portent for the gems to come. The Victor Light Opera Company recorded a medley of highlights from the score in 1930. A complete cast recording of *Have a Heart* was made by the Comic Opera Guild in 2005.

HAYWORTH, Rita [née Margarita Carmen Cansino]. (1918–1987) Film performer. Columbia Pictures' reigning star of the 1940s, the redheaded beauty exuded a sensual quality in all her roles, such as the Argentine beauty Maria Acuña in Kern's *You Were Never Lovelier* (1942); yet she still could play the all-American girl, as with the aspiring model Rusty Parker in Kern's *Cover Girl* (1944). Hayworth was born in Brooklyn, the daughter of professional dancers from Spain who had performed in the *Ziegfeld Follies,* and was taught to dance at an early age, making her professional debut when she was twelve years old. While performing in nightclubs, Hayworth was signed by Hollywood and made her screen debut in 1935 but did not get much recognition until her performance in the melodrama *Only Angels Have Wings* (1939). She was soon one of the screen's hottest stars appearing in dramas, comedies, and musicals. Her best musical roles were the Broadway actress Sheila Winthrop in *You'll Never Get Rich* (1941), the femme fatale *Gilda* (1946), the society dame Vera Simpson in *Pal Joey* (1957), and in the already mentioned *You Were Never Lovelier* and *Cover Girl.* Hayworth's other musical credits include *Under the Pampas Moon* (1935), *Paddy O'Day* (1935), *Music in My Heart* (1940), *My Gal Sal* (1942), *Tonight and Every Night* (1945), *Down to Earth* (1947), *Affair in Trinidad* (1952), and *Miss Sadie Thompson* (1953). Her singing was frequently dubbed but Hayworth's dancing was the important thing, especially when paired with **Fred Astaire** or **Gene Kelly**. She continued to make films into the 1970s. Biographies: *If This Is Happiness: A Biography of Rita Hayworth,* Barbara Leming (1991); *Being Rita Hayworth: Labor, Identity, and Hollywood Stardom,* Adrienne L. McLean (2004).

HEAD OVER HEELS. A musical comedy by Edgar Allan Woolf (book and lyrics), Jerome Kern (music). [23 November 1918, George M. Cohan Theatre, 100 performances] Produced by Henry W. Savage, directed by George Marion, choreographed by Julian Mitchell, musical direction by

Harold Levey. Producer Savage created *Head Over Heels* as a vehicle for the alluring Hungarian star Mitzi Hajos who he billed simply as "Mitzi," the moniker she used for the rest of her career. The plot was far from original or clever: the European acrobat Mitzi Bambinetti (Mitzi) is the headliner in her family's circus act so when she falls in love with the dashing American Edward Sterling (Irving Beebe) and he gives her a ring, the family decides to go with her when Mitzi takes a boat to America. Once there she is shattered to learn that the philandering Sterling can barely recall her (or the ring), but she finds true love with Sterling's partner Robert Lawson (Boyd Marshall). Although Mitzi's acrobatics were more talked about than shown, the star charmed audiences with her singing and dancing and helped the show run three months. Woolf's libretto and lyrics were routine but Kern's music was sometimes enchanting. There is a jazz influence in "I Was Lonely" and "Funny Little Something," a Middle-European sound can be detected in "Mitzi's Lullaby," and "The Big Show" was a lively two-step. Musicologists have determined that much of the music for *Head Over Heels* was written for and discarded from earlier shows.

"Heaven in My Arms (Music in My Heart)" is an enchanting ballad by Kern and **Oscar Hammerstein** from the short-lived Broadway musical *Very Warm for May* (1939). The romantic number was sung by three apprentices— Johnny (**Jack Whiting**), May (Frances Mercer), and Carol (Hollace Shaw)—at Winnie's Barn, a summer stock theatre. Kern's flowing music is distinctive, repeating part of the verse in the refrain. Hammerstein's lyric is a casual but heartfelt declaration of love while dancing. The show was Kern's last on Broadway and much of the score has been unjustly neglected, including this number, which was dropped when *Very Warm for May* was turned into the film *Broadway Rhythm* (1944). Harold Lang recorded the song in the 1970s, and two decades later a distinctive quintet recording was made featuring Hugh Panaro, Rebecca Luker, George Dvorsky, Jeanne Lehman, and Lydia Milá. More recent recordings include a solo by Philip Chaffin and a duet version by Susan Watson and Danny Carroll.

"Here Am I" is an optimistic ballad by Kern and **Oscar Hammerstein**, one of the team's most unusual, if lesser known, songs. It was introduced by beer-hall singer Addie Schmidt (**Helen Morgan**) and her pal Dot (Violet Carson) in the Broadway musical *Sweet Adeline* (1929). Kern's music is very unusual in its structure and has a striking F-sharp beginning even though the song is written in the key of E-flat. Also of interest are the remarkable harmonies used throughout. In Hammerstein's lyric, the two women patiently wait for the man they love to return to them, confident that they have not been abandoned. **Irene Dunne** played Addie and sang the song as a solo in the 1935 movie version of *Sweet Adeline*. Both Morgan and Dunne recorded the ballad. Conductor John McGlinn reconstructed the original stage orchestrations in 1992 and recorded the number with Judy Kaye and Rebecca Luker singing the duet. Noteworthy solo recordings of "Here Am I" was made by Christina Lind and Karen Wyman.

HIGH, WIDE AND HANDSOME. A movie musical by **Oscar Hammerstein**, George O'Neill (screenplay); Jerome Kern (music); Hammerstein (lyrics). [1937, Paramount] Produced by Arthur Hornblow, Jr., directed by **Rouben Mamoulian**, choreographed by LeRoy Prinz, musical direction by Boris Morros, orchestrations by **Robert Russell Bennett**.

Plot: In the western hills of Pennsylvania in 1859, the farmer Peter Cortlandt takes in the itinerant medicine man Doc Watterson, his daughter Sally, and their sidekick Mac. When Peter discovers oil on his land, he attempts to build a pipeline to bring the oil out of the hills, but the railroad robber baron Walt Brennan opposes him every step of the way. A romance between Peter and Sally blossoms, then is disrupted. In the film's climatic scene, Sally brings along the personnel from a traveling circus, dwarfs and elephants included, to drive away the railroad goons and allow Peter to complete his pipeline.

This exciting, sprawling musical piece of Americana was Kern and Hammerstein's best original film musical. The screenplay painted a broad panorama of frontier life, including medicine shows, backwoods saloons, a circus, riverboat entertainment, and country square dances, and employed a rich set of supporting characters, particularly Dorothy Lamour as the knowing saloon singer Molly. The songs were more integrated into the story than in most previous movie musicals, helped by Hammerstein's plotting and Mamoulian's expert direction. Kern's music captures the vigorous spirit of the frontier, ranging from quaint folk songs to rousing chorus numbers. Standouts in the score are the farewell ballad "Can I Forget You?," the

HIGH, WIDE AND HANDSOME. A visual and musical piece of Americana, this 1937 pioneer movie musical offered what is considered Kern and Oscar Hammerstein's finest screen score. Irene Dunne (center) finds adventure and romance in the wilds of western Pennsylvania, all depicted with masterful atmosphere by director Rouben Mamoulian. Dorothy Lamour (in the striped dress) shed her sarong from that same year's *The Hurricane* and was just as fetching in a pioneer gal's dress. *Paramount Pictures/ Photofest ©Paramount Pictures*

CAST FOR *HIGH, WIDE AND HANDSOME*

Character	Performer
Sally Watterson	**Irene Dunne**
Peter Cortlandt	**Randolph Scott**
Molly	**Dorothy Lamour**
Joe Varies	**Akim Tamiroff**
Red Scanlon	Charles Bickford
Doc Watterson	Raymond Walburn
Samuel	Ben Blue
Maurice (Mac)	William Frawley
Grandma Cortlandt	Elizabeth Patterson
Walt Brennan	Alan Hale

delicate "The Folks Who Live on the Hill," the raffish "Allegheny Al," the riverboat ditty "The Things I Want," and the anthem-like title song. The creators and the studio were very proud of the expensive but classy movie, and reviews were laudatory, yet *High, Wide and Handsome* did modest box office and never paid off its high price tag. Looking at the movie today, one can see elements of both ***Show Boat*** (1927) and *Oklahoma!* (1943) in the musical, yet it has a distinction and quality of its own.

Recording: The film soundtrack recording is far from complete, but the highlights of the score are there. It was rereleased on an LP with the movie soundtrack for ***Sweet Adeline***. The movie itself is hard to find, not yet being available on DVD.

HIGH, WIDE AND HANDSOME SONGS

"**High, Wide and Handsome**"
"To Fool a Simple Maiden"
"**Can I Forget You?**"
"Will You Marry Me Tomorrow, Maria?"
"**The Folks Who Live on the Hill**"
"Jenny Dear"
"**The Things I Want**"
"**Allegheny Al**"

"High, Wide and Handsome" is the rollicking anthem to the rugged Pennsylvania wilderness and the title song for the 1937 pioneer musical scored by Kern and lyricist **Oscar Hammerstein**. Sally Watterson (**Irene Dunne**) sang the rousing number as part of her father's medicine show. "High, Wide and Handsome" has been recorded on several occasions and in different styles, from a dance arrangement by Gus Arnheim's Orchestra to swing versions by Edgar Hayes (vocal by Bill Darnell) and the Tempo King's Swing Combo to a western approach by Tex Ritter. A solo disc by Warren Galjour is in a pleasing ballad format.

HITCHY-KOO 1920. A musical revue by Glen MacDonough, **Anne Caldwell** (sketches and lyrics); Jerome Kern (music). [19 October 1920, New Amsterdam Theatre, 71 performances] Produced by Raymond Hitchcock, directed and choreographed by Ned Wayburn, musical direction by Cassius Freeborn, orchestrations by **Frank Saddler**. Unlike most composers in his day, Kern rarely wrote the score for revues, though his songs were sometimes interpolated into others' scores for revues. Producer Hitchcock had previously presented shows titled *Hitchy-Koo* in 1917, 1918, and 1919 so this one was billed as Raymond Hitchcock's *Hitchy-Koo 1920.* The show tended toward the nostalgic: there was a spoof of an old-time melodrama, a salute to "Old New York," a number about "Buggy Riding," and an innocent ditty titled "Ding Dong, It's Kissing Time." Hitchcock starred with singing star **Julia Sanderson** and newcomer Grace Moore, and the press thought it was all very pleasant if not sensational. The 1920 edition of Hitchcock's series struggled to run two months but did better on tour. Nevertheless, it was the last revue in the series to play New York.

HOLLYWOOD, Kern in. Most Broadway songwriters had a love-hate relationship with Tinsel Town and the movies. Cole Porter and Irving Berlin were usually pleased with what Hollywood did with their songs, but most of the others were not and only turned to the West Coast out of necessity (especially during the Depression) or for the easy money (most any time). Kern also had his difficulties with Hollywood, but for the most part he fared well there. Kern's first connection with Hollywood was in 1929 when a silent film version of Edna Ferber's novel *Show Boat* was filmed, and because of the success of the Broadway musical version, the studio wanted to add some songs to the completed picture. Kern and lyricist **Oscar Hammerstein** did not write any new material for the film and

KERN IN HOLLYWOOD

Original movie musicals:

Men of the Sky (1931)
I Dream Too Much (1935)
Swing Time (1936)
High, Wide and Handsome (1937)
Joy of Living (1938)
One Night in the Tropics (1940)
You Were Never Lovelier (1942)
Cover Girl (1944)
Can't Help Singing (1944)
Centennial Summer (1946)

Films based on Kern stage works:

Show Boat (1929, 1936, 1951)
Sally (1929)
Sunny (1930, 1941)
The Cat and the Fiddle (1934)
Music in the Air (1934)
Roberta (1935) and as *Lovely to Look At* (1952)
Sweet Adeline (1935)
Broadway Rhythm (1944) based on *Very Warm for May*

their cooperation was minimal, as it frequently was when Hollywood made movies from Kern's Broadway musicals. Kern's first original score for the movies was with lyricist **Otto Harbach** for a First National movie about World War I flying aces tentatively titled *Stolen Dreams*. The writing of the score and the production process went smoothly, and Kern returned to New York in 1930. But with so many movie musicals flooding the market, moviegoers lost interest in the new genre and the studios panicked. First National retitled the film as *Men of the Sky* (1931) and cut all the songs, leaving only some Kern music as background. Kern's first full movie score was finally heard in *I Dream Too Much* (1935), and over the next decade he composed eight more movie musicals, the two biggest hits being *Swing Time* (1936) and *Cover Girl* (1944). Many of Kern's stage works were filmed by Hollywood with mixed results. On some occasions Kern wrote new songs for the screen version, such as the 1936 movie version of *Show Boat*. At other times, other songwriters' work was interpolated into the movie. The most glaring example is the screen version of *Very Warm for May* (1939), which came to the screen as *Broadway Rhythm* (1944) with little of Kern's music surviving the transition. Kern was still alive during the preparation and filming of his biopic *Till the Clouds Roll By* (1946), but the movie was released after his death. Also released after his passing was *Centennial Summer* (1946), the 1951 remake of *Show Boat*, and the 1952 remake of *Roberta* called *Lovely to Look At*.

HOPE, Bob [né Leslie Townes Hope]. (1903–2003) Stage, film, and television performer. Hope was one of the English-speaking world's favorite entertainers, and Broadway and Hollywood musicals were part of his long and illustrious career, which took flight with his Broadway performance as American bandleader Huckleberry Haines in Kern's *Roberta* (1933). Hope was born in Eltham, England, and came to America at the age of four and grew up in Cleveland. He worked as a clerk, newsboy, soda jerk, and even a boxer before going into show business as a song-and-dance man on the variety circuit. Hope's wisecracking, self-deprecating style of comedy caught on, and by the late 1920s he was featured in the Broadway revues *The Ramblers* (1926), *Ups-a-Daisy* (1928), and *Ballyhoo of 1932*, and the book musicals *Sidewalks of New York* (1927) and *Smiles* (1930). After getting recognition with *Roberta*, he starred in *Say When* (1934), *Ziegfeld Follies* (1936), and *Red, Hot and Blue* (1936). Hope made his screen debut in *Big Broadcast of 1938* and never returned to Broadway, concentrating on films, his own radio program, television specials, and personal appearances over the next fifty years. On screen he was featured in the musicals *College Swing* (1938), *Give Me a Sailor* (1938), and *Thanks for the Memory* (1938) before teaming up with Bing Crosby for *Road to Singapore* (1940), followed by six more *Road* pictures over the next twenty-two years. Hope's other memorable musicals include *Louisiana Purchase* (1941), *Let's Face It!* (1943), *The Paleface* (1948), *Fancy Pants* (1950), *The Lemon Drop Kid* (1951), *Son of Paleface* (1952), *The Seven Little Foys* (1955), *Beau James* (1957), *I'll Take Sweden* (1967), and specialty bits in *Star Spangled Rhythm* (1942), *Duffy's Tavern* (1945), *Scared Stiff* (1953), *The Five Pennies* (1959), and *The Muppet Movie* (1979). Hope made many other films, but by the 1970s he concentrated on television specials and concerts, playing at hundreds of venues across the country and in Great Britain. He was also known for and decorated for entertaining American and British troops during every conflict from World War II to the Persian Gulf War in the 1990s. Although Hope became an institution of sorts and was highly awarded and revered as the ultimate patriotic American during his later years, he always kept his sarcastic persona, spoofing political figures and world problems, and retaining his vaudeville-like delivery. He wrote several comic memoirs, including *They Got Me Covered* (1941), *Have Tux, Will Travel* (1954), *I Owe Russia $1,200* (1963), *The Last Christmas Show* (1974), *The Road to Hollywood:*

My 40-Year Love Affair with the Movies (1977), and *Don't Shoot, It's Only Me* (1990). Biographies: *Bob Hope: The Road Well-Traveled,* Lawrence J. Quirk (2000); *Bob Hope: A Life in Comedy,* William Robert Faith (2003).

"How'd You Like to Spoon with Me?" is the song that brought Kern his first recognition in New York. When the British musical *The Earl and the Girl* was imported to Broadway in 1905, a handful of songs were interpolated into Ivan Caryll's London score. The hit of the evening was this saucy duet that Kern wrote with lyricist Edward Laska. Actually, the songwriters had completed the number a few years earlier, but prospective producers thought that "spoon" was too vulgar a word for theatre audiences. In *The Earl and the Girl*, the duet was sung by Georgia Caine and Victor Morley, supported by six beautiful girls on flowered swings who swung out over the audience. The catchy music is simple and uncomplicated and the lyric sly and only slightly naughty. The song quickly caught on with the public, and sheet music sales were healthy, giving Kern his first hit song. Interest in "How'd You Like to Spoon with Me?" was revived when a young and fetching Angela Lansbury sang it with the chorus in the Kern biopic *Till the Clouds Roll By* (1946). In 1971 the number was interpolated into a London revival of *Show Boat* where it was performed by Frank (Kenneth Nelson) and Ellie (Jan Hunt). Among those who made recordings of the ditty are the Haydn Quartet, Andrea Marcovicci, Sandy Stewart, Tracy Powell, Jane Lanier with Laura Hornberger, Kim Criswell, and the Audubon Quartet.

ROBERTA. Bob Hope (far left) found his first recognition on Broadway as the bandleader Huckleberry Haines in this 1933 Kern musical. He played the comic sidekick to Ray Middleton (center) who was caught up in intrigues with Lyda Roberti and Sydney Greenstreet. Hope made his first movie the next year, but when *Roberta* was filmed in 1935 Fred Astaire played Hope's stage role. *Photofest*

"I AM" SONGS by Kern. One of the important innovations that came with the development of the integrated musical is the "I am" or "I want" song. This number usually comes very early in the score and gives a major character the opportunity to express his or her wishes or dreams, allowing the audience to gain empathy with the person. Introducing and establishing a definite character through a song would become commonplace after Rodgers and Hammerstein's *Oklahoma!* (1943). That is not to say that the "I am" song did not exist before that influential work. Characters in the Gilbert and Sullivan operettas had introduced themselves to audiences with such numbers as "A Wand'ring Minstrel, I" and "I Am the Pirate King." George M. Cohan had sung "(I'm a) Yankee Doodle Dandy" in his *Little Johnny Jones* (1904) to present the patriotic jockey Johnny to audiences. In Kern's **Princess Theatre Musicals** in the 1910s, some efforts were made to introduce characters musically. Put-upon Eddie Kettle sings of his diminutive size in **"Thirteen Collar"** in *Very Good Eddie* (1915); the playboy Ted sings "I'm Here, Little Girls, I'm Here" to advertise his charm in *Have a Heart* (1917) and elevator operator Billy compares himself to **"Napoleon"** in the same show; the wistful Lou Ellen proclaims she wants to be "An Old-Fashioned Wife" in *Oh, Boy!* (1917); and the betrothed Mollie opens *Oh, Lady! Lady!!* (1918) with "I'm to Be Married Today." Other "I am" songs in Kern's musical comedies include Mrs. White's lament "Left All Alone Blues" from *The Night Boat* (1920), Sally's heartfelt **"Look for the Silver Lining"** in *Sally* (1920), Dorothy's wishful "I Want to Be There" from *Dear Sir* (1924), and Aunt Minnie's nostalgic **"Yesterdays"** in *Roberta* (1933). With *Show Boat* (1927), Kern and librettist-lyricist **Oscar Hammerstein** had much richer characters to work with and offered numbers that introduced Ravenal (**"Where's the Mate for Me?"**), Joe (**"Ol' Man River"**), Julie (**"Can't Help Lovin' Dat Man"**), and even Ellie (**"Life Upon the Wicked Stage"**). Among the "I am" songs Kern wrote for Hollywood are **"I Won't Dance"** from *Roberta* (1935), **"The Things I Want"** in *High,*

Wide and Handsome (1937), **"I'm Old Fashioned"** in *You Were Never Lovelier* (1942), and **"Make Way for Tomorrow"** from *Cover Girl* (1944).

I DREAM TOO MUCH. A movie musical melodrama by James Gow, Edmund North, Allan Scott (screenplay); **Dorothy Fields** (lyrics); Jerome Kern (music). [1935, RKO]. Produced by **Pandro S. Berman**, directed by John Cromwell, choreography by Hermes Pan, musical direction by Max Steiner, orchestrations by **Robert Russell Bennett**.

Plot: Annette Monard, a simple girl from the French provinces, is discovered by impresario Paul Darcy and taken to Paris. Once there her voice is trained while her heart is stolen by the idealistic Johnny Street, a young composer struggling to break into the opera business. They marry, but Annette becomes famous and he doesn't, so she foregoes her career to devote her energies to promoting his. Hollywood came up with what it thought was a happy ending: Johnny's opera is turned into a musical comedy that becomes a hit with Annette as the leading lady.

After opera singer Grace Moore scored a triumph in Columbia's *One Night of Love* (1934), RKO and producer Berman attempted to do the same thing with Metropolitan Opera diva Lily Pons. The script and score were tailored to her operatic talents, resulting in her first and best film, proving that the diminutive star could act as well as sing. In addition to the expected opera arias, the score included some marvelous new numbers by Kern and Fields: the swinging "I Got Love," the lullaby "The Jockey on the Carousel," and

CAST FOR *I DREAM TOO MUCH*

Character	Performer
Annette Monard	**Lily Pons**
Johnny Street	Henry Fonda
Roger Briggs	**Eric Blore**
Paul Darcy	Osgood Perkins
Hubert Dilley	Lucien Littlefield
Gwendolyn Dilley	Lucille Ball
Darcy's Pianist	Mischa Auer

the entrancing title song. The movie was a hit but Pons's three subsequent efforts were not so popular, so she gave up on Hollywood.

I DREAM TOO MUCH SONGS

"I Dream Too Much"
"The Jockey on the Carousel"
"I Got Love"
"I'm the Echo (You're the Song That I Love)"
"Bell Song" from Delibes's *Lakmé*
"Caro Nome" from Verdi's *Rigoletto*

Recording: Pons is the only one heard on the film soundtrack recording, which was later rereleased as an LP with the soundtrack of Grace Moore's opera movie *One Night of Love*.

"I Dream Too Much" is the entrancing title song by Kern and lyricist **Dorothy Fields** from the 1935 screen vehicle for Metropolitan Opera star **Lily Pons**. The confessional song about dreaming "too much alone" was sung by Annette Monard (Pons) and a chorus on stage as part of a musical written by her husband Johnny Street (Henry Fonda) and was reprised at the end of the film. When producer **Pandro Berman** heard the song, he changed the movie's title from *Love Song* to that of the waltzing ballad. Wishing to show off Pons's coloratura opera talents, Kern composed expansive and demanding music that musicologist David Ewen notes "is of special interest for its chromatic harmonies and for the leap of a minor ninth in the melody." Pons recorded the song, as did the orchestras of Leo Reisman and Paul Weston, the Jimmy Knepper Sextet, the Mike Wofford Trio, Eric Parkin, New York Swing, Hildegarde, and Marni Nixon. In the revue *Jerome Kern Goes to Hollywood*, David Kernan, Liz Robertson, and Elaine Delmar sang it in London in 1985, and the next year Scott Holmes performed it with Delmar and Robertson on Broadway. "I Dream Too Much" was heard on the soundtrack of the film *Alice* (1990).

"I Got Love" is opera star **Lily Pons**'s attempt to sing a swing number in the Kern musical film *I Dream Too Much* (1935), and though some found her singing of the jazzy song with Andre Kostelanetz's Orchestra in a Parisian cafe successful, others used this song as a reason for dubbing the movie *I Scream Too Much*. Although Kern had difficulty accepting the new swing sound as a legitimate form of music, he wrote "I Got Love" with a low-down sound that complemented **Dorothy Fields**'s grasping lyric. Karen Ziemba sang the number in a sarcastic manner in the Broadway musical *Never Gonna Dance* (2003). Rebecca Luker made a distinctive recording of the song in 2012.

"I Have the Room Above Her" is the lyrical romantic ballad that Kern and lyricist **Oscar Hammerstein** wrote for the 1936 screen version of *Show Boat*. Gambler-turned-actor Gaylord Ravenal (**Allan Jones**) sang the song from his room on the show boat *Cotton Blossom* to Magnolia Hawks (**Irene Dunne**) who is at the window of her room below his, and then the two joined in a lovely duet. Kern's music beautifully climbs the scale in fits and starts while Hammerstein's lyric is simple, succinct, and endearing. The song has sometimes been interpolated into stage revivals of *Show Boat*, and in the revue *Jerome Kern Goes to Hollywood* David Kernan sang it in London in 1985 and Scott Holmes performed it on Broadway the next year. Sometimes listed as "I Have the Room Above," the song was given solo recordings by Cy Young, **Howard Keel**, and Mandy Patinkin, and a lovely duet version by Mark Jacoby and Rebecca Luker who played Gaylord and Magnolia in the 1994 Broadway revival of *Show Boat*. There is a delectable recording of the number by jazz drummer Paul Motian.

"I Might Fall Back on You" is a vaudeville turn for the *Cotton Blossom* performers Ellie (**Eva Puck**) and Frank (**Sammy White**) in *Show Boat* (1927). The lively polka number, in which a flirtatious gal puts off her suitor until she has played the field, pastiches the kind of duo act that was popular in the nineteenth century. **Oscar Hammerstein**'s lyric is sassy and light, and the number provides one of *Show Boat*'s most comic moments. The song was dropped from the 1936 screen version but was sung and danced by **Marge** and **Gower Champion** in the 1951 remake. Playful duet versions of the number were recorded by Janet Pavek with Kevin Scott, Paige O'Hara with David Garrison, and Dora Bryan with Geoffrey Webb; Andre Previn made an instrumental recording of the song.

"I Was Alone" is a melancholy ballad that Kern and lyricists **Oscar Hammerstein** and **Otto Harbach** interpolated into the 1930 screen version of their Broadway hit *Sunny*. **Marilyn Miller,** re-creating her stage role as circus performer Sunny Peters who stows away on a ship heading to New York, sang the lonely number twice in the film.

"I Won't Dance" is a scintillating rhythm song that Kern and lyricist **Dorothy Fields** wrote for the 1933 movie version of *Roberta*. Bandleader Huckleberry Haines **(Fred Astaire)** sang the tangy refusal to Lizzie Gatz **(Ginger Rogers)** as they danced in a Paris nightclub, and then Astaire broke into a fiery tap solo. It was Astaire who requested a faster and more jumping number for *Roberta*'s near-operatic score, and Kern obliged him with one of his few rhythm songs. The result was, as theatre historian Gerald Mast put it, "bizarrely meandering" with a simple and catchy main theme but a very tricky release, "perhaps the most difficult release Kern ever wrote," according to musicologist Alec Wilder, because it jumps from the key of C to A-flat then to D-flat to B. The melody was not entirely original. Kern and lyricist **Oscar Hammerstein** had written a similar number for the short-lived London musical *Three Sisters* (1934), but Fields's new lyric sent the song in a whole new direction. It is one of her finest lyrics: snappy, sensual, and slightly ambiguous. She even makes a reference to "The Continental," the song and dance made popular the year before by Astaire and Rogers in the film *The Gay Divorcee*. "I Won't Dance" became a big hit, helped by Eddy Duchin's best-selling recording. Other notable recordings include those by Blossom Dearie, Margaret Whiting, Leo Reisman, Van Alexander, Oscar Peterson, Ella Fitzgerald, Jane Monheit, Peggy Lee, Sylvia McNair, Betty Buckley, the Audubon Quartet, a sassy duet version by Kaye Ballard and Jack Cassidy, and Frank Sinatra whose recording was heard in the film *What Women Want* (2000). Van Johnson and Lucille Bremer sang and danced to "I Won't Dance" in the Kern biopic *Till the Clouds Roll By* (1946), and it was performed by **Marge** and **Gower Champion** in the remake of *Roberta* called *Lovely to Look At* (1952). The song was also heard on the soundtrack for the movies *Warm Springs* (2005), *Gray Matters* (2006), and *Step Up 3D* (2010). On stage the number was sung by Liz Robertson in the revue *Jerome Kern Goes to Hollywood*, which played in London in 1985 and on Broadway in 1986, and by Noah Racey and the company of the Broadway musical *Never Gonna Dance* (2003).

"I'll Be Hard to Handle" is a jaunty comic song from Kern's Broadway musical *Roberta* (1933) sung by the plucky Clementina Scharwenka (**Lyda**

Roberti) about her independent ways. Kern's music is typical of the new jaunty flavor of 1930s song, suggesting both a jazz influence and a bluesy vamping that makes it sexy. Although **Otto Harbach** wrote the lyrics for the rest of *Roberta*'s score, he asked Kern if his nephew Bernard Dougall could break into show business by providing a lyric for one number. Kern gave him the sheet music for "I'll Be Hard to Handle," and Dougall wrote the sassy, playful lyric. (It was the only song hit of Dougall's career.) In the 1935 film version of *Roberta*, the number was given a revised lyric by **Dorothy Fields** and was sung by **Ginger Rogers** who then danced to the music with **Fred Astaire**. In the 1952 remake, titled *Lovely to Look At*, "I'll Be Hard to Handle" was sung and danced by Ann Miller and a male chorus in a New York nightclub. Liz Robertson sang the number in the 1986 London revue *Jerome Kern Goes to Hollywood* and reprised it the next year when the show opened on Broadway, and Deidre Goodwin and Eugene Fleming performed it in the Broadway musical *Never Gonna Dance* (2003). Among those who have recorded "I'll Be Hard to Handle" are Robertson, Paul Lawrence, Ella Fitzgerald, Rebecca Luker, and Kaye Ballard.

"I'm Old Fashioned" is the bewitching ballad by Kern and lyricist **Johnny Mercer** that was introduced in the film *You Were Never Lovelier* (1942) by Argentine beauty Maria Acuña (**Rita Hayworth** dubbed by Nan Wynn) to American Robert Davis (**Fred Astaire**); the two then dance to Xavier Cugat's Orchestra in a Buenos Aires garden. The lyric lists old-fashioned favorites such as moonlight and the sounds of raindrops, yet the tone is never mawkish or trite. (Mercer once stated that this lyric came closest to his personal philosophy of life.) Kern's music, a carefully disguised waltz, has been described by musical historian Gerald Bordman as "an imaginative series of theme and variations, all played out in a range of just over an octave." In fact, the refrain has unusually few notes, none shorter than a quarter note. The music is also a masterwork of building up melody and harmony in an effortless but captivating way. The oft-recorded ballad has received memorable discs by Cugat, Astaire (whose recording was heard in the 1971 movie *A Safe Place*), Glen Gray and the Casa Loma Orchestra (vocal by Kenny Sargent), jazz pianist Beegie Adair, Cassandra Wilson, Ella Fitzgerald, Kiri Te Kanawa, Judy Garland, Susan Watson, Sylvia McNair, Robert Morse, John Coltrane, Margaret Whiting, Chet Baker, the Glenn

Miller Orchestra, Helen Merrill, the Audubon Quartet, Mandy Patinkin, Jack Jones, Eileen Farrell, Barbara Carroll, Rebecca Luker, Sandy Stewart, and Dorothy Kirsten. "I'm Old Fashioned" was sung by Dianne Wiest in the film *Hannah and Her Sisters* (1986) and was heard on the soundtracks of *Rocket Gibraltar* (1988) and *Reign Over Me* (2007). Elaine Delmar performed it in the revue **Jerome Kern Goes to Hollywood** in London in 1985 and on Broadway in 1986, and Nancy Lemenager sang it in the Broadway musical *Never Gonna Dance* (2003).

"In Egern on the Tegern See" (1932) is a pastiche of an old-style operetta number that Kern and lyricist **Oscar Hammerstein** wrote for the Broadway musical *Music in the Air* (1932). The retired Bavarian opera singer Lilli Kirschner (Ivy Scott) is coaxed into singing her big number from an old operetta, and she obliges with this nostalgic aria filled with images of moonlight on the water and soft caressing breezes. The number was not included in the 1934 movie version of *Music in the Air* but was sung by Muriel O'Malley in the 1951 Broadway revival. Jane Pickens, Jeanne Lehman, and Nancy Andrews each made effective recordings of it. There was also a very jazzy piano version by Eddie Duchin, which was frowned upon by Kern. "In Egern on the Tegern See" was spoofed in the Off-Broadway pastiche musical *Little Mary Sunshine* (1962) with a song titled "In Izzenshnooken on the Lovely Essenzook Zee."

"In Love in Vain" is the lyrical ballad of unrequited love that Kern and lyricist Leo Robin wrote for the nostalgic period movie **Centennial Summer** (1946). Philadelphian Julia Rogers (**Jeanne Crain**, dubbed by Louanne Hogan), upset that the Frenchman Phillippe is more interested in her sister than herself, sang the torchy song and was joined by her sister's neglected beau Ben (William Eythe). Recordings of the ballad include those by Margaret Whiting, Andrea Marcovicci, Lena Horne, Danny Carroll, Betty Madigan, Sandy Stewart, Ralph Sharon Trio, Paul Weston, the Mike Wofford Trio, Helen Merrill, Allison Crowe, Bobby Darin, Susannah McCorkle, Mildred Bailey, Sarah Vaughan, Joni Jones, Melissa Errico, and Barbara Carroll.

"In the Heart of the Dark" is a gentle ballad from the unsuccessful musical **Very Warm for May** (1939), Kern's last Broadway production. The nocturnal reverie was sung by summer stock apprentice Carol (Hollace Shaw) and later reprised by Liz (Frances Mercer) in the show. The number was not used in the 1944 screen adaptation called *Broadway Rhythm*. The music, with its repeated notes and quarter-note triplets, is very atypical of Kern and recalls a Cole Porter kind of melody, just as the romantic lyric by **Oscar Hammerstein** is reminiscent of Porter's "All Through the Night." Among the artists to record "In the Heart of the Dark" are Barbara Cook, Warren Galjour, Reid Shelton, Dale Kristien, Andrea Marcovicci, Lorna Dallas, Eric Parkin, and a trio version by Heidi Blickenstaff, Kate Baldwin, and Philip Chaffin.

"I've Told Ev'ry Little Star" (1932) is the simple but absorbing ballad from the Kern–**Oscar Hammerstein** operetta *Music in the Air* (1932) where it served as the central motif in the plot. The old Bavarian music teacher Dr. Lessing (**Al Shean**) and the young schoolmaster Karl Reder (**Walter Slezak**) write a song called "I've Told Ev'ry Little Star" based on a melody they have heard a bird singing. The timid Karl first sings the affectionate number as part of the Edendorf Choral Society recital. Later Karl and his sweetheart Sieglinde (Katherine Carrington) sing it as a duet when they audition the song for a music publisher in Munich. Hammerstein's lyric is particularly touching, with the singer asking why he has told all of nature and all his friends about his love but he hasn't told her. According to backstage legend, Kern got the main musical phrase for the song from a bird he heard singing outside his window while visiting Nantucket. In the 1934 film version of *Music in the Air*, the song was sung by **Gloria Swanson**, June Lang (dubbed by Betty Hiestand), **John Boles**, Douglass Montgomery (dubbed by James O'Brien), and the chorus. It was also sung by Elisabeth Welch in the revue *Jerome Kern Goes to Hollywood* in London in 1985 and on Broadway in 1986. The ballad had successful recordings by Mary Ellis (who sang it in the 1933 London production of *Music in the Air*), Eddy Duchin, Bing Crosby, Sonny Rollins, Margaret Whiting, Pat Boone, Peggy King, Joan Morris and William Bolcom, Dorothy Kirsten, Cannonball Adderley, Stanley Black, Annie Ross, Jane Pickins, **Irene Dunne**, Jane Powell, and others, and in 1961 Linda Scott made a single that hit the Top Ten. "I've Told Ev'ry Little Star" was also heard in the film *Mulholland Drive* (2001).

JEROME KERN GOES TO HOLLYWOOD. A musical revue by David Kernan and Dick Vosburgh; score by **Oscar Hammerstein**, **Dorothy Fields**, **Ira Gershwin**, **Otto Harbach**, **Johnny Mercer**, etc. (lyrics); Jerome Kern (music). [23 January 1986, Ritz Theatre, 13 performances] Produced by Arthur Canton, Bonnie Nelson Schwartz, etc.; directed by Kernan; musical direction by Peter Howard. What was an intimate musical revue in a small London theatre in 1985 celebrating the centenary of Kern's birth looked like a formal recital in the mid-sized Broadway house, and despite the talented performers (Elaine Delmar, Scott Holmes, Liz Robertson, Elisabeth Welch) and superlative songs, few critics could recommend the program. With no particular chronology or thematic structure, the revue featured forty songs that Kern wrote for films and Broadway songs that were later heard in films, making the revue's title somewhat inaccurate. Familiar favorites, such as **"Ol' Man River"** and **"Smoke Gets in Your Eyes,"** were joined by some lesser-known numbers, like **"Just Let Me Look at You"** and **"Can I Forget You?"** Critics applauded the cast, though most of the praise was for the seventy-seven-year-old veteran Welch. The musical arrangements were well executed, particularly the duet, trio, and quartet versions of some of the numbers. With no money reviews and little interest on the part of the public, the revue closed within two weeks. The original London revue was recorded in 1985 with the same cast, except for producer-director David Kernan singing the songs that Holmes later did on Broadway. It is a very satisfying CD (though it contains only a little over half of the songs) and has a cozy, unpretentious feeling that was missing in New York. Among the highlights are Welch's renditions of **"Why Was I Born?,"** Delmar's **"Remind Me,"** and a lovely choral medley of **"They Didn't Believe Me"** and **"All the Things You Are."**

"The Jockey on the Carousel" is a sentimental lullaby that the French girl Annette Monard (**Lily Pons**) and a male chorus sing to cheer up a lonely child at a Parisian fairground as they ride a merry-go-round in Kern's movie operetta *I Dream Too Much* (1935). **Dorothy Fields**'s narrative lyric tells the tale of a carousel jockey who is always chasing after his sweetheart on the horse ahead of him but never seems to get any closer. Kern's music is adventurous as it shifts moods and leaps through different key changes, such as a five-sharped key of B that Kern knew was the sort of thing that discouraged sheet music sales. Met opera star Pons recorded "The Jockey on the Carousel" and there have been discs by the orchestras of Paul Whiteman, Morton Gould, and Andre Kostelanetz, but the song has been little heard since the 1960s.

JONES, Allan. (1907–1992) Stage and film singer, actor. A personable tenor who appeared in several film musicals between 1935 and 1945, perhaps his finest performance was as Gaylord Ravenal in the 1936 screen version of Kern's *Show Boat*. Jones was born in Scranton, Pennsylvania, the son of a coal miner, and worked in the mines himself as a young man. He later studied music at Syracuse University and in Paris, then returned to America where he toured in musicals and made a few appearances in Broadway shows. Jones made his film debut in *Reckless* (1935) and was noticed for his crooning in the Marx Brothers' *A Night at the Opera* (1935) and *A Day at the Races* (1937). Other notable musicals include *The Firefly* (1937) in which he first sang his signature song "The Donkey Serenade," *The Great Victor Herbert* (1939), *The Boys from Syracuse* (1940), Kern's *One Night in the Tropics* (1940), and *When Johnny Comes Marching Home* (1942). No character he played had the depth and complexity of the gambler Ravenal in *Show Boat*, and Jones's singing of **"Make Believe," "You Are Love,"** and **"I Have the Room Above Her"** (written for Jones for the movie) are highlights in the classic film. His later years were spent in concerts and nightclubs, making recordings, and appearing on television specials. He is the father of popular singer Jack Jones.

JOY OF LIVING. A movie musical comedy by Gene Towne, Graham Baker, Allan Scott (screenplay); **Dorothy Fields** (lyrics); Jerome Kern (music). [1938, RKO] Produced by Tay Garnett, Felix Young; directed by Tay Garnett; musical direction by Frank Tours; orchestrations by **Robert Russell Bennett.**

CAST FOR *JOY OF LIVING*

Character	Performer
Maggie Garret	**Irene Dunne**
Dan Brewster	Douglas Fairbanks, Jr.
Minerva Garret	Alice Brady
Dennis Garret	Guy Kibbee
Harrison	Jean Dixon
Potter	**Eric Blore**
Salina Garret Pine	Lucille Ball

Plot: Broadway star Maggie Garret is too uptight to enjoy life, although her wacky relatives and other parasites are sure having a great time. It takes the Boston banking heir Dan Brewster to teach Maggie to live by doing Donald Duck impersonations for her, taking her to a beer hall and a skating rink, and whisking her off to a South Seas island.

A screwball comedy with music, *The Joy of Living* suffered from a weak plot but was saved by a strong score and fine performances. Dunne gives one of her funniest performances in a musical, Douglas Fairbanks is a delightful foil for her, and the supporting cast reads like a Who's Who of favorite Hollywood character actors: Guy Kibbee, Lucille Ball, Alice Brady, Eric Blore, Billy Gilbert, Franklin Pangborn, Mischa Auer, Fuzzy Knight, Jean Dixon, and Warren Hymer. They all deserved a better script than the one producer-director Tay Garnett offered them. Kern and Fields came up with three sparkling songs: the swinging lullaby "You Couldn't Be Cuter," the farewell ballad "What's Good About Good Night?," and the flowing "Just Let Me Look at You," which was used throughout the film as a leitmotif.

JOY OF LIVING SONGS

"Just Let Me Look at You"
"What's Good About Good Night?"
"A Heavenly Party"
"You Couldn't Be Cuter"

Recording: The film soundtrack, which has only Dunne's numbers, is difficult to find, but the movie is on DVD.

"Just Let Me Look at You" is the languid ballad by Kern and lyricist **Dorothy Fields** that was used throughout the backstage movie musical *Joy of Living* (1938). Broadway star Maggie Garret (**Irene Dunne** in her last musical film) rehearsed the new song at home before it was to be added to her hit show. She reprised it later in her limo where Dan Brewster (Douglas Fairbanks, Jr.), who was hitching a ride on the vehicle's luggage rack, listened to her dreamily. Finally Maggie sang it seductively to the judge in a courtroom scene. Fields's sunny lyric claims that one speechlessly in love can only look with adoration at one's beloved. Kern's music has been described by musicologist Alec Wilder as "a beautiful, uncluttered song which proceeds from melodic point to point in one long flowing line." Musical historian Stanley Green has pointed out that the song melody recalls Tchaikowsky's "None But the Lonely Heart." Recordings of note include those by Warren Galjour, George Reinholt, Paul Weston's Orchestra, Sandy Stewart, Al Bowlly, and a trio version by Heidi Blickenstaff, Kate Baldwin, and Philip Chaffin. Liz Robertson sang "Just Let Me Look at You" in the revue *Jerome Kern Goes to Hollywood*, which played London in 1985 and on Broadway in 1986.

"Just You Watch My Step" is the eager anthem of the go-getter college kids in Kern's collegiate musical *Leave It to Jane* (1917). Student Stub Talmadge (**Oscar Shaw**) is chided by his sweetheart, the athletic coed Bessie Tanner (Ann Orr), about his laziness so he sings this spirited number with the chorus about how he will find fortune and fame one day. Kern's music is infectious and toe-tapping, and **P. G. Wodehouse** wrote the zippy lyric in which Stub argues that Henry Ford, Andrew Carnegie, J. P. Morgan, and other giants of industry started with as little as he has. Angelo Mango led the song in the long-running 1959 Off-Broadway revival of *Leave It to Jane* and recorded it as well.

"Ka-lu-a" is a pseudo-Hawaiian ballad from the Broadway musical *Good Morning, Dearie* (1921) that involved Kern in a lawsuit over plagiarism. Society dandy Billy Van Cortlandt (**Oscar Shaw**) and a chorus of girls sang the romantic memory song about a moonlit night in the tropics. Hawaiian songs had been quite the rage for the previous six years but "Ka-lu-a" proved to be one of the most popular. Kern's music is languid yet intoxicating, and **Anne Caldwell**'s lyric conjures up exotic images of island love. The number was a best-seller in sheet music and piano rolls, and orchestras across America were soon playing it. Songwriter Fred Fisher took out an ad on the front page of *Variety* stating that the bass line in "Ka-lu-a" was exactly like that in his 1919 song hit "Dardanella," and he sued Kern and the show's producers for $1 million. The 1924 trial was a sensation in which it was revealed that Fisher had not actually written the music for "Dardanella" but only purchased the rights to it and provided the lyric. The star witness for Kern was renowned composer Victor Herbert who demonstrated to the court that the bass section in question could be traced back to classic origins and had also been used by Schumann, Weber, and Wagner. Fisher lost his case. "Ka-lu-a" was used in Kern's London musical *The Cabaret Girl* (1922) where it was sung by **Dorothy Dickson** and the girls' chorus with the contentious bass theme dropped for legal reasons. In the movie biopic *Till the Clouds Roll By* (1945), Kern (Robert Walker) played "Ka-lu-a" on the piano as one of his first compositions, and it was picked up by the orchestra on the soundtrack. Although the ballad fell out of favor by World War II, a record by jazz violinist Joe Venuti revived interest in the song in the 1950s. Other discs include those by Andy Williams, Marty Robbins, Andre Kostelanetz, Paul Whiteman, Stanley Black, and Spike Hughes. The number has sometimes been listed as "Kalua" and "Kailua."

KEEL, Howard [né Harold Clifford Leek]. (1919–2004) Film and stage singer, actor. A stalwart, full-voiced baritone in many Hollywood musicals, he played gambler Gaylord Ravenal in the 1951 version of *Show Boat* and the American Tony Naylor in Paris in Kern's *Lovely to Look At* (1952). Keel was born in Gillespie, Illinois, and grew up in California where he later worked as an aircraft salesman. Keel started singing in clubs and at aircraft sales conventions, and eventually went professional and performed in California stock theatres. He made his Broadway debut as a replacement for Billy Bigelow in *Carousel* in 1945 and reprised the role in a 1957 Broadway revival. In 1946 he took over the role of Curly in *Oklahoma!* on Broadway, played it in the original 1947 London production, and repeated his performance on tour. Keel got to originate only two roles on Broadway—in the short-run musicals *Saratoga* in 1959 and *Ambassador* in 1972—but he was very busy in Hollywood where he made an impressive debut playing Frank Butler in *Annie Get Your Gun* (1950), as well as leading parts in *Lovely to Look At*, *Show Boat*, *Calamity Jane* (1953), *Kiss Me, Kate* (1953), *Seven Brides for Seven Brothers* (1954), *Rose Marie* (1954), *Deep in My Heart* (1954), and *Kismet* (1955). Keel continued to sing on television, in clubs and concerts, and in stock revivals into the 1990s.

KELLY, Gene [né Eugene Curran Kelly]. (1912–1996) Film and stage dancer, singer, actor, choreographer, director. The cinema's preeminent dancer-choreographer, he made a big splash on Broadway before going to Hollywood where his first challenging role was hoofer Danny Maguire in Kern's *Cover Girl* (1944). A native of Pittsburgh, Pennsylvania, the son of a sales executive and a former actress, he was educated at Penn State and the University of Pittsburgh in economics. Kelly had taken dance lessons as a child, and as a young adult worked as a dance instructor to support himself while he tried to get acting jobs in New York. He made his Broadway debut in the chorus of *Leave It to Me!* (1938) and the next year was featured in the revue *One for the Money* while he choreographed nightclub acts and revues in Manhattan. Kelly was first noticed on Broadway in the non-musical *The Time of Your Life* (1939) in which he played the desperate Harry the Hoofer. That part got him the leading role of the unscrupulous Joey Evans in *Pal Joey* (1940), which made him famous. After choreographing the Broadway musical *Best Foot Forward* (1941), Kelly went to Hollywood where he made his screen debut in the musical *For Me and My Gal* (1942), followed by one of the most spectacular careers in movie history. He performed, choreographed, and directed film musicals for the next twenty-five years, shining in such classics as *Cover Girl, Anchors Aweigh* (1945), *Words and Music* (1948), *On the Town* (1949), *An American in Paris* (1951), and *Singin' in the Rain* (1952). He also acted in non-musicals, such as *The Three Musketeers* (1948) and *Inherit the Wind* (1960). Oddly, when he returned to New York to direct *Flower Drum Song* in 1958, he did not choreograph the production (the dances were staged by Carol Haney), nor was he involved with the 1961 film version. Kelly's athletic dancing, imaginative choreography, innovative use of cinema effects in movie musicals, and astute direction made him a giant in the American film musical. Biographies: *Gene Kelly*, Clive Hirschhorn (1985); *Gene Kelly: A Life of Dance and Dreams*, Alvin Yudkoff (2001).

LA BELLE PAREE. A musical extravaganza by Edgar Smith (book), Edward Maddern (lyrics), Frank Tours, Jerome Kern (music). [20 March 1911, Winter Garden Theatre, 104 performances] Produced by the Shubert Brothers, directed by J. C. Huffman, William J. Wilson. Although it was the first Broadway musical to have a substantial part of its score composed by Kern (seven songs) and it introduced Al Jolson to the legitimate theatre, *La Belle Paree* brought little fame to either man as the critics wrote mostly about the lovely new Winter Garden Theatre. Although it was a revue, the show had a thin plot about the Widow McShane (Arthur Cunningham in drag) who is pursued by ambitious and amorous suitors as she tours Paris. Stella Mayhew, who played the widow's maid, was the featured star, and newcomer Jolson (in blackface) was her boyfriend. It was so late in the show when Jolson got to sing that most of the critics had already left the theatre to make their newspapers' deadlines. But audiences were thrilled when Jolson and Mayhew sang Kern's "Paris Is a Paradise for Coons," and by the end of the run the producing Shuberts knew they had a new star. Jolson was featured in many subsequent Shubert shows at the Winter Garden, but this was his only musical with Kern. Other notable Kern songs in the show include the Scottish ditty "The Edinboro Wriggle," the rag "De Goblin's Glide," and the operatic spoof "Sing Trovatore."

LADY, BE GOOD. A movie musical by Jack McGowan, Kay Van Riper, John McClain (screenplay); **Arthur Freed**, **Oscar Hammerstein** (lyrics); Roger Edens, Jerome Kern (music). [1941, MGM] Produced by Arthur Freed, directed by Norman Z. McLeod, choreographed by Busby Berkeley (uncredited), musical direction by George Stoll, orchestrations by George Bassman, Conrad Salinger, Leo Arnaud. The Gershwins' jazzy Broadway musical *Lady, Be Good!* (1924) came to the screen barely recognizable, but it brought acclaim to Kern and Hammerstein's lovely song **"The Last Time I Saw Paris."** MGM kept the Gershwins' title song and "Fascinating

Rhythm," tossed out the rest of the stage score and plot, and substituted a dull story about songwriters Dixie Donegan (Ann Sothern) and Eddie Crane (Robert Young) who are romantic as well as professional partners. When success goes to their heads, the couple breaks up, followed by a series of reconciliations and further partings that try the patience of even the most forgiving movie musical fan. Eleanor Powell, as a character who hardly entered the plot, gave the film its only winning moments, such as a lavish production number that featured her, eight grand pianos, and a hundred men in white tie and tails tapping to "Fascinating Rhythm." Also effective was Sothern's rendition of "The Last Time I Saw Paris," which was interpolated into the film and won the Oscar for Best Song. Also in the score were "Your Words and My Music" and "You'll Never Know" by Roger Edens and Arthur Freed. Norman Z. McLeod directed without much energy, and the supporting cast included Lionel Barrymore, **Red Skelton**, John Carroll, Virginia O'Brien, Dan Dailey, Reginald Owen, and **Phil Silvers**, all of whom had been better and would be again in other films. The film soundtrack is fairly complete and includes Sothern's singing of "The Last Time I Saw Paris."

"Lafayette" is the spirited march that Kern and lyricist **Dorothy Fields** wrote for the film remake of *Roberta* titled *Lovely to Look At* (1952). American theatrical producers Al Marsh (**Red Skelton**), Tony Naylor (**Howard Keel**), and Jerry Ralby (**Gower Champion**) arrive in Paris and announce to the dead French general of the song title that they, as in the famous quote, "are here!" During the number the threesome toured and danced through some city streets and tried out some French phrases and habits, but with little success. The music was a trunk tune by Kern, who had died seven years before the film was made.

LAMOUR, Dorothy [née Mary Leta Dorothy Slaton]. (1914–1996) Film and stage performer. Typecast as an exotic, primitive jungle princess when she donned a sarong in non-musical films, the dark-haired, sultry beauty appeared in over thirty movie musicals, most fondly remembered as the beautiful distraction in the seven **Bob Hope**–Bing Crosby *Road* pictures, but she gave one of her best performances as the saucy saloon gal Molly in Kern's *High, Wide and Handsome* (1937). Lamour was born in New Orleans and won beauty contests and sang in bands before making her

Hollywood debut as a chorus girl in the musical *Footlight Parade* (1933). When she appeared in a sarong in the non-musical *Jungle Princess* (1936), she was widely noticed and was similarly clothed in such films as *The Hurricane* (1937), *Typhoon* (1940), *Aloma of the South Seas* (1941), and others. Lamour's early musicals were *College Holiday* (1936), *Swing High, Swing Low* (1937), *High, Wide and Handsome*, *Thrill of a Lifetime* (1937), *Big Broadcast of 1938*, *Her Jungle Love* (1938), *Tropic Holiday* (1938), *St. Louis Blues* (1939), and *Man About Town* (1939), but it was in *Road to Singapore* (1940) that her exotic persona was used in a satirical, musical way and she revealed a playful side rarely seen before. She costarred with Hope and Crosby in six of the *Road* musical comedies and made a cameo in the final entry, *The Road to Hong Kong* (1962). Among her other musical credits are *Johnny Apollo* (1940), *Moon Over Burma* (1940), *The Fleet's In* (1942), *Beyond the Blue Horizon* (1942), *Star Spangled Rhythm* (1942), *Dixie* (1943), *Riding High* (1943), *And the Angels Sing* (1944), *Rainbow Island* (1944), *Duffy's Tavern* (1945) *Variety Girl* (1947), *Slightly French* (1949), and *Here Comes the Groom* (1951). In the 1950s Lamour acted on television and occasionally turned to the stage. She continued to perform into the late 1980s. Autobiography: *My Side of the Road* (1980).

"The Land Where the Good Songs Go" is the enchanting song by Kern and lyricist **P. G. Wodehouse** about a magical place "on the other side of the moon" where life is idyllic and all the best music can be heard. The lovely number was sung by Elizabeth Brice and Charles King in *Miss 1917* (1917), but when that show failed to find an audience the number was added to the score of Kern's *Oh, Boy!* during its run that same year. George Gershwin recorded a piano roll of the song early in his career. "The Land Where the Good Songs Go" was sung by Lucille Bremer (dubbed by Trudy Erwin) and the chorus in the Kern biopic *Till the Clouds Roll By* (1946). It was also sung (and recorded) by the cast of a popular New York concert titled *The Land Where the Good Songs Go* in 2012. Noteworthy recordings of the ballad were made by Hal Cazalet, Peggy King, and Pamela Myers.

"The Last Time I Saw Paris" is a Kern–**Oscar Hammerstein** standard that was not written for a play or a film, which was very unusual for either songwriter. Hammerstein was so upset when the Nazis occupied Paris in

1940 that he was moved to write a lyric about the much-cherished city. He showed it to Kern who composed a lilting waltz melody that captured the pictures Hammerstein described: lovers walking in the park, birds singing, honking taxicabs, laughter from the sidewalk cafes, and so on. (This writing procedure was also unusual: Kern always insisted on writing the music first and then having a lyric fashioned to fit it.) Kate Smith introduced the ballad on the radio, and a movie producer heard it, liked it, and interpolated it into the film *Lady, Be Good* (1941) where it was sung by Ann Sothern. It won the Academy Award for Best Song even though it was not written for any movie; several complained (none more forcefully than Kern and Hammerstein) and the Academy changed the rules so that such a case would not happen again in the future. Among the many memorable recordings of the ballad are those by Smith, Lanny Ross, Hildegarde, Sophie Tucker, Tony Martin, Robert Clary, Skitch Henderson, Joni James, jazz pianist Beegie Adair, Kiri Te Kanawa, Sonny Rollins, the Four Freshmen, Andrea Marcovicci, Charles Busch, and Noel Coward, to whom the authors dedicated the song. Dinah Shore sang "The Last Time I Saw Paris" in the Kern film biopic *Till the Clouds Roll By* (1946), it was heard on the soundtrack and performed by Odette in French in *The Last Time I Saw Paris* (1954), and **Bob Hope** sang it in *Paris Holiday* (1958). In the revue *Jerome Kern Goes to Hollywood*, David Kernan sang it in London in 1985 and Scott Holmes performed it on Broadway the next year.

LEAVE IT TO JANE. A musical comedy by **Guy Bolton** (book), **P. G. Wodehouse** (book and lyrics), Jerome Kern (music). [28 August 1917, Longacre Theatre, 167 performances] Produced by William Elliott, **F. Ray Comstock**, Morris Gest; directed by **Edward Royce**; choreographed by David Bennett; musical direction by John McGhie; orchestrations by **Frank Saddler**.

Plot: In order to win the big football game, Jane Witherspoon, the daughter of the president of Atwater College, flirts and coerces the All-American halfback Billy Bolton not to enroll at the rival Bingham College but to come to Atwater and join their team. He does, Atwater wins the big game, and Billy wins Jane. The comic subplots include the romance of the football-crazy students Stub Talmadge and Bessie Tanner, the efforts of the landlady's daughter Flora Wiggins to financially and romantically secure

CASTS FOR *LEAVE IT TO JANE*

Character	1917 Broadway	1959 Off-Broadway
Jane Witherspoon	Edith Hallor	Kathleen Murray
Billy Bolton	Robert Pitkin	Art Matthews
Flora Wiggins	Georgia O'Ramey	Dorothy Greener
Stub Talmadge	**Oscar Shaw**	Angelo Mango
Ollie Mitchell	Rudolf Cutten	George Segal
Matty McGowan	Dan Collyer	Monroe Arnold
Harold Bub Hicks	Olin Howland	Ray Tudor

the ex-boarder Harold Hicks, and the scheme of the students to keep Billy's father from finding out that his son has switched over to Atwater.

Although not technically a **Princess Theatre Musical** because it did not play at the Princess Theatre, the bouncy collegiate show had the same creators as the famous musical series and fulfilled all its goals to present literate musical comedies with contemporary characters. (The Princess was already occupied by the smash hit **Oh, Boy!**) Bolton and Wodehouse's libretto was based on the 1904 comedy *The College Widow*, and the slight but useful storyline allowed for ample song and dance opportunities; the score used those opportunities to present such delightful numbers as the bouncy "Just You Watch My Step," the comic "Cleopatterer," the sultry "The Siren's Song," the optimistic "The Sun Shines Brighter," and the celebratory title song. The superior cast was also adulated by the press, and *Leave It to Jane* ran five months in the large house. The show was also popular on the road where three touring companies performed it across the nation. Yet the musical was deemed too American for London so there was no West End transfer. Inexplicably, Hollywood never made a screen version of *Leave It*

LEAVE IT TO JANE SONGS

"A Peach of a Life"
"Wait Till Tomorrow"
"Just You Watch My Step"
"Leave It to Jane"
"The Crickets Are Calling"
"There It Is Again"
"Cleopatterer"
"What I'm Longing to Say"
"Sir Galahad"
"The Sun Shines Brighter"
"The Siren's Song"
"I'm Going to Find a Girl"

to Jane either before or after sound came in. (Silent movie versions of *The College Widow* were made in 1915 and 1927.)

A 1958 Off-Broadway revival of *Leave It to Jane* ran a surprising two years. It was directed by Lawrence Carra with vivacious choreography by Mary Jane Doerr. Fortunately the production was recorded, and it remains the most complete recording of this important and timeless musical. A 1985 revival at the Goodspeed Opera House in Connecticut (with Rebecca Luker as Jane) was so well received that it set out on tour with the hopes of arriving on Broadway as the Goodspeed's previous production of *Very Good Eddie* had in 1976. But business was not strong enough to risk a New York mounting.

Recordings: The Victor Light Opera Company recorded a medley of the score's highlights in 1930s. The 1958 Off-Broadway cast recording is more complete and superior in every way.

"Leave It to Jane" is the catchy title song from Kern's 1917 collegiate musical that sang the praises of Jane Witherspoon (Edith Hallor), the school president's daughter who is as resourceful as she is admired. Atwater College students Stub Talmadge (**Oscar Shaw**) and Bessie Tanner (Mary Orr) decide that Jane is just the person to solve the dilemma of getting footballer Billy Bolton (Robert G. Pitkin) to play on their team. The two praise Jane in song, she responds with modest agreement, and the other Atwater students join in the merry number. **P. G. Wodehouse**'s lyric is spirited and fun, and Kern's music is particularly contagious because of a simple 4/4 time that has a subtle syncopation in its melody and countermelody. The music for "Leave It to Jane" was first used in the number "Whistling Dan" in the Kern musical *90 in the Shade* (1915) where it was sung by Marie Cahill and the company, but it was little noticed and Kern rightfully felt such a scintillating melody ought to be given a second hearing. June Allyson performed the number on screen with the chorus in the Kern biopic *Till the Clouds Roll By* (1945), and Kathleen Murray played Jane and sang it in the successful 1959 Off-Broadway revival of *Leave It to Jane*.

LEROY, Mervyn. (1900–1987) Film director and producer. A versatile Hollywood showman, he was a shrewd producer who also excelled in directing many kinds of films, including the Kern musicals *Sweet Adeline*

LEAVE IT TO JANE. Although this 1917 tuneful collegiate musical comedy was a solid success on Broadway, there was no London production or screen version. Yet when *Leave It to Jane* was revived Off-Broadway in 1959, it ran a surprising two years. Kathleen Murray (center) played Jane in that production. She is pictured here with coeds Bessie (Joy Claussen, left) and Flora (Dorothy Greener) as they flatter the college president (Jon Richards) who just happens to be Jane's father. *Photofest*

(1935) and *Lovely to Look At* (1952). LeRoy was born in San Francisco and as a boy saw his family business destroyed by the famous earthquake of 1906. He sold newspapers on the street then went into show business, first as a singer in vaudeville and then in the movies where he worked his way up from the wardrobe department to cameraman to director in 1927. LeRoy made his name directing some hard-hitting melodramas for Warner Brothers, such as *Little Caesar* (1931) and *I Am a Fugitive from a Chain Gang* (1932). At the same time he was turning out musicals such as *Little Johnny Jones* (1930), *Show Girl in Hollywood* (1930), *Gold Diggers of 1933*, and *Sweet Adeline.* By 1937 LeRoy was also producing for MGM and presented such musicals as *The King and the Show Girl* (1937), *Mr. Dodd Takes the Air* (1937), *Fools for Scandal* (1938), *The Wizard of Oz* (1939), and *At the Circus* (1939). After World War II he concentrated on non-musicals but still directed *Lovely to Look At, Million Dollar Mermaid* (1952), *Latin Lovers* (1953), and both produced and directed *Rose Marie* (1954) and *Gypsy* (1962). Autobiography: *Mervyn LeRoy: Take One* (1974).

"Let's Begin" is the slightly swinging song about recognizing that flirtation has turned to love, written by Kern and lyricist **Otto Harbach** for the Broadway show *Roberta* (1933). Harbach wrote several different lyrics for the number so that it could be used throughout the show. George Murphy and the ensemble sang it as the opening number, and it was later reprised three times: by Ray Middleton and **Bob Hope** and the male chorus, then as a duet by Hope and **Tamara**, and finally as a quartet by Hope, Middleton, **Lyda Roberti**, and Sydney Greenstreet. **Dorothy Fields** wrote some additional lyrics for the 1935 screen version of *Roberta,* where it was sung as a mock duet by **Fred Astaire** and Candy Candido (in a falsetto voice) and then was danced by Astaire, Candido, **Ginger Rogers**, and Gene Sheldon. Liz Robertson sang "Let's Begin" in the revue *Jerome Kern Goes to Hollywood*, which played London in 1985 and on Broadway in 1986. Recordings of note were made by Ella Fitzgerald, Anita O'Day, Tony Bennett, Jackie Cain, Margaret Whiting, Barbara Carroll, Eric Parkin, Rebecca Luker with Graham Rowat, and Jack Cassidy with Joan Roberts.

"Life Upon the Wicked Stage" is a sparkling comic song from *Show Boat* (1927) in which the showgirl Ellie (**Eva Puck**) and the chorus girls lament the rigors of show business, explaining that it is not as romantic as the public imagines. Kern's bouncy melody and **Oscar Hammerstein**'s shrewd lyric recall the sassy musical comedy numbers from the **Princess Theatre Musicals** a decade earlier. Of particular interest is the song's frothy lyric filled with clever rhyming, something Hammerstein usually eschewed in his work. (Hammerstein wrote the lyric after Dorothy Jacobson, who would become his second wife, told him about her frustrating career as an actress.) Kern's music is practically comic in his spirited, carefree manner, and "Life Upon the Wicked Stage" is *Show Boat*'s funniest number. Although the song was not used in the 1929 and 1936 screen versions of *Show Boat*, the number was given a hilariously droll interpretation by Virginia O'Brien in the *Show Boat* section of the Kern biopic *Till the Clouds Roll By* (1945) and was sung and danced by **Marge** and **Gower Champion** in the 1951 movie remake of *Show Boat*. Paige O'Hara sang it in John McGlinn's comprehensive recording of *Show Boat* in 1988 and there have also been notable recordings by Blossom Dearie, Janet Pavek, Carole Cook, Colette Lyons, Allyn Ann McLerie, Dora Bryan, Dorothy Stanley and Elaine Stritch, Tracey Miller, Fay DeWitt, Jan Hunt, and Caroline O'Connor. The song was listed in the 1927 theatre program as "Life on the Wicked Stage," and it is sometimes labeled that way, but the lyric uses "upon" rather than "on," and that is the most used title for the number.

LIST SONGS by Kern. An old and favored technique for structuring a theatre song, particularly a comic one, is to list a series of examples, names, or items. Sometimes called a "laundry list song," the number is hopefully more interesting because of its listing. A master of the list song was Cole Porter whose "You're the Top" and "Brush Up Your Shakespeare" are still model examples of the type. But list songs go back long before Porter and sometimes showed up in Kern musicals. For example, lyricist **Oscar Hammerstein** created lists in the Kern songs **"The Things I Want"** and **"The Last Time I Saw Paris,"** P. G. Wodehouse used the device in such numbers as **"You Never Knew About Me"** and "Greenwich Village," and **Johnny Mercer** came up with a charming list for **"I'm Old Fashioned."**

LONDON STAGE, Kern on the. Few American composers for Broadway were as active in the London theatre as Kern. He first visited London in 1903, and as a young man he saw a handful of his songs interpolated into West End shows. By 1916 he was writing the full scores for British musicals, often with British writers and producers. In addition to five shows that premiered in London, seven of Kern's New York hits were produced in the West End, most of them more than once over the years. Kern was one of the few American creators of musicals who was well known to the British because of his many hit songs, some of which first became popular on the London stage. Yet Kern's love for the British was more than professional. He met his future wife Eva Leale in England, and he had many close ties there with people both in show business and outside of it. Between 1920 and 1935, hardly a year passed without Kern making his annual trip to London.

Unlike on Broadway, hit musicals in London during the first three decades of the twentieth century were often recorded using members of the original cast. (This would not become common practice in the States until the mid-1940s.) So Kern's affection for England in the 1920s and 1930s must have been further multiplied by hearing his songs not only in music halls, ballrooms, and nightclubs, but on record and radio as well.

KERN ON THE LONDON STAGE

Original London musicals:

Theodore & Co. (1916)
The Cabaret Girl (1922)
The Beauty Prize (1923)
Blue Eyes (1928)
Three Sisters (1934)
Jerome Kern Goes to Hollywood (1985)

Broadway musicals in the West End:

Very Good Eddie (1918, 1976)
Oh, Boy! retitled *Oh, Joy!* (1919)
Sally (1921) and retitled *Wild Rose* (1942)
Sunny (1926)
Show Boat (1928, 1943, 1971, 1990, 1998)
The Cat and the Fiddle (1932)
Music in the Air (1933)

"Long Ago (and Far Away)" is arguably the last great song Kern wrote, and although lyricist **Ira Gershwin** never liked it all that much, it was the biggest seller of Gershwin's career. The enchanting ballad was sung by the heartsick entertainer Danny McGuire (**Gene Kelly**) in an empty nightclub in the film *Cover Girl* (1944) while his sidekick Genius (**Phil Silvers**) played the piano and the unseen model Rusty Parker (**Rita Hayworth**) looked on. Near the end of the movie Kelly and Hayworth (dubbed by Martha

Mears) briefly reprised the number. Told by the film's producer to "Keep it simple," Gershwin labored through several drafts before he wearily submitted the lyric about a long-past dream that finally comes true. It is an atypically simple lyric for a Gershwin song but perfectly phrased all the same. Another strength of the ballad is Kern's music, which keeps returning to the same musical theme, something rarely done in popular music. As musicologist Alec Wilder notes, "Kern daringly restates his principal idea a minor third higher after only eight measures . . . I was convinced that this device would be too much for the public ear, but not so." In fact, "Long Ago (and Far Away)" sold 600,000 copies of sheet music the first year. Among the many recordings of the song are those by Bing Crosby, Perry Como, Helen Forrest and Dick Haymes, jazz pianist Beegie Adair, Chet Baker, Carmen Dragon, Dorothy Kirsten, Oscar Peterson, Kiri Te Kanawa, Judy Garland, Jo Stafford, Joan Morris and William Bolcom, Guy Lombardo (vocal by Tony Craig), Glenn Miller, Marni Nixon, Eddie Fisher, Les Brown (vocal by Doris Day), Bob Dylan, Billy Eckstine, Tommy Dorsey, Rosemary Clooney, Vera Lynn, Frank Sinatra, Mel Tormé, Robert Goulet, Eydie Gorme, Johnny Mathis, and Englebert Humperdinck. **Kathryn Grayson** sang the ballad in the Kern biopic *Till the Clouds Roll By* (1946), Crosby's recording was heard in the film *Someone to Love* (1987), Stafford's rendition was played in *Bugsy* (1991), and Miller's recording was heard in *The Grass Harp* (1995). On stage, the cast of the revue *Jerome Kern Goes to Hollywood* sang it in London in 1985 and on Broadway the next year.

"Look for the Silver Lining" is the best-selling song from Kern's Broadway hit *Sally* (1920) and one of the great optimistic ballads of its era. The melody was first heard in the song "Catamaran" in Kern's failed musical *The King of Cadonia* (1910). With a new lyric by B. G. DeSylva about finding the sunny side of life, it was heard in the Kern musical *Zip Goes a Million* that closed out of town in 1919. The next year it was sung in *Sally* by millionaire Blair Farquar (Irving Fisher) to the downhearted dishwasher Sally (**Marilyn Miller**) who then joins him in singing it. DeSylva provided an unembellished, hopeful lyric, and Kern composed a seemingly simple, almost hymn-like, melody. The harmonics are uncomplicated and the music has few jumps, but the few that are there are subtle and almost subliminally effective. Using mostly quarter, half, and whole notes, Kern created an unforgettable melody that is not predictable or trite. The popularity of "Look for the Silver Lining" is possibly due to its delectable ambiguity: it conjures up impressions of longing and sadness as much as it instills a feeling of hope and joy. The number is also purely theatrical in that it requires no scenery or costumes to create the dramatic situation. **Dorothy Dickson** played Sally in the 1921 West End production and introduced the number in London with Gregory Stroud as Blair, and Jesse Matthews sang it as Sally in the 1942 London revival. On screen it was sung by Miller in the 1929 version of *Sally*, Judy Garland in the Kern biopic *Till the Clouds Roll By* (1945), and June Haver in the Marilyn Miller biopic *Look for the Silver Lining* (1949). The song was also heard on the soundtrack of *The Great Ziegfeld* (1936), *Jack & Sarah* (1995), *L.A. Confidential* (1997), and *Man of the Century* (1999). The cast of the revue *Jerome Kern Goes to Hollywood* sang the ballad in London in 1985 and on Broadway the next year. Among the many recordings over the years are those by Kiri Te Kanawa, Andrea Marcovicci, Connee Boswell, Chet Baker, Aretha Franklin, Joan Morris and William Bolcom, Susannah McCorkle, Rod McKuen, and Margaret Whiting.

"The Lorelei" is a merry trio about the Rhine maiden who sang to passing ships, luring men to their destruction, as performed in Kern's Broadway hit *Sally* (1920). **Anne Caldwell** wrote the wry lyric to Kern's gently rocking music, and the song was intended for *The Night Boat* (1920) but was dropped during rehearsals. In *Sally* it was sung by Otis (**Walter Catlett**), Rosalind (Mary Hay), and Jimmie (Stanley Ridges). Kim Criswell is among the very few to record the song. The number is not to be confused with a 1928 Noel Coward song and a 1933 George and **Ira Gershwin** song with the same title and about the same Germanic folk legend.

LOVE DUETS by Kern. Whether it's a musical comedy, operetta, revue, or musical play, every Broadway show is expected to include at least one love song. The very essence (and biggest challenge) of songwriting for the theatre is to find fresh situations and methods for expressing love. This task often falls on the lyricist who must find interesting words to fit to the romantic music. **Oscar Hammerstein**, for example, created a fresh approach when the lovers first meet in *Show Boat* (1927) and pretend to know each other better with the number **"Make Believe."** Among the many notable love duets by Kern and his lyric collaborators are **"The Touch of Your Hand," "Whip-**

Poor-Will," "You Are Love," "Nodding Roses," "Till the Clouds Roll By," "Heaven in My Arms," "Nesting Time in Flatbush," "Don't Ever Leave Me," "The Song Is You," and "Why Do I Love You?"

LOVE O' MIKE. A comedy with music by Sydney Smith, Augustus Thomas, Jr. (book); **Harry B. Smith** (lyrics); Jerome Kern (music). [15 January 1917, Shubert Theatre, 233 performances] Produced by **Elisabeth Marbury**, Lee Shubert; directed by J. H. Benrimo; musical direction by Frank Tours; orchestrations by **Frank Saddler**. In one of those rare cases in which a musical was a flop during its tryout tour but a hit on Broadway, *Love o' Mike* began as a Shubert product titled *Girls Will Be Girls*. Elisabeth Marbury, who had helped found the **Princess Theatre Musical** series, was coproducer, and when the show was in trouble she was instrumental in saving it. The title, cast members, songs, and plot were greatly altered, and what opened on Broadway was a pleasing piece of ridiculous fluff. The whole musical takes place during one day at a house party at Mrs. Marvin's country estate in Bronxville. The life of the party is the British lord Michael Kildare (Lawrence Grossmith) who not only charms all the girls but becomes a hero when he rescues several inhabitants during a local tenement fire. The males at the party seethe with jealousy and plan their own stunt to impress the women, but the conniving butler Bif Jackson (George Hassell) waylays the plot and Mike comes out on top, winning the heart of Vivian (Vivian Wessell). In minor roles were newcomer Peggy Wood and, showing off their dancing skills, Gloria Goodwin and **Clifton Webb**. The hit song of the musical was the lyrical duet "It Wasn't My Fault" (which came from the 1915 Kern flop *90 in the Shade*), but also pleasing were the sassy dance number "It's in the Book," the plaintive ballad "I Wonder Why," the Scottish parody "Hoot Mon," and the wistful "A Lonesome Little Tune." *Love o' Mike* was a surprise hit, running seven months, but ironically did not do well on its subsequent road tour, folding in two weeks. In the 1930s the Victor Light Opera Company recorded a medley of the score's highlights.

LOVELY TO LOOK AT. See *Roberta*.

"Lovely to Look At" is the enchanting tribute to beauty that Kern and lyricist **Dorothy Fields** interpolated into the 1935 screen version of *Roberta*.

It was their first collaboration, although Fields wrote the lyric to Kern's lead sheet before she ever met the composer. The result was a haunting, intoxicating song and the birth of one of the finest songwriting teams in the history of Hollywood musicals. The number was heard over the opening credits of the movie, then princess-in-disguise Stephanie (**Irene Dunne**) sang it, then **Fred Astaire** and **Ginger Rogers** danced to it. Told that the number must serve as a love song and also be used for the film's fashion show finale, Fields came up with an elegant lyric that sits on Kern's dreamy melody effortlessly. The song's refrain is unusually short (only sixteen measures), and when asked why, Kern replied, "That was all I had to say." But the last four measures are very complex and the studio feared the song was too difficult to become popular. To their surprise, the cascading love song was at the top of *Your Hit Parade*'s listing, Eddy Duchin's recording was number one on the charts, and the ballad was nominated for an Oscar. The 1952 remake of *Roberta* was titled **Lovely to Look At** because of the song, which was sung by American tourist Tony Naylor (**Howard Keel**) as he appeared in the imagination of Paris designer Stephanie (**Kathryn Grayson**); the two reprised the number at the end of the movie. The ballad was also heard in the films *In Person* (1935), *Bright Lights, Big City* (1988), *Another Woman* (1988), and *Meet Joe Black* (1998). Other recordings of note include those by Astaire, Gordon MacRae, Leo Reisman, Stanley Black, Oscar Peterson, the Audubon Quartet, jazz violinist Joe Venuti, Andrea Marcovicci, Paul Weston, George Feyer, the Mike Wofford Trio, and a duet version by Stephen Douglass and Joan Roberts. Elisabeth Welch sang "Lovely to Look At" in the revue *Jerome Kern Goes to Hollywood*, which played London in 1985 and on Broadway in 1986.

LUCKY. A musical comedy by **Otto Harbach** (book and lyrics), Jerome Kern (music), Bert Kalmar, Harry Ruby (music and lyrics). [22 March 1927, New Amsterdam Theatre, 71 performances] Produced by **Charles Dillingham**; directed by **Hassard Short**; choreographed by David Bennett, Albertina Rasch; musical direction by Gus Salzer; orchestrations by **Robert Russell Bennett**. In his efforts to rival the showman **Florenz Ziegfeld**, producer Dillingham and Kern concocted a lavish spectacular that would offer dazzling sets and costumes, songs by a handful of composers, top stars, ballets staged by Rasch, and even Paul Whiteman conducting his famous orchestra. The result was a glossy bore that left critics cold and failed to impress audiences. The tale was set in Ceylon where the pearl diver Lucky (Mary Eaton) plies her trade for the thief Barlow (Paul Everton) who claims to be her father. The American pearl buyer Jack Mansfield (Joseph Santley) falls in love with Lucky, rescues her from the bondage of Barlow, and brings her to New York where she finds success as a cabaret dancer. Such talented performers as **Walter Catlett**, Ruby Keeler, Skeets Gallagher, and Ivy Sawyer were wasted in underdeveloped secondary characters. The scenery and costumes were indeed lush and expensive looking, and the dancing (which required two choreographers) was on a massive scale. The score was generally disappointing, with both Kern's and his collaborators' songs offering little outside of routine. As for Kern himself, a low point in his career and personal problems at home converged on his temperament, and his behavior during the preparation for *Lucky* could only be described as deplorable. He insisted on full credit and royalties for the score even though he only wrote a small percentage of the songs, he had Harbach locked out of rehearsals and took over libretto revisions himself, and when Dillingham was taken ill Kern took charge of the tryout period with a dictator-like fervor. Because such behavior was out of character for Kern, his friends and collaborators later forgave him and worked with him again. As for *Lucky*, the expensive show struggled to find an audience and closed deep in the red after nine weeks.

MacDONALD, Jeanette [Anna]. (1901–1965) Film and stage singer, actress. One of filmdom's favorite sopranos, she played the American composer Shirley Sheridan in Brussels in the screen version of Kern's *The Cat and the Fiddle* (1934). Born and educated in Philadelphia, she studied voice in New York before landing her first Broadway job in the chorus of Kern's *The Night Boat* (1920). Soon the delicate blonde beauty was playing ingenue roles in operettas and musical comedies, including *Tip-Toes* (1925) and *Sunny Days* (1928). Few of these shows were hits, and MacDonald never became a stage star. In 1929 she signed a film contract and never returned to the theatre. From her first film, *The Love Parade* (1929) with Maurice Chevalier, MacDonald was a sensation, going on to star in over two dozen musicals before retiring twenty years later to concentrate on concerts and recordings. She also costarred with Chevalier in *One Hour with You* (1932), the innovative musical *Love Me Tonight* (1932), and *The Merry Widow* (1934), but she is most remembered for her eight movies with Nelson Eddy, including *Naughty Marietta* (1935), *Rose-Marie* (1936), *Maytime* (1937), *Sweethearts* (1938), *New Moon* (1940), and *I Married an Angel* (1942). Her other screen musicals include *The Vagabond King* (1930), *The Cat and the Fiddle*, *The Firefly* (1937), *Bitter Sweet* (1940), and *Cairo* (1941). While she was sometimes dubbed the "Iron Butterfly" for her cold beauty and super-human voice, MacDonald was beloved by audiences, and her partnership with Eddy formed the most popular singing duo in the history of Hollywood. Autobiography: *Jeanette MacDonald Autobiography: The Lost Manuscript*, Sharon Rich, ed. (2004); biographies: *The Jeanette MacDonald Story*, Robert Parish (1976); *Hollywood Diva: Biography of Jeanette MacDonald*, Edward Baron Tirk (2000).

"Make Believe" is the rhapsodic duet from the Kern–**Oscar Hammerstein** classic **Show Boat** (1927) and one of the American musical theatre's greatest love songs. The young and impressionable Magnolia Hawks (**Norma Terris**) and riverboat gambler Gaylord Ravenal (**Howard Marsh**) have just met and are immediately attracted to each other. Rather than break into a gushing duet, as accepted in operetta, the two tease each other and pretend to be lovers singing to each other. The subtext is clear and the moment is, lyrically, musically, and character-wise, thrilling. Kern's music is very melodic with wonderful harmonic surprises, such as interesting triplets in the refrain. Hammerstein's lyric is both passionate and playful. Sometimes listed as "Only Make Believe," the song was heard in two screen versions of *Show Boat*, sung by **Irene Dunne** and **Allan Jones** in the 1936 movie and by **Kathryn Grayson** and **Howard Keel** in the 1951 remake. Grayson also sang it with Tony Martin in the Kern biopic *Till the Clouds Roll By* (1946), and the song can be heard on the soundtrack of the films *Another Woman* (1988) and *Bullets Over Broadway* (1994). In the 1985 London revue and 1986 Broadway revue *Jerome Kern Goes to Hollywood*, the number was sung as a solo by Liz Robertson. Among the many duet recordings of "Make Believe" are those by Edith Day and Howett Worster (of the 1928 London production of *Show Boat*), Robert Merrill and Patrice Munsel, Barbara Cook and Stephen Douglass, Cook with John Raitt, Frederica von Stade and Jerry Hadley, and Rebecca Luker with Mark Jacoby. Notable solo recordings were made by Frank Sinatra, Deanna Durbin, Bing Crosby, Jo Stafford, Kelly Harland, Lee Wiley, Tony Martin, Barbra Streisand, Peggy Lee, Andrea Marcovicci, and James Melton.

"Make Way for Tomorrow" is the vibrant song about an optimistic future that Kern wrote with lyricists **Ira Gershwin** and **E. Y. Harburg** for the fashion magazine movie musical *Cover Girl* (1944). Struggling entertainer Danny McGuire (**Gene Kelly**), his sidekick Genius (**Phil Silvers**), and model Rusty Parker (**Rita Hayward** dubbed by Martha Mears) sang the up-lifting number as they left their favorite late-night diner and pranced down a Brooklyn street, using brownstone stoops, garbage can lids, and other found objects in their ingenious dancing. The three friends also reprised the song briefly at the end of the film. Kern's music is a merry march that continues to rise throughout the song while the Gershwin-Harburg lyric has fun with clichés about smiles, clouds, and sunshine. "Make Way for Tomorrow" was sung by the cast of the revue *Jerome Kern Goes to Hollywood* in London in 1985 and on Broadway the next year, and Barbara Cook, Bobby Short, and Cy Young made a playful trio recording of the number in the 1970s.

MAMOULIAN, Rouben. (1898–1987) Stage and film director. An extraordinary director of plays and musicals and one of the most visual of all Broadway artists, he directed the Kern film musical *High, Wide and Handsome* (1937). Mamoulian was born in Tiflis, in the Georgian state of Russia, to an Armenian family. His father was a bank president so Mamoulian was educated in Paris and at the University of Moscow for a law career. While in Moscow he dropped law and enrolled at Evgeny Vakhtangov's Third Studio, a school connected with the Moscow Art Theatre. A theatre company he organized in his hometown in Georgia traveled to England in 1920 and Mamoulian stayed to study theatre at the University of London. First coming to America in 1923, he directed opera at the Eastman School of Music in Rochester, New York, before making his Manhattan directorial debut with the Theatre Guild production of *Porgy*. As his reputation grew, Mamoulian was invited to direct films in Hollywood, but he continued to return to the stage and directed some outstanding musicals of his era, such as *Porgy and Bess* (1935), *St. Louis Woman* (1946), and *Lost in the Stars* (1949). It was Mamoulian's masterful direction of *Oklahoma!* (1943) and *Carousel* (1945) that crowned his career, treating these innovative works as serious drama while retaining a musical persona as well. Mamoulian's film career was just as impressive, directing cinema favorites such as *Applause* (1929), *Dr. Jekyll and Mr. Hyde* (1932), *Love Me Tonight* (1932), and *Golden Boy* (1939). He was particularly talented at handling a large number of actors, turning crowd scenes into focused and theatrical paintings. Mamoulian's background in art and music served him well and few productions were as visually vibrant as his, bringing a European sense of decor to American works. This is particularly true with the evocative movie *High, Wide and Handsome*, which has an epic feel yet is intimate and detailed as well. Biographies: *Rouben Mamoulian*, Tom Milne (1969); *Reinventing Reality: The Art and Life of Rouben Mamoulian*, Mark Spergel (1993).

MARBURY, Elisabeth. (1856–1933) Stage agent and producer. While most of her career was promoting the work of playwrights, her suggestion for the format of the **Princess Theatre Musicals** made her an important producer as well. The daughter of a famous New York attorney, she was encouraged by producer Daniel Frohman to become an authors' agent. Most of her early clients were foreign playwrights, such as Victorien Sardou, Oscar Wilde, William Somerset Maugham, and James M. Barrie. Marbury is believed to have been the first agent to negotiate a percentage of box office receipts for her clients. She later began to represent important American artists, including Clyde Fitch, Rachel Crothers, and Kern. In connection with Kern, it was she who apparently suggested to producer **F. Ray Comstock** that the small Princess Theatre be turned into a house for intimate musicals, thus creating the stage for the Princess Theatre Musicals that helped make Kern, **Guy Bolton**, and **P. G. Wodehouse** famous. She coproduced two of the musicals in the series, *Nobody Home* (1915) and *Very Good Eddie* (1915), then later presented Kern's *Love o' Mike* (1917). Marbury also produced a handful of plays and revues between 1915 and 1930. Autobiography: *My Crystal Ball* (1924); biography: *Ladies and Not-So-Gentle Women: Elisabeth Marbury, Anne Morgan, Elsie de Wolfe, Anne Vanderbilt and Their Times*, Alfred Allan Lewis (2001).

MARCH SONGS by Kern. Marches, both military and circus, were popular in American operettas and no musical spectacle would be complete without a glittering display of a marching chorus. The very first musical, *The Black Crook* (1866), offered the "March of the Amazons," followed by such memorable numbers over the decades as the "Evangeline March" from *Evangeline* (1874), "March of the Toys" from *Babes in Toyland* (1903), "The Mascot of the Troop" from *Mlle. Modiste* (1905), "Tramp! Tramp! Tramp!" from *Naughty Marietta* (1910), and "Students' March Song" from *The Student Prince* (1924). Musical comedy was not so interested in parades, but the march tempo was still a favorite in theatre scores. George M. Cohan, for example, used march time for such popular songs as "Yankee Doodle Dandy" and "Over There." Since Kern wished to move the American musical away from the European model, he mostly avoided the march tempo. Yet it is still to be heard in such numbers as "Roll On, Rolling Road," **"There's a Hill Beyond a Hill,"** "Out of the Blue," and **"Make Way for Tomorrow."**

MARSH, Howard. (?–1969) Stage performer. A handsome tenor with a lyrical voice, he originated the role of the gambler Gaylord Ravenal in Kern's *Show Boat* (1927). Marsh managed to keep details of his youth, including his birth year, a secret, but it has been confirmed that he was born in Bluffton, Indiana, and was on the New York stage by 1917 in *The Grass Widow*. The next year he was a replacement for Rudolfo in *Maytime* and appeared in the revue *Greenwich Village Follies* (1920) before getting attention as Baron Franz Schober in *Blossom Time* (1921). Marsh found fame as the original Prince Karl Franz in *The Student Prince* (1924) and secured his career as Ravenal in *Show Boat*. His other musical credits include *Cherry Blossoms* (1927), *The Well of Romance* (1930), a revival of *Robin Hood* (1932), and several Gilbert and Sullivan operettas. In 1932 Marsh retired from the stage and became a banker in New Jersey.

McDANIEL, Hattie. (1895–1952) Film, stage, and television performer. Although she will be forever remembered as Mammy in *Gone with the Wind* (1939), the round African American character actress was memorable in many stage and screen performances and got her best musical film role as the riverboat cook Queenie in the 1936 screen version of Kern's **Show Boat**. McDaniel was born in Wichita, Kansas, the daughter of a Baptist preacher and his church-singing wife, and sang as a child. She was a band vocalist before making her screen debut in 1932 and was quickly noticed for her large size, expressive eyes, and firm voice. McDaniel rarely got to play anything but maids and other servile types, but she usually shone with dignity and humor. After *Gone with the Wind*, her best movie performance was in *Show Boat* (1936). She also lit up such screen musicals as *I'm No Angel* (1933), *Harmony Lane* (1935), *The Little Colonel* (1935), *Music Is Magic* (1935), *Carefree* (1938), *Merry-Go-Round of 1938*, *Thank Your Lucky Stars* (1946), and *Song of the South* (1946). McDaniel performed in different media and broke social barriers in each one. She was the first African American to sing on network radio, the first to win an Academy Award (for *Gone with the Wind*), the first to star in her own television series (*Beulah*), and the first to be buried in Los Angeles' exclusive Rosedale Cemetery. Biographies: *Hattie: The Life of Hattie McDaniel*, Carlton Jackson (1993); *Hattie McDaniel: Black Ambition, White Hollywood*, Jill Watt (2007).

MENJOU, Adolphe [Jean]. (1890–1963) Film performer. With his precise mustache, suave demeanor, and well-tailored clothes, the debonair character actor had one of Hollywood's longest screen careers (1914 to 1960) with two dozen musicals, including Kern's **You Were Never Lovelier**

(1942) in which he played the rich Argentine Eduardo Acuña. Menjou was born in Pittsburgh, the son of a hotel manager, and was educated at military school and then Cornell University toward an engineering career. Instead he worked at various odd jobs and performed in vaudeville before appearing in some silent films, interrupting his career to serve in World War I. Returning to the movies after the war, Menjou soon found himself a matinee idol on the silent screen and the heartthrob lover or urbane playboy in such films as *Through the Back Door* (1921), *The Three Musketeers* (1921), and *A Woman of Paris* (1923). With the arrival of sound, he continued to play dapper types, even if they were older in years, in over eighty talkies, including such musicals as *Fashions in Love* (1929), *Morocco* (1930), *New Moon* (1930), *Little Miss Marker* (1934), *Gold Diggers of 1935, Broadway Gondolier* (1935), *One in a Million* (1936), *One Hundred Men and a Girl* (1937), *The Goldwyn Follies* (1938), *Syncopation* (1942), *You Were Never Lovelier*, *Sweet Rosie O'Grady* (1943), *Step Lively* (1944), *My Dream Is Yours* (1949), *Dancing in the Dark* (1949), and *Bundle of Joy* (1956). Autobiography: *It Took Nine Tailors* (1948).

MERCER, Johnny [né John Herndon Mercer]. (1909–1976) Stage and film lyricist, composer, singer. A favorite songwriter in Hollywood and on Broadway, he collaborated with Kern on the film ***You Were Never Lovelier*** (1942). Mercer was born in Savannah, Georgia, and as a youngster had ambitions to be a singer. He went to New York and got some singing jobs, was a vocalist with bands touring across the country, and started writing lyrics. Some of his songs were heard in the Broadway revues *Garrick Gaieties* (1930) and *Blackbirds of 1939*, but he had better luck in Hollywood writing scores for such musicals as *Old Man Rhythm* (1935), *To Beat the Band* (1935), *Ready, Willing and Able* (1937), *Varsity Show* (1937), *Hollywood Hotel* (1937), *Cowboy from Brooklyn* (1938), *Garden of the Moon* (1938), *Going Places* (1938), and *Naughty But Nice* (1939) with such composers as Richard A. Whiting and Harry Warren. Mercer collaborated with Hoagy Carmichael on the score for the Broadway musical *Walk with Music* (1940) and for the next thirty years would work on both coasts with various composers, writing hit songs for both successful and unsuccessful shows. With Harold Arlen, he scored the Broadway musicals *St. Louis Woman* (1946), *Saratoga* (1959), and the films *Blues in the Night* (1941), *Star Spangled*

Rhythm (1942), *The Sky's the Limit* (1943), and *Here Come the Waves* (1944). With Gene de Paul, he wrote the songs for the Broadway musical satire *Li'l Abner* (1956) and the movies *Seven Brides for Seven Brothers* (1954) and *You Can't Run Away from It* (1956). Mercer sometimes wrote both music and lyrics, as with the Broadway show *Top Banana* (1951) and the movie musical *Daddy Long Legs* (1955). With Kern he came up with a delectable score for *You Were Never Lovelier*. His other Broadway credits are *Texas, Lil Darling* (1949) and *Foxy* (1964) and his other Hollywood musicals include *You'll Find Out* (1940), *Second Chorus* (1940), *You're the One* (1941), *The Fleet's In* (1942), *True to Life* (1943), *The Harvey Girls* (1946), *Dangerous When Wet* (1953), *Merry Andrew* (1958), and *Darling Lili* (1969). He also wrote many memorable theme songs for non-musical films, such as "Moon River," and "Days of Wine and Roses." Mercer possessed an estimable talent for writing idiomatic lyrics filled with regional slang and folksy familiarity. He never gave up on his singing, making many recordings over the years of his own and others' songs, and he was a co-founder of Capitol Records in 1942. His work was celebrated in the Broadway revue *Dream* (1997). Autobiography: *Portrait of Johnny: The Life of John Herndon Mercer*, with Gene Lees (2006); biography: *Skylark: The Life and Times of Johnny Mercer*, Philip Furia (2004).

MILLER, Ann [née Lucille Ann Collier]. (1923–2004) Film and stage performer. One of Hollywood's most accomplished tap dancers, the dark-haired, apple-cheeked singer-actress rarely played leading roles on screen but was memorable as second leads, such as the sassy nightclub entertainer Bubbles Cassidy in the Kern movie **Lovely to Look At** (1952). Miller was born in Chireno, Texas, and grew up in Southern California where she took dance lessons as a child and later got jobs dancing in nightclubs. She was only a teenager when she was cast in such movie musicals as *New Faces of 1937, Life of the Party* (1937), *Radio City Revels* (1938), *Having Wonderful Time* (1938), *Too Many Girls* (1940), *Hit Parade of 1941* (1940), *Melody Ranch* (1940), *Time Out for Rhythm* (1941), and *Go West, Young Lady* (1941). Although Miller got better roles in *True to the Army* (1942), *Priorities on Parade* (1942), *Reveille with Beverly* (1943), *What's Buzzin', Cousin?* (1943), *Carolina Blues* (1944), *Eadie Was a Lady* (1945), and *The Thrill of Brazil* (1946), she didn't get wide recognition until she danced with **Fred Astaire** in *Easter Parade* (1948). She was better billed and more recognized in *The Kissing Bandit* (1948), *On the Town* (1949), *Texas Carnival* (1951), *Two Tickets to Broadway* (1951), *Lovely to Look At*, *Small Town Girl* (1953), *Kiss Me, Kate* (1953), *Deep in My Heart* (1954), *Hit the Deck* (1955), and *The Opposite Sex* (1956). Throughout her career Miller performed in musicals on the stage. She made her Broadway debut in the revue *George White's Scandals* (1939), then decades later was a replacement for *Mame* in 1967. Miller costarred with Mickey Rooney in the popular Broadway salute to burlesque, *Sugar Babies* (1979) and later toured in the show. She also acted on stage in *Anything Goes; Hello, Dolly!; Follies;* and other musicals regionally and on tour. Miller was still performing into the 1990s.

MILLER, Marilyn [née Mary Ellen Reynolds]. (1898–1936) Stage and film performer. One of the brightest stars of Broadway musicals in the 1920s, her two best roles were in Kern musicals: the optimistic dishwasher *Sally* (1920) and the circus bareback rider *Sunny* (1925). Miller was born in Evansville, Indiana, and at the age of five started performing in the family's vaudeville act, touring the world for a decade before being discovered in London by producer Lee Shubert. He cast her in three editions of *The Passing Show* (1914, 1915, and 1917); she then went on to star in the *Ziegfeld Follies* (1918 and 1919). The petite blonde's effervescent dancing and singing made her a beloved favorite in both revues and book musicals, as with *Sally, Sunny,* and *Rosalie* (1928). Her other musical credits include *The Show of Wonders* (1916), *Fancy Free* (1918), and *Smiles* (1930), and she got to reprise her *Sally* on screen in 1929 and her *Sunny* in 1930. After filming *Her Majesty Love* (1931), Miller returned to Broadway in the legendary revue *As Thousands Cheer* (1933) before her premature death at the age of thirty-seven. Although she played optimistic heroines who found a Cinderella-like happiness at the end of her musicals, Miller's short life was far from a fairy tale, with three unhappy marriages and a destructive alcohol addiction. A sanitized version of her life was portrayed in the movie bio-musical *Look for the Silver Lining* (1947) in which June Haver played Miller, and Judy Garland portrayed her briefly in the Kern biopic **Till the Clouds Roll By** (1946). Biography: *The Other Marilyn*, Warren G. Harris (1985).

SALLY. The reigning dancing star on Broadway in the 1920s, Marilyn Miller found her best role as the Cinderella-like Sally who rises from dishwasher to *Ziegfeld Follies* queen in Kern's 1920 musical romance. Ziegfeld himself produced *Sally,* and not surprisingly, he saw that his star was well clothed, as seen in this photo from the production. *Photofest*

"Mis'ry's Comin' Aroun'" is a stirring spiritual number from *Show Boat* (1927) that was cut in the Washington out-of-town tryouts in order to trim the four-and-a-half-hour show. Kern's haunting music is oppressive and has the foreboding of a storm about it. **Oscar Hammerstein**'s lyric, like that for **"Ol' Man River,"** is written in Negro dialect and has a resignation about it, knowing that trouble is coming and anyone who has done wrong will now have to suffer. More complex than a Negro spiritual, "Mis'ry's Comin' Aroun'" has a classical air about it and foreshadows some of the choral singing in George Gershwin's later *Porgy and Bess* (1935). The number was sung by Julie (**Helen Morgan**), Queenie (**Tess Gardella**), and the African American chorus for only one performance, and it must have bothered Kern greatly when it was deleted. He used some of the music for the Overture (written after the song was cut) and insisted that it be included in the published vocal score of the show. "Mis'ry's Comin' Aroun'" was heard as background music in both the 1936 and 1951 screen versions of *Show Boat*. The number has been used in some revivals of *Show Boat*, such as the 1994 production on Broadway where it was sung by Gretha Boston (Queenie) and the chorus. The song is sometimes listed as "Mis'ry's Comin' 'Round" although the lyric clearly uses "aroun'."

MISS INFORMATION. A "little comedy with little music" by Paul Dickey, Charles W. Goddard (book), Elsie Janis (lyrics), Jerome Kern (music). [5 October 1915, George M. Cohan Theatre, 47 performances] Produced by **Charles Dillingham**, directed by Robert Milton, musical direction by Harold Vicars. *Miss Information* was a vehicle for the popular singer-comedienne Elsie Janis who donned various disguises throughout the evening and sang a handful of songs by Kern and herself. The thin plot that surrounded Janis concerned the wealthy, publicity-hungry Mrs. Calwalder (Annie Esmond) who gives her jewels to her son Jack (Howard Estabrook) to hide while she claims that jewel thieves have invaded her house. The pretend theft is reported by all the newspapers, but Mrs. Calwalder's plan backfires when a gang of real crooks steals the jewels from Jack. Janis played a telephone operator called Dot From Nowhere who not only solves the crime but wins Jack's heart. Kern and Janis wrote four of the production's seven songs and a young Cole Porter penned one of the others. Since the show was mostly a comedy, few critics or audience members paid much attention to the music. Thinking the score deserved a second hearing, Kern rewrote three of his numbers and retained the zesty **"Some Sort of Somebody"** for *Very Good Eddie* that opened two months later. As for *Miss Information*, Janis and her many fans allowed the show to run nearly six weeks.

MISS 1917. A musical revue by **P. G. Wodehouse** (sketches and lyrics), **Guy Bolton** (sketches), Jerome Kern, Victor Herbert (music). [5 November 1917, Century Theatre, 72 performances] Produced by **Charles Dillingham**, **Florenz Ziegfeld**; directed by Ned Wayburn; choreographed by Adolph Bohm; musical direction by Robert Hood Bowers. Rival producers Dillingham and Ziegfeld combined forces to produce this mammoth revue in the huge Century Theatre with a large cast featuring such stars (and future stars) as Lew Fields, Irene Castle, **Vivienne Segal**, Lilyan Tashman, Bessie McCoy Davis, Gus Van and Joe Schenck, Marion Davies, George White, Ann Pennington, Bert Savoy and Joe Brennan, and Charles King. In addition to its star power, *Miss 1917* had ravishing sets by Joseph Urban (in one scene the leaves fell from trees to indicate the coming of autumn) and some pleasing songs, most memorably Kern's **"The Land Where the Good Songs Go"** that was written for *Oh, Boy!* that same year but was not used. Despite some rave notices, *Miss 1917* did not draw enough patrons to fill the large, out-of-the-way Century Theatre, and the expensive revue folded in nine weeks. Since *Oh, Boy!* was still running, Kern wisely interpolated "The Land Where the Good Songs Go" into that hit **Princess Theatre Musical** where it gained some notoriety.

MISS SPRINGTIME. A musical comedy by **Guy Bolton, Herbert Reynolds, P. G. Wodehouse** (book and lyrics); Emmerich Kalman, Jerome Kern (music). [25 September 1916, New Amsterdam Theatre, 227 performances] Produced by Marc Klaw, Abe Erlanger; directed by Herbert Gresham; choreographed by Julian Mitchell; musical direction by Charles Previn. Kalman's Hungarian-set operetta was Americanized by Reynolds and **Princess Theatre Musicals** songwriters Bolton, Wodehouse, and Kern, yet the show was decidedly European in setting and tone. In the village of Pilota, the newspaper editor Paul Pilgrim (Charles Meakins) is in love with the beautiful Rosika Wenzel (Hungarian prima donna Sari Petrass) and promises to bring the famous singer Rudolfo Marta (George MacFarlane) to sing with her at the musical festival. When Rudolfo refuses, Paul's friend Robin (John E. Hazzard) gets the itinerant photographer Jo Varady (who is Rudolfo in disguise) to impersonate the famous singer. Rosika falls for Rudolfo and Paul has to win her back. The hit song from the show was Kalman's "Throw Me a Rose," which was used throughout the musical very effectively, but Kern provided a handful of new numbers that pleased, in particular the sweet ballad "Some One" and the comic ditty "Saturday Night." The authors originally titled the musical *Little Miss Springtime* and some songs were actually published under that name before the show opened. Producer Erlanger was furious, stating no production of his could be called "little" and had the piece retitled *Miss Springtime*. The production, designed by Joseph Urban, was indeed far from little yet the cast was able to shine and both the press and the public welcomed the escapist entertainment for a profitable seven months, followed by a successful tour. The Victor Light Opera Company recorded a medley of highlights from the score in the 1930s.

MOOREHEAD, Agnes [Robertson]. (1906–1974) Stage, television, and film performer. The sharp-featured character actress usually played haughty or neurotic women on stage and in films but comic ladies on television and in musicals; all of these elements can be seen in her performance as the domineering Parthy Hawks in the 1951 screen version of ***Show Boat***. Moorehead was born in Clinton, Massachusetts, the daughter of a minister, and educated at Muskingum College in Ohio, the University of Wisconsin, and Bradley University before becoming a high school English teacher and directing the school plays. She had performed in ballet as a child and was a professional dancer in her teens. Each summer when she wasn't teaching, Moorehead returned to the stage in summer theatres and in vaudeville. Eventually she gave up teaching, studied acting at the American Academy of Dramatic Arts, and made her Broadway debut in a play in 1929. She was also performing on national radio with Orson Welles who made Moorehead a member of his Mercury Theatre troupe in 1940. When Welles went to Hollywood, he brought his players with him and Moorehead made her screen debut as his mother in *Citizen Kane* (1941). After giving a superb performance in *The Magnificent Ambersons* (1942), she was established in Hollywood and over the next thirty years appeared in dozens of films, almost always in supporting roles. Although she was not a singer, Moorehead was featured in such musicals as *Summer Holiday* (1948), *Show Boat*, *Main Street to Broadway* (1953), *Those Redheads from Seattle* (1953), *The Opposite Sex* (1956), *Meet Me in Las Vegas* (1956), and *The Singing Nun* (1966). She became a familiar face on television because of the series *Bewitched* (1964–1972) and appeared on many other programs as well, such as the TV musical version of Kern's *Roberta* (1955). Moorehead returned to Broadway on occasion, as in the musical *Gigi* (1973), and frequently toured in readers' theatre programs, one-woman shows, and poetry readings. Biographies: *I Love the Illusion: The Life and Career of Agnes Moorehead*, Charles Tranberg and Herbie J. Pilato (2007); *My Travels with Agnes Moorehead, The Lavender Lady*, Quint Benedetti (2010).

"More and More" is the Oscar-nominated ballad by Kern and lyricist **E. Y. Harburg** about an ever-growing feeling of love that is overwhelming one. Senator's daughter Caroline (**Deanna Durbin**) sang the intoxicating song to cardsharp Johnny Lawlor (**Robert Paige**) in a moonlit frontier setting in the movie *Can't Help Singing* (1944). Film historian Roy Hemming states that "More and More" was the best song Durbin ever got to introduce in any of her movies. Kern's music is unusually expansive, and as musical theatre historian Gerald Bordman notes, it "never repeats itself, moving along on an ABCD frame . . . yet the song is tied together by variations on the initial theme." Kern's last hit song during his lifetime, "More and More" was on *Your Hit Parade* for fifteen weeks. The ballad was recorded by Durbin and many others, the top sellers being discs by Tommy Dorsey (vocal by Bonnie Lou Williams) and Perry Como.

MORGAN, Frank [né Francis Phillip Wupperman]. (1890–1949) Stage and film performer. The colorful and much-recognized character actor could play jovial types, menacing ones, or a combination of both, as with his conniving producer Alphonse Daudet in Kern's movie musical *The Cat and the Fiddle* (1934). The native New Yorker was the son of a wealthy manufacturer, and he tried a handful of different jobs before he decided to follow in his elder brother Ralph's footsteps and become an actor. After training at the American Academy of Dramatic Arts, Morgan made his Broadway debut in a minor role in a 1914 revival of *A Woman Killed with Kindness*. He also started making films at the same time, managing both a stage and movie career until the 1930s when he devoted all his time to Hollywood. Of Morgan's two dozen Broadway credits, only a handful were musicals, but he shone as King Cyril in *Rosalie* (1928) and as various characters in the famous revue *The Band Wagon* (1931). His other stage musicals included Kern's *Rock-a-Bye Baby* (1918), *Her Family Tree* (1920), and *Hey Nonny Nonny!* (1932). In Hollywood Morgan quickly became a familiar face and was known for his nervous chuckle and wide-eyed double takes. He appeared in over seventy films, mostly at MGM, including twenty-one musicals although usually he did not sing. His most famous role was Professor Marvel/Wizard in *The Wizard of Oz* (1939), but he also shone as the Mayor in *Hallelujah, I'm a Bum* (1933), the frustrated Governor in *Naughty Marietta* (1935), the promoter Billings in *The Great Ziegfeld* (1936), the King in *Rosalie* (1937), and the boozy Uncle Sid in *Summer Holiday* (1948). Morgan's other screen musicals include *Queen High* (1930), *Broadway to Hollywood* (1933), *The Cat and the Fiddle, Dimples* (1936), *Sweethearts* (1936), *Broadway Melody of 1940, Hullabaloo* (1940), and *Yolanda and the Thief* (1945). His brother Ralph Morgan (1883–1956) was a popular stage and screen actor, usually playing villains, and his niece was the busy stage-film-television actress Claudia Morgan (1912–1974).

MORGAN, Helen [née Helen Riggins]. (1900–1941) Stage and film singer, actress. One of America's great torch singers, her two best roles were in Kern musicals: the tragic mulatto Julie LaVerne in *Show Boat* (1927) and the saloon singer Addie Schmidt in *Sweet Adeline* (1929). Born in Danville, Ohio, she worked in a biscuit factory and as a manicurist before she started to sing in Chicago nightclubs and in vaudeville. She made her Broadway debut in *George White's Scandals* (1925) before finding the role of her career in *Show Boat*. Her renditions of **"Can't Help Lovin' Dat Man"** and **"Bill"** made her famous, and she reprised them in the 1929 part-talkie version of *Show Boat* before appearing as Julie in the celebrated 1936 film version. Kern and **Oscar Hammerstein** wrote *Sweet Adeline* with her in mind, and she introduced the torchy standard **"Why Was I Born?"** in the Broadway success. That same year Morgan triumphed in the film musical *Applause*, then in 1932 she played Julie once again in the Broadway revival of *Show Boat*. Her bouts with alcohol and depression harmed her career, and after a few more appearances on screen, in revues, and in clubs, she

SHOW BOAT. Easily the finest of the three screen versions of the Kern-Hammerstein classic, the 1936 *Show Boat* boasted a superior cast, many of them giving their finest screen performances. Irene Dunne (center) as Magnolia grew from a romantic teenager to a mature performer and mother. Helen Morgan (far right) reprised her tragic Julie from the original Broadway production six years earlier. Paul Robeson as Joe and Hattie McDaniel as Queenie provided both humor and gravity to the story. *Universal Pictures/ Photofest ©Universal Pictures*

died of cirrhosis of the liver at the age of forty-one. Although Morgan might be described as a saloon singer, she was atypical of the type, being small and frail with a high but delicate soprano voice. Few performers have been able to convey such heartbreak and vulnerability in their singing as she did. Ann Blyth portrayed Morgan and Gogi Grant provided her singing vocals in the biopic *The Helen Morgan Story* (1957). Biography: *Helen Morgan: Her Life and Legend*, Gilbert Maxwell (1975).

"A Mormon Life" is a shrewd comic number from the short-lived Kern musical ***Dear Sir*** (1924) that showed the promise of young lyricist **Howard Dietz** in his first Broadway score. The vaudevillian Andrew Bloxom (**Walter Catlett**) and a chorus of girls sang the ribald number about how dandy it would be to live the life of a multi-wived Mormon. Dietz's lyric is sparkling, rhyming "bigamy" with "polygamy" and "make a pig o' me."

MUSIC IN THE AIR. An operetta by **Oscar Hammerstein** (book and lyrics), Jerome Kern (music). [8 November 1932, Alvin Theatre, 342 performances] Produced by Peggy Fears and A. C. Blumenthal (uncredited), directed by Hammerstein and Kern, musical direction by Victor Baravalle, orchestrations by **Robert Russell Bennett**.

   Plot: In the Bavarian town of Edendorf, the elderly music teacher, Dr. Walther Lessing, and his pupil Karl Reder have written a song together titled "I've Told Ev'ry Little Star." Joined by Karl's sweetheart Sieglinde, who is also Lessing's daughter, and the Edendorf Walking Club, they set

CASTS FOR MUSIC IN THE AIR

Character	1932 Broadway	1934 film	1951 Broadway
Karl Reder	**Walter Slezak**	Douglass Montgomery	Mitchell Gregg
Sieglinde	Katherine Carrington	June Lang	Lillian Murphy
Dr. Walther Lessing	**Al Shean**	Al Shean	**Charles Winninger**
Frieda Hatzfeld	**Natalie Hall**	**Gloria Swanson**	Jane Pickens
Bruno Mahler	Tullio Carminati	**John Boles**	Dennis King

out for Munich to get their song published, but the big city nearly devours them. The predatory prima donna Frieda Hatzfeld goes after Karl and the lusty composer Bruno Mahler pursues Sieglinde, writing an opera for her to star in. The inexperienced Sieglinde turns down both his sexual and musical advances and accepts a job as understudy to the temperamental Frieda. When the diva cannot perform on opening night of the opera, Sieglinde takes her place and, contrary to cliché, fails to impress the audience. Fed up with the big time in Munich, Lessing, Sieglinde, and Karl return to tranquil Edendorf to make music the way they like.

Since the golden era of European-type operetta on Broadway waned with the coming of the Depression, Hammerstein and Kern worked at adapting the old form into a more modern piece. The settings may have recalled those former days, but the story was set in contemporary times, and the worn devices of disguised princes and Cinderella-like rises to fame were discarded for a more realistic story. Yet where the show most succeeded was in the score, which blended the pleasantly warm music of the past with more pertinent lyrics that led to a new kind of operetta sound. The standout hits of the musical were the lilting "I've Told Ev'ry Little Star" and the expansive "The Song Is You," but also memorable were the march "There's a Hill Beyond a Hill" and the nostalgic "In Egern on the Tegern See." Critical reaction was positive, as was audience appeal, and *Music in the Air* had a healthy run on Broadway and on the road. The London production in 1933, also staged by Kern and Hammerstein, was a hit as well. A 1951 Broadway revival, staged by Hammerstein and produced by his brother Reginald, featured a fine cast headed by Mitchell Gregg (Karl), Lillian Murphy (Sieglinde), **Charles Winninger** (Lessing), Dennis King (Bruno), and Jane Pickens (Frieda). Hammerstein made a few changes in the script, such as setting the story in Switzerland to avoid lingering anti-German feelings from the war, and the reviews were complimentary; but

MUSIC IN THE AIR SONGS

"Melodies of May"
"I've Told Every Little Star"
"There's a Hill Beyond a Hill"
"And Love Was Born"
"I'm Coming Home"
"I'm Alone"
"I Am So Eager"
"One More Dance"
"Night Flies By"
"When Spring Is in the Air"
"In Egern on the Tegern See"
"The Song Is You"
"We Belong Together"

Broadway audiences were not in the mood for European-style operetta and the production only ran seven weeks.

Film version: Music in the Air. A movie musical by Howard Young, Billy Wilder (screenplay), Oscar Hammerstein (lyrics), Jerome Kern (music). [Twentieth Century-Fox 1934] Produced by Erich Pommer, directed by Joe May, choreographed by Jack Donohue, musical direction by Louis De Francesco. Although four songs from the stage score (including the hit "The Song Is You") were dropped for the screen version, it was a remarkably faithful screen adaptation that not only captured the spirit of the original but avoided the Hollywood clichés that were so tempting, such as turning Sieglinde (June Lang, dubbed by Betty Hiestand) into a Bavarian Ruby Keeler and having her become a star. The smart screenplay focused more on the romantic jealousy between the diva Frieda (Gloria Swanson) and her lover Bruno (John Boles). Douglass Montgomery (dubbed by James O'Brien) was Karl, and Al Shean reprised his role as Lessing. The screen *Music in the Air* opens up the stage action effectively, even starting with an arial shot of the Bavarian Alps and then discovering Edendorf nestled in the mountains, foreshadowing the famous opening of the movie of *The Sound of Music* (1965). All in all, it is one of the best film treatments of a Kern-Hammerstein stage work.

Recordings: No Broadway cast recording was made, but Mary Ellis, who played Frieda in the 1933 London production, recorded a handful of the songs that same year. The film soundtrack recording contains the highlights of the score, as does a 1949 radio broadcast with Gordon MacRae and Jane Powell. Jane Pickens of the 1951 Broadway revival also recorded some of the songs. The album was released on CD as was the 1952 radio broadcast recording.

"My Houseboat on the Harlem" is a deliciously sarcastic song for the comic leads **Walter Catlett** and Kathlene Martyn in *Dear Sir* (1924), the Kern musical that introduced lyricist **Howard Dietz** to Broadway. The vaudevillian Andrew Bloxom (Catlett) and his sweetie Sukie (Martyn) mocked those popular duets in which the lovers sing about the humble little cottage they will live in together. Their houseboat docked on the Harlem River is stuck in the mud and life there is filled with the horrors of urban living. Although *Dear Sir* was a quick flop, critics noticed Dietz's clever lyrics in this and other numbers, and his career was launched.

"Napoleon" is a patter song from Kern's *Have a Heart* (1917) and **P. G. Wodehouse**'s first major comic number in a Broadway show. The pint-sized elevator operator Henry (Billy B. Van), who is instrumental in getting the lovers together and exposing a forger, sang the ditty, which outlines the many reasons for the French general's greatness, despite the fact that he was short and stingy and had other less-than-noble attributes. Kern had originally written the music for *Miss Springtime* (1916), but it was the new lyric by Wodehouse that made the number a comedy delight. Soon after *Have a Heart* opened, Van made a recording of the song, a very unusual practice for that period.

"Nesting Time in Flatbush" is a cozy comic number from the **Princess Theatre Musical** *Oh, Boy!* (1917) that spoofed all those "let's settle down together in . . ." songs of the period, in particular the popular "When It's Apple Time in Normandy." The comic leads Jackie Sampson (Anna Wheaton) and Jim Marvin (Hal Forde) sang the tongue-in-cheek number about how happy they will be married and living in poverty on Flatbush Avenue in Brooklyn. Kern's music is a syncopated foxtrot and the lyric by **P. G. Wodehouse** is delicious fun. In the original theatre program the duet was listed as "Nesting Time," but it was later published and most known by the full title. A charming duet recording was made by Heidi Blickenstaff and Philip Chaffin in 2012.

NEVER GONNA DANCE. See *Swing Time*.

"Never Gonna Dance" is the dark and broodingly romantic song of denial that Kern and lyricist **Dorothy Fields** provided for one of **Fred Astaire** and **Ginger Rogers**'s most alluring musical numbers. Gambler Lucky Garnett (Astaire) sang the song to dance teacher Penny Carroll (Rogers) in the film *Swing Time* (1936), claiming to forego dancing if he cannot dance with her. The two of them glided into a dance in an empty nightclub, where they tried to part ways yet were pulled back together by the music. (The dance sequence reportedly took forty-eight takes to get right.) Musical theatre historian Gerald Bordman describes the music as "a smoky, sometimes wailing rhythm number that resorts to the tempo and key changes that Kern so loved." Fields's lyric is also a marvel, with phrases like "la belle, la perfectly swell romance" that song historian Philip Furia comments "combined the colloquial with the romantic . . . [that] perfectly characterizes Astaire and Rogers." The lyric also refers to Rogers' character name Penny, and it remained that way for the published version of "Never Gonna Dance." The creative team was so pleased with the scene that the movie was slated to be titled *Never Gonna Dance*, but the studio feared than an Astaire and Rogers film that sounded like it had no dancing would keep audiences away. The number served as the title song for the Broadway musical version of *Swing Time* called ***Never Gonna Dance*** (2003) where it was sung and danced by Nancy Lemenager (Penny) and Noah Racey (Lucky). Two distinctive recordings of the song were made by Andrea Marcovicci and Bobby Short.

THE NIGHT BOAT. A musical comedy by **Anne Caldwell** (book and lyrics), Jerome Kern (music). [2 February 1920, Liberty Theatre, 313 performances] Produced by **Charles Dillingham**, directed by Fred G. Latham, choreographed by Ned Wayburn, musical direction by Victor Baravalle, orchestrations by **Frank Saddler**.

Plot: The restless husband Bob White occasionally escapes from his wife Hazel and his overbearing mother-in-law Mrs. Maxim by saying he has to captain a night boat from Manhattan up the Hudson River to Albany. Of course he goes nowhere near the river but spends the night partying in the city. When Mrs. Maxim insists that she and her daughter accompany Bob on one of his night excursions, he has to borrow a boat and a captain's uniform. Luckily the real captain aboard the boat is named Robert Smith and it looks like Bob will get away with the deception, but mishaps aboard the boat result in Bob's confessing the truth and promising to behave. The subplot dealt with Hazel's boisterous sister Barbara and her flirtations with the affable Freddie Ides.

CAST FOR *THE NIGHT BOAT*

Character	Performer
Bob White	John E. Hazzard
Mrs. Hazel White	Stella Hoban
Barbara Maxim	**Louise Groody**
Freddie Ides	Hal Skelly
Captain White	Ernest Torrence
Mrs. Maxim	Ada Lewis

Based on Alexandre Bisson's French farce *Le Controeur des wagons-lits*, *The Night Boat* was a joyous romp with a sassy plot, fun characters, and some wonderful songs. Although producer Dillingham insisted on interpolating some song standards about rivers, Kern matched them with some sparkling numbers of his own. The comic lament "Left All Alone Again Blues," the quick-step "Whose Baby Are You?," the Scottish spoof "I Love the Lassies," and the catchy "Good Night Boat" were among the high points of the unjustly neglected score. Although they were in secondary roles, Groody and Skelly shone most brightly and their rendition of "Whose Baby Are You?" and stopped the show each night. The press applauded Caldwell's playful script and lyrics as well as Kern's tuneful music, and *The Night Boat* was one of the major hits of the season. Dillingham foolishly closed the show after nearly a year to free the Liberty Theatre for an operetta that failed. But *The Night Boat* was very successful on tour, and it is surprising that no London production or film version followed.

Recording: Unfortunately there is no complete recording of the score for *The Night Boat*,

THE NIGHT BOAT SONGS

"Some Fine Day"
"Whose Baby Are You?"
"Left All Alone Again Blues"
"Good Night Boat"
"I'd Like a Lighthouse"
"Catskills, Hello"
"Don't You Want to Test Me?"
"I Love the Lassies"
"River Song Medley" (by various songwriters)
"A Heart for Sale"
"Girls Are Like a Rainbow"

only a medley of highlights made by the Victor Light Opera Company in the 1930s.

"The Night Was Made for Love" is a sweeping love serenade from Kern's operetta *The Cat and the Fiddle* (1931) where it was used throughout the evening as a form of leitmotif. The musical began with the strolling guitarist Pompineau (Metropolitan Opera star George Meader) singing the romantic ballad to set a soft, romantic mood, and it was reprised in various spots thereafter, acting as a recurring theme song. **Otto Harbach**'s lyric is lush and poetic, but it is Kern's arioso music that soars. Although its range is within two octaves, there are sweeping arpeggios and fanciful triplets that make the song so rich. In London the number was introduced by Henry Leoni in the 1932 production of *The Cat and the Fiddle*. In the 1931 screen version, **Jeanette MacDonald** sang "The Night Was Made for Love" as she played the piano, then reprised it with **Ramon Novarro**. A memorable recording of the ballad was made by Elisabeth Welch.

90 IN THE SHADE. A musical comedy by **Guy Bolton** (book); **Harry B. Smith**, Clare Kummer (lyrics); Jerome Kern (music). [25 January 1915, Knickerbocker Theatre, 40 performances] Produced by Daniel V. Arthur, directed by Robert Milton, choreographed by Julian Alfred, musical direction by John McGhie. This early Kern musical was a vehicle for stars Marie Cahill and Richard Carle, yet it afforded the young composer an opportunity to get noticed by the critics. The plot by Bolton (it was his first collaboration with Kern) was slight but useful in handling the songs and comedy. In the Philippines, Willoughby Parker (Carle) is quite the man about town, and the saucy Donna Estrada, known as the Hot Tamale (Jean Newcombe), has her eye on him for marriage. But Willoughby is secretly engaged to Polly Bainbridge (Cahill) who unexpectedly shows up in the Philippines. Helping to keep Willoughby's secret is his friend Bob Mandrake (Edward Martindell) who falls for Polly, she returns his affections, and Willoughby gets the Tamale. Comic singer Cahill had some songs by Clare Kummer interpolated into the show, even though these went against the character of Polly. Kern's music was tuneful and pleasing, although none of the songs became hits. He later reused several melodies from *90 in the Shade* for other musicals. Cahill's career was waning, and her marquee value was no longer strong enough to keep the poorly reviewed show from folding after a month.

"Nobody Else But Me" is the last song composed by Kern, written for the 1946 Broadway revival of *Show Boat*. Kern's music is bouncy and easygoing with a slight swing to it, and **Oscar Hammerstein**'s zesty lyric celebrates the fact that, with all of one's faults, a sweetheart thinks one is grand and wishes for no one else. Jan Clayton and the chorus introduced the song in the stage revival, and it was interpolated into many subsequent productions and recordings of *Show Boat*. Among the many memorable discs made of "Nobody Else But Me" were those by Paul Weston (vocal by Lou Dinning), Stan Getz, Helen Merrill, Sylvia Syms, Dinah Shore, Morgana King, Mitzi Gaynor, Tony Bennett, Gogi Grant, Mabel Mercer, and more recently, Barbara Cook, Barbara Carroll, Andrea Marcovicci, Sandy Stewart, Sylvia McNair, Kristin Chenoweth, Bobby Short, and Susan Watson with Danny Carroll.

NOBODY HOME. A musical comedy by **Guy Bolton**, Paul Rubens (book); **Herbert Reynolds**, Schulyer Greene, **Harry B. Smith** (lyrics); Jerome Kern (music). [20 April 1915, Princess Theatre, 135 performances] Produced by

CAST FOR *NOBODY HOME*

Character	Performer
Tony Miller	Adele Rowland
Violet Briton	Alice Dovey
Vernon Popple	George Anderson
Freddy Popple	Lawrence Grossmith
Rolondo D'Amorini	Charles Judels
Mrs. D'Amorini	Maude Odell
Jack Kenyon	Lillian Tucker
Polly Polka	Marion Davies
Trilby Tango	Marion Dale
Tessie Trot	Gertrude Waixel
Dolly Dip	Helen Clarke

Elisabeth Marbury, F. Ray Comstock; directed by J. H. Benrimo; choreographed by Dave Bennett; musical direction by Max Hirschfeld; orchestrations by **Frank Saddler**.

Plot: In order to marry his beloved Violet Briton, man-about-town Vernon Popple must get permission from her overbearing aunt and the aunt's temperamental Italian husband Rolondo. Vernon's staid brother Freddy needs a place to stay in Manhattan and is offered an apartment by actress Tony Miller, Vernon's former lover, who is going on tour. Freddie, Vernon, and Violet all show up at the apartment on the same day, joined by the aunt and Rolondo who are looking to rent the place. The confusion is further complicated when Tony returns unexpectedly and much has to be sorted out before Vernon and Violet get permission to wed and Freddy ends up with Tony.

Nobody Home was the first of what became known as the **Princess Theatre Musicals**, a series of small, modern, and very influential shows that brought fame to Kern. Producers Marbury and Comstock commissioned Bolton and Kern to rework Paul Rubens's British musical *Mr. Popple of Ippleton* but were lacking funds to mount a large production in a Broadway musical house. The 299-seat Princess Theatre, built for one-act plays and small dramas, was struggling to find an audience so Marbury and Comstock announced that the intimate theatre would be presenting new, innovative, and smart musical comedies in the space. *Nobody Home* was indeed small, though critics, who were delighted with the cast and the score, felt the book was far from innovative or even commendable. But the novelty of the concept and the strong entertainment value on stage were enough to please audiences for four months. While several songs from the original London production remained and found favor, the brightest moments in the score were by Kern and his American lyricists. The standouts of the Kern songs were the sprightly rag "The Magic Melody," the waltzing "In Ar-

> ### *NOBODY HOME* SONGS
>
> "You Know and I Know"
> "Cupid at the Plaza"
> "In Arcady"
> "The Magic Melody"
> "Ten Little Bridesmaids"
> "Bed, Wonderful Bed"
> "Another Little Girl"
> "Any Old Night (Is a Wonderful Night)"
> "The San Francisco Fair"

cady," the slaphappy ditty "Another Little Girl," and the dancing duet "You Know and I Know." When *Nobody Home* caught on, the producers moved it to the larger Maxine Elliot Theatre where it enabled them to make a profit. There were also three road companies that set out on tour, and one of these ran into 1917. Marbury and Comstock were convinced that they had found a successful formula for the Princess Theatre and immediately began planning for more (and better) shows there.

Recording: The only known recording of the score is a medley of highlights made by the Victor Light Opera Company in the 1930s.

"Nodding Roses" is a delicious waltz duet from *Very Good Eddie* (1915), the landmark **Princess Theatre Musical** that first brought Kern wide recognition. Dick Rivers (**Oscar Shaw**) and Elsie Lilly (Ann Orr) finally are united near the end of the contemporary musical and sing this ditty about taking a cue from the roses and saying "yes" to marriage. Only the refrain is a waltz; the verse is in a comic 4/4 time. Also, as a sly comment, Kern inserted some musical phrases from the recent *Der Rosenkavalier* into the piano accompaniment. The lyric, which is just shy of satirical, is by **Herbert Reynolds** and Schuyler Green. "Nodding Roses" was sung by Walter Williams (Dick) and Veronica Brady (Elsie) in the 1918 London production of *Very Good Eddie* and by David Christmas (Dick) and Cynthia Wells (Elsie) in the 1975 Broadway revival.

NOVARRO, Ramon [né José Ramón Gil Samaniegoes]. (1899–1968) Film performer. One of the most romantic and popular "Latin lovers" of the silent screen, he appeared in five musicals after talkies came in, including Kern's *The Cat and the Fiddle* (1934) in which he played the struggling composer Victor Florescu. Born in Durango, Mexico, at the age of fifteen he moved to Los Angeles where he worked as a singing waiter and then sang in vaudeville before getting cast in his first film in 1917. By 1922 he was a famous romantic leading man, starring in such silents as *The Prisoner of Zenda* (1922), *Scaramouche* (1923), *Ben-Hur* (1926), *The Student Prince* (1927), and *The Pagan* (1929). Novarro made the transition to sound without difficulty and made many films in the 1930s, including the musicals *In Gay Madrid* (1930), *The Cat and the Fiddle,* and *The Night Is Young* (1935). By the 1940s he was no longer considered a dashing leading man and played character parts in films and on television until his death by homicide at the age of sixty-eight. Biographies: *Ramon Novarro*, Allan R. Ellenberger (2009); *Beyond Paradise: The Life of Ramon Novarro*, André Soares and Anthony Slide (2010).

OH, BOY! A musical comedy by **Guy Bolton**, **P. G. Wodehouse** (book and lyrics); Jerome Kern (music). [20 February 1917, Princess Theatre, 463 performances] Produced by **Ray Comstock**; William Elliott; directed by **Edward Royce**; musical direction by Max Hirschfield; orchestrations by **Frank Saddler**.

Plot: Without telling his wealthy, domineering Quaker guardian-aunt Penelope, George Budd has married Lou Ellen and doesn't know how to break the news. His playboy pal Jim Marvin and his girl Jackie invade George's apartment when the Budds are away and are surprised by an impending visit from the aunt. The Budds return to find Jackie pretending to be Lou Ellen, and then when other country club friends come by, Jackie masquerades as the aunt herself. By the time the real aunt arrives on the scene, all deceptions and confusions are revealed for a happy ending with George and Lou Ellen officially matched and Jim and Jackie engaged.

Arguably the finest of the **Princess Theatre Musicals**, this high-spirited musical comedy bubbled with silly goings-on and scintillating songs. The plot not only moved quickly and efficiently but the dialogue sparkled in a sassy, irreverent way rarely seen in musicals up to that time. The characters

CASTS FOR *OH, BOY!* AND *OH, JOY!*

Character	Broadway 1917	London 1919 (Oh, Joy!)
Lou Ellen Carter	Marie Carroll	Dot Temple
Jim Marvin	Hal Forde	Billy Leonard
Jackie Simpson	Anna Wheaton	Beatrice Lillie
George Budd	Tom Powers	Tom Powers
Jane Packard	Marion Davies	Isabel Jeans
Judge Carter	Frank McGinn	
Penelope Budd	**Edna May Oliver**	

may have been broad but they were likable, and their shenanigans were almost logical in a breezy way. It was all lovable nonsense punctuated by such delicious songs as the contagious "Till the Clouds Roll By," the cozy duet "Nesting Time in Flatbush," the coy "An Old-Fashioned Wife," the beguiling "The Land Where the Good Songs Go," and the romantic but wry "You Never Knew About Me." The raves from the press adulated the authors and the cast, and the merry show ran over a year, the most successful of all the Princess musicals. Five road companies of *Oh, Boy!* crisscrossed the nation, one of them remaining in Chicago for twenty-three weeks. A British version, retitled *Oh, Joy!*, opened in London in 1919 and ran 167 performances, giving Beatrice Lillie her first triumph in a book musical. A silent screen version of *Oh, Boy!* was released in 1919, and even without spoken dialogue or songs the movie played well as a farce. The cast included Creighton Haley (George), June Caprice (Lou Ellen), Zena Keefe (Jackie), and Flora Finch (Penelope), and it was directed by Albert Capellani. A talkie version was never made, and surprisingly, the musical has never received a Broadway revival.

Recordings: Members of the original London cast of *Oh, Joy!* recorded much of the score in 1919, and the Victor Light Opera Company made a record of highlights of the score in 1938. The most complete recording is the two-CD version of the Comic Opera Guild's 2005 production, which has twenty songs and was recorded with a live audience.

OH, BOY! SONGS

"Let's Make a Night of It"
"You Never Knew About Me"
"A Package of Seeds"
"An Old-Fashioned Wife"
"A Pal Like You"
"Till the Clouds Roll By"
"A Little Bit of Ribbon"
"The First Day of May"
"Koo-La-Loo"
"Rolled Into One"
"Oh, Daddy, Please"
"Nesting Time in Flatbush"
"Words Are Not Wicked"
"Flubby Dub, the Cave-Man"

OH, I SAY! A musical comedy by Sidney Blow, Douglas Hoare (book); **Harry B. Smith** (lyrics); Jerome Kern (music). [30 October 1913, Casino Theatre, 68 performances] Produced by the Shubert Brothers, directed by J. C. Huffman, choreographed by Julian Alfred, musical direction by Alfred Bendell, orchestrations by **Frank Saddler**. The second Broadway show in

TILL THE CLOUDS ROLL BY. Six years before Gene Kelly got wet *Singin' in the Rain,* Ray McDonald did his own dancing and splashing in the title number of the 1946 film *Till the Clouds Roll By.* The number depicted was supposedly from Kern's small-scale, intimate Princess Theatre musical *Oh, Boy!* (1917), but on screen McDonald and June Allyson were quite clearly in a vast and rain-filled MGM soundstage. *MGM/Photofest ©MGM*

which Kern provided the complete score, *Oh, I Say!* was a typical piece of 1920s fluff that was distinguished by some of its music. The plot, based on the French farce, which in turn had been turned into a British comedy, involved a situation that was used in later Kern musicals: several characters converging on one apartment. When the French actress Sidonie de Mornay (Cecil Cunningham) announces she is going on tour, her maid Claudine (Clara Palmer) sublets their Paris apartment to the young newlywed couple Marcel (Charles Meakins) and Suzette Durant (Alice Yorke), unaware that Marcel and Sidonie were once lovers. Suzette's father (Walter Jones) hires Sidonie to perform at a function he throws for the young couple so she stays in Paris and is reunited with Marcel at the apartment. The usual complications sustain the action until a happy ending. The score had quite a range, from the ragtime "Katydid" and the tango "I Can't Forget Your Eyes" to the waltzing "Each Pearl a Thought" and the lively polka "I Know and She Knows." Although very pleasing, none of the songs became hits and Kern remained unrecognized for another two years. The Victor Light Opera Company recorded a medley of highlights from the score in 1938.

OH, LADY! LADY!! A musical comedy by **Guy Bolton**, **P. G. Wodehouse** (book and lyrics); Jerome Kern (music). [1 February 1918, Princess Theatre, 219 performances] Produced by **F. Ray Comstock**, William Elliott; directed by Robert Milton, **Edward Royce**; musical direction by Max Hirschfield; orchestrations by **Frank Saddler**.

CAST FOR *OH, LADY! LADY!!*

Character	Performer
Mollie Farrington	**Vivienne Segal**
Willoughby Finch	Carl Randall
Spike Hudgins	Edward Abeles
May Barber	Carroll McComas
Hale Underwood	Harry C. Browne
Cyril Twombley	Reginald Mason
Clarette Cupp	Jeanne Sparry
Mrs. Farrington	Margaret Dale

Plot: Willoughby Finch is about to be wed to Mollie Farrington when the Farrington jewels are stolen and suspicion falls on Willoughby's valet Spike, a former jewel thief. Also complicating the situation is the arrival of May Barber from Ohio to deliver some lingerie for Mollie. It seems May was once engaged to Willoughby, and her presence so upsets Mollie that she calls off the wedding. It takes Spike to find the jewel thieves and to get Molly and Willoughby back together again.

The last of the Bolton-Wodehouse-Kern collaborations for the **Princess Theatre Musical** series, this intimate, contemporary show reflected the spirit of the innovative series. Efforts were made by Bolton to keep the plot plausible even if it was silly. The nimble score featured the rhapsodic "Moon Song," the spirited two-step "Before I Met You," the dreamy "When the Ships Come Home," the comic number "Not Yet," and the sarcastic "Greenwich Village." The best song written for the show was "Bill," but it did not fit in the production and was discarded before opening; Kern used it nine years later in **Show Boat**. Reviews for *Oh, Lady! Lady!!* were exemplary. The cast was praised for its dancing as well as singing and comic performances, and the score by the famous team was cited as one of their best. Ironically, none of the songs became standards, and the show is most remembered as the one for which "Bill" was written. Initially box office was so strong that after four and a half months the producers moved the musical to the larger Casino Theatre. But it only lasted two more months there, and the two road companies of *Oh, Lady! Lady!!* were not profitable. More unfortunate, the team of Bolton, Wodehouse, and Kern broke up as each went his own way. Although two or even all three would briefly reunite for later projects, their glory days at the Princess Theatre were over. No film version, silent or sound, was made of the piece,

OH, LADY! LADY!! SONGS

"I'm to be Married Today"
"Not Yet"
"Do It Now"
"Our Little Nest"
"Little Ships Come Sailing Home"
"Oh, Lady! Lady!!"
"You Found Me and I Found You"
"Moon Song"
"Waiting Around the Corner"
"The Sun Starts to Shine Again"
"Before I Met You"
"Greenwich Village"
"A Picture I Want to See"
"It's a Hard, Hard World for a Man"
"Bill" (cut)

but years later Wodehouse reworked the plot into his novel *The Small Bachelor,* which was filmed in 1927.

Recording: The only known recording of *Oh, Lady! Lady!!* is a medley version made by the Victor Light Opera Company in 1938.

"Ol' Man River" is arguably the greatest theatre song in America, for it is surely one of the most enduring, recognized, and beloved. The ballad by Kern and **Oscar Hammerstein** is used throughout *Show Boat* (1927) as a kind of leitmotif but also stands firmly on its own and has retained its power decade after decade. **Jules Bledsoe**, as the African American stevedore Joe, introduced the ballad in the original production, but the song is most associated with **Paul Robeson** who sang it in the London production, in revivals, on film, and in his concerts for many years. Essentially a folk song, "Ol' Man River" is, as Hammerstein described it, a "song of resignation with protest implied." This ambiguity is what makes the song so haunting. Joe and the African American coworkers along the Mississippi River lament their oppression, yet they can't help being in awe of the mighty river that is indifferent to mankind's troubles. The ballad was at first mistaken for an authentic Negro spiritual because Kern's music captures a Southern folk flavor that few theatre songs before or since have attained. It was the first number that Kern and Hammerstein wrote for the score, and when they played it for Edna Ferber, she overcame her objections to musicalizing her novel and gave the authors permission to proceed with the show. "Ol' Man River" is not a complex song musically and has no major jumps in the melody, although it does have a wide range (an octave and a sixth) with a high ending that has always proven a challenge to singers. The release is actually a section of the verse repeated, so musically the ballad is very tight and unified. Lyrically, it is Hammerstein's master achievement. He avoids lengthy phrases and hard endings (sumpin', nothin', rollin') and employs few rhymes. Instead he uses a series of identities (or near rhymes) and scattered soft multisyllable rhymes to capture the steady, rolling feel of the river flowing by. Just as the Mississippi gives unity to Ferber's sprawling novel, "Ol' Man River" gives unity to the musical *Show Boat.* The song is reprised several times and even shows up in altered forms, as in the opening **"Cotton Blossom"** theme, which is "Ol' Man River" played in reverse and sped up to a banjo-strumming tempo. On the screen, the song was sung by Bledsoe in the 1929 part-talkie version of *Show Boat,* by Robeson in the 1936 classic film, by Caleb Peterson and reprised by Frank Sinatra in the Kern biopic *Till the Clouds Roll By* (1946), and by **William Warfield** in the 1951 remake of *Show Boat.* It was also heard on the soundtracks for the movies *Whoopee!* (1927), *The Great Ziegfeld* (1936), *The Miniver Story* (1950), *Nightdreams* (1981), *Old Explorers* (1990), *The Mask* (1994), and *Fantastic Mr. Fox* (2009). Of the hundreds of recordings over the decades, those most famous and popular were Robeson's 1932 record and best-sellers by Bing Crosby (with the Paul Whiteman Orchestra) and Sinatra. The song was given an unusual female trio version by Elisabeth Welch, Liz Robertson, and Elaine Delmar in the London revue *Jerome Kern Goes to Hollywood* (1985); the trio reprised the number in the Broadway version of the show the next year.

OLIVER, Edna May [neé Edna May Nutter]. (1883–1942) Stage and screen performer. A commanding, horse-faced character actress who often stole every scene she was in, she originated the role of the cantankerous Parthy Ann Hawks in Kern's *Show Boat* (1927). Oliver was born in Malden, Massachusetts, a descendant of John Quincy Adams. She quit school at the age of fourteen to pursue an acting career and was on Broadway by 1916. The next year she found recognition as the formidable Quaker Aunt Penelope in Kern's *Oh, Boy!* (1917). While appearing on Broadway throughout the 1920s, Oliver made her first silent film in 1923, soon playing outspoken relatives, spinsters, duchesses, and other authoritative characters. Her last stage role was the domineering Parthy in the original production of *Show Boat* and again in the 1932 Broadway revival. For the next ten years she shone in Hollywood talkies, playing memorable character types in such films as *Little Women* (1933), *David Copperfield* (1935), *A Tale of Two Cities* (1935), *Romeo and Juliet* (1936), *Drums Along the Mohawk* (1939), and *Pride and Prejudice* (1940).

"Once in a Blue Moon" is a graceful lullaby by Kern and lyricist **Anne Caldwell** that has fallen into oblivion but is greatly admired by music scholars. It was written for the fairy-tale musical *Stepping Stones* (1923) where it was sung by various princes and fantasy characters played by Roy Hoyer, Evelyn Herbert, John Lambert, Lilyan White, and Ruth White. The song is captivatingly simple, with a sweet lyric that turns cynical in the last line and a melody that barely extends outside of a single octave. Although the renowned song stylist Mabel Mercer sang the lullaby over the years in order to revitalize interest in it, the song remains mostly a forgotten gem. Andrea Marcovicci made a lovely recording of it in 1992.

ONE NIGHT IN THE TROPICS. A movie musical by Gertrude Purcell, Charles Grayson (screenplay); **Dorothy Fields**, **Otto Harbach**, **Oscar Hammerstein** (lyrics); Jerome Kern (music). [Universal 1940] Produced by Leonard Spigelgass, directed by A. Edward Sutherland, choreographed by Larry Ceballos, musical direction by Charles Previn, orchestrations by Frank Skinner.

Plot: The insurance salesman Jim Moore makes his playboy friend Steve Harper buy a policy promising to marry his fiancée Cynthia Merrick by a certain date. When the predatory Mickey Fitzgerald chases after Steve, Cynthia breaks off the engagement and goes to the fictional Caribbean island of San Marcos with her Aunt Kitty. Jim, Steve, and Mickey pursue Cynthia to the island where Jim and Cynthia fall in love. The gangster Roscoe stands to lose a fortune if the wedding doesn't take place so he tries to force the ceremony, but on the wedding day Steve marries Mickey, making the insurance policy null and void. The comic relief came in the form of two henchmen, played by Abbott and Costello, who are employed by Roscoe.

CAST FOR *ONE NIGHT IN THE TROPICS*

Character	Performer
Jim Moore	**Allan Jones**
Cynthia Merrick	Nancy Kelly
Abbott	Bud Abbott
Costello	Lou Costello
Steve Harper	**Robert Cummings**
Aunt Kitty Marblehead	Mary Boland
Roscoe	William Frawley
Mickey Fitzgerald	Peggy Moran
Escobar	Leo Carillo

It may have had a silly and improbable excuse for a plot, but the West Indies musical offered some masterful songs by Kern, Hammerstein, Fields, and Harbach, all of which were written four years earlier for an unproduced musical called *Riviera*. Unfortunately the songs were lost in the inept shenanigans going on, and it took years for the scintillating rhumba "Remind Me," the heartfelt "Your Dream (Is the Same as My Dream)," and the lovely "You and Your Kiss" to find any notoriety. Universal lost a bundle on the lavish film but eventually had the last laugh: producer Spigelgass hired two radio comics, Bud Abbott and Lou Costello, to play the henchmen in the movie and the team immediately clicked with audiences. They would go on to make twenty-eight more movies for the studio and save the company from bankruptcy.

Recording: While there is no soundtrack recording of *One Night in the Tropics*, copies of the movie on DVD are not too difficult to find.

ONE NIGHT IN THE TROPICS SONGS

"You and Your Kiss"
"Remind Me"
"Back in My Shell"
"Your Dream (Is the Same as My Dream)"
"Farandola"
"Simple Philosophy"

PAIGE, Robert [né John Arthur Page]. (1910–1987) Film and television performer. Often paired with singer-actress Jane Frazee, the handsome leading man of Hollywood musicals was usually stuck in B movies but still had some shining moments, as when he played the robust pioneer Johnny Lawlor in Kern's *Can't Help Singing* (1944). Paige was born in Indianapolis, Indiana, to British parents and attended West Point Academy until he left to pursue an acting career. He began as a radio singer and then an announcer. After appearing in a few film shorts, Paige made his feature debut in 1935 and gradually moved to romantic leads. In his twenty-two screen musicals he was partnered with Frazee seven times, yet his most memorable performance was in the **Deanna Durbin** vehicle *Can't Help Singing* in which he joined her in introducing **"Californ-i-ay"** and the title song. Paige's other musical credits include *Cain and Mabel* (1936), *The Lady Objects* (1938), *Dancing on a Dime* (1941), *San Antonio Rose* (1941), *Hellzapoppin'* (1941), *What's Cookin'?* (1942), *Pardon My Sarong* (1942), *Get Hep to Love* (1942), *Hi Buddy* (1943), *Cowboy in Manhattan* (1943), *Crazy House* (1943), *Follow the Boys* (1944), *Shady Lady* (1945), and *Bye Bye Birdie* (1963). In addition to many non-musicals, Paige was a familiar face on television both as an actor and a quiz show host.

PASTICHE SONGS by Kern. Any musical number that echoes the style, either musically or lyrically, of an earlier era is said to pastiche the past. Such songs can be written to spoof the past or to recapture the period for the setting of the new work. Since Kern grew up listening to the songs of the 1890s, years later he was able to capture that style in such songs as **"I Might Fall Back on You," "Sure Thing,"** "Goodbye My Lady Love," and **"All Through the Day."** The various African American styles of music were pastiched in such Kern numbers as **"Gallavantin' Aroun'," "Cinderella Sue," "Can't Help Lovin' Dat Man," "Bojangles of Harlem,"** and **"Ol' Man River."** Kern had fun pastiching Hawaiian ballads with **"Ka-lu-a,"**

backcountry tunes with **"Allegheny Al,"** old-time operetta in **"In Egern on the Tegern See,"** tribal numbers with **"Bongo on the Congo,"** a college alma mater with **"Tulip Time in Sing Sing,"** and exotic ancient Egypt with **"Cleopatterer."**

PERSONAL CHARACTERISTICS of Kern. Judging from interviews of his friends and collaborators, Kern was a complex person and one of conflicting qualities. Kern the composer was serious, hard-working, businesslike, impatient, demanding, stubborn, and on a few occasions very difficult. He did not consider himself a Tin Pan Alley hack and took theatre songwriting very seriously, even when working on the lightest of musical comedies. He could be kind and generous while working on a show, just as he had moments of egotism and unreasonable behavior. On the other hand, there was a quixotic and even pixie-like quality to the man himself. The biographies are filled with examples of this lighter and even silly side of Kern. He enjoyed practical jokes and teasing his collaborators by demanding impossible things and then breaking out into laughter when he knew he had fooled them. He knew how to relax and enjoy life and could not properly be described as a workaholic like Richard Rodgers. He had his hobbies (particularly collecting rare books and antiques) and pursued them aggressively, but those who knew him could see he got real joy out of buying and possessing something special. Evidently he was a devoted husband to his (only) wife Eva. They married young and remained happy together until his death without a breath of talk about infidelity or neglect. Kern was also a patient and loving father to his daughter Betty who, as an adult, was actively involved in Kern's work before and after his death. He could not be put on a pedestal as a saint but instead was very human, and both his failings and attributes brought him many close friends. Kern was also generous in his praise of others. When critic Alexander Woollcott asked him what place Irving Berlin had in American music, Kern replied: "Irving Berlin has no place in American music. He *is* American music." The show business community was quite sincere when they mourned Kern's premature passing, and the loss was a personal as well as professional one. See also **Eulogy** for Kern and **Working Methods**.

"Pick Yourself Up" is a swinging polka that Kern and lyricist **Dorothy Fields** wrote for **Fred Astaire** and **Ginger Rogers** to perform in the movie

Swing Time (1936), and it made for an unusual musical scene. Gambler Lucky Garnett (Astaire) told dancing instructor Penny (Rogers) that he knew nothing about hoofing and required lessons, whereupon he performed an ingenious routine with her filled with elegant mistakes and rhythmic pratfalls. The lyric suggests one get up, dust oneself off, and "start all over again." Fields wrote the lyric first (very unusual in collaborations with Kern), and the composer used an old Bohemian musical motif to match her rapid-fire words. The result is one of Kern's finest rhythm songs and one of the most intricate *pas de deux* for Astaire and Rogers. Astaire recorded the song with Johnny Green's Orchestra and there were also discs by Rosemary Clooney, Benny Goodman, Mel Tormé, Anita O'Day, Nat King Cole, Ella Fitzgerald, Frank Sinatra, Dianne Reeves, Diana Krall, Sylvia McNair, and an improvisational rendition by the George Shearing Trio, which made the song a favorite with jazz musicians such as Oscar Peterson and Beegie Adair. "Pick Yourself Up" was heard on the soundtrack for the films *Dirty Rotten Scoundrels* (1988), *Home for the Holidays* (1995), and *Nanny McPhee Returns* (2010). The number was featured in three Broadway shows: in the revue *Jerome Kern Goes to Hollywood*, Liz Robertson and Elaine Delmar sang it in London in 1985 and on Broadway the next year; Clevant Derricks, Larry Marshall, Mel Johnson, Jr., Alan Weeks, and Alde Lewis, Jr. performed it in *Big Deal* (1986); and it was sung by Noah Racey and Nancy Lemenager then reprised by Peter Gerety and Karen Ziemba in *Never Gonna Dance* (2003).

PONS, Lily [neé Alice Josephine Pons]. (1904–1976) Film and opera performer. One of the Metropolitan Opera's favorite coloraturas, the petite, dark-haired singer was courted by Hollywood after the success of opera singer Grace Moore on the screen; Pons made a thrilling screen debut as the struggling singer Annette Monard in Kern's *I Dream Too Much* (1935). Pons was born in Draguignan, France, of Italian and French ancestry, and entered the Paris Conservatoire at the age of thirteen. After World War I her career took off, singing in the leading opera houses in Europe and making her Met debut in 1931. Over the next thirty years Pons would give 280 performances at the celebrated Manhattan opera house. She played character parts in the movie musicals *I Dream Too Much*, *That Girl from Paris* (1936), and *Hitting a New High* (1937), then performed as herself in

Carnegie Hall (1947). While Pons's movie career did not take off as hoped, she was very popular on the radio and was beloved for her many concerts entertaining the troops during World War II. She was married to Andre Kostelanetz (1901–1980) who conducted many of her performances. Biography: *Lily Pons: A Centennial Portrait*, James A. Drake and Kristin Beall Ludecke (2003).

PREMINGER, Otto. (1905–1986) Film and stage director, actor, producer. A severe German character actor who later became one of Hollywood's most successful directors, he helmed six musicals, including Kern's **Centennial Summer** (1946), which he also produced. Born in Vienna, Austria, the son of a high-level politician, he studied law at the University of Vienna before turning to the theatre and working as an actor and assistant for Max Reinhardt. Preminger directed his first film in Germany in 1931 then came to America in 1935 to restage the drama *Libel* on Broadway and stayed, directing plays and then learning more about movies, in California. Hollywood cast him as Teutonic heavies in several films, and then he became just as famous as a director for *Laura* (1944), which he also produced. Preminger's other hits include *The Moon Is Blue* (1953), *Carmen Jones* (1954), *The Man with the Golden Arm* (1955), *Saint Joan* (1957), *Anatomy of a Murder* (1959), *Porgy and Bess* (1959), and *Advise and Consent* (1962). Preminger continued to act, direct, and produce into the 1980s. Autobiography: *Preminger* (1978); biographies: *Otto Preminger: The Man Who Would Be King*, Foster Hirsch (2007); *The World and Its Double: The Life and Work of Otto Preminger*, Chris Jujiwara (2009).

PRINCESS THEATRE MUSICALS. A short-lived (1915–1919) but extremely influential series of intimate musical comedies, they were very popular in their day, brought wide recognition to Kern, and foreshadowed the shape of Broadway shows of the future. The musicals were presented in Manhattan's Princess Theatre, a 299-seat venue that was considered too small for traditional stage shows. Literary agent **Elisabeth Marbury** and theatre owner **F. Ray Comstock** had an idea for a series that would feature small, contemporary musicals by new composers, performed by a resident company of actors. It was planned to be the world's first musical repertory theatre, but the shows that followed were not done in repertory, and the cast differed from musical to musical. Yet the series was successful as an alternative to the large-scale operettas and lavish musical revues that dominated Broadway at the time. Because of the small stage, the shows could not have large chorus lines or opulent scenery, and the size of the orchestra pit limited the number of musicians to eleven players. The first entry in the series was Kern's *Nobody Home* (1915) with a libretto by **Guy Bolton** and lyrics by Schuyler Greene. Aside from its small scale, the musical comedy about young lovers and mistaken identity was not much different from the standard fare of the day. But the second entry, the same team's *Very Good Eddie* (1915), was a major hit and a literate, witty musical comedy of manners that somewhat integrated the songs into the plot. Less successful was *Go to It* (1916) with a score by John Golden and **Anne Caldwell. P. G. Wodehouse** joined Kern and Bolton for the next Princess musical, *Oh, Boy!* (1917), and the illustrious team of Bolton, Wodehouse, and Kern was born. The series would reach its goal of expert modern musical comedy in the shows by this trio, who blended story, character, and song together in a charming and surprisingly intelligent way. Although officially not part of the series because it played at another theatre, the team's *Leave It to Jane* (1917) had all the superior qualities of the Bolton-Wodehouse-Kern shows. Their *Oh, Lady! Lady!!* (1918) was another hit in the series, but it was the last at the Princess Theatre by the popular triumvirate. Louis Hirsch took over the composing for *Oh, My Dear!* (1918), and although it was mildly popular, Kern's music was greatly missed. The final Princess Theatre offering, *Toot Sweet* (1919), with a score by Richard A. Whiting and Ray Egan, was an unsuccessful revue that departed from the series' initial intention. The bold experiment ended after only seven shows in four years, but the Princess Musicals were fondly remembered and inspired the next generation of songwriters such as Richard Rodgers, Lorenz Hart, Cole Porter, and others who later acknowledged the series as the reason they first pursued musical theatre.

PUCK, Eva (1892–1979) and **Sammy WHITE** (1894–1960). Stage and film performers. The husband and wife team played the married showboat performers Ellie and Frank Shultz in the original Broadway production of Kern's *Show Boat* (1927) and reprised their performances in the 1932 revival. A native New Yorker, Puck performed in vaudeville before getting cast in a small role on Broadway in *Irene* (1919). Born in Providence, Rhode Island, White made his Broadway debut at the age of six and by the time he was an adult he was singing and dancing in such revues as *Shubert Gaieties* (1919) and *The Passing Show of 1921*, as well as playing character parts in comedies and musicals. Puck and White appeared together in vaudeville, were featured in the film short *Eva Puck and Sammy White* (1923), and performed as a team on Broadway in *The Greenwich Follies* (1923) before getting cast in *Show Boat*. Because the couple divorced in 1933, White played opposite **Queenie Smith** in the 1936 film version of *Show Boat*. Twelve years later he reprised his Frank opposite Clare Alden in the 1946 Broadway revival. Puck retired from show business in the 1930s, but White continued to act in movies up until 1960, the year he died. Among his feature film credits are *Cain and Mabel* (1936), *Swing Your Lady* (1938), *Pat and Mike* (1952), *The Bad and the Beautiful* (1952), *About Mrs. Leslie* (1954), and *The Helen Morgan Story* (1957), in which he played himself.

"Put Me to the Test" is the song of determination that nightclub hoofer Danny McGuire (**Gene Kelly**) sang as he danced on stage with a dummy in a dress shop in the Kern movie musical *Cover Girl* (1944), soon replacing the mannequin with **Rita Hayworth**. Later in the film Danny reprised the number with sidekick Genius (**Phil Silvers**) and a male chorus on the back of a military truck as they clowned around and did jazz, Hawaiian, and boogie-woogie versions of the song. "Put Me to the Test" began as a list song by the Gershwin brothers written for the film *Damsel in Distress* (1937), but only George Gershwin's music was used for a dance routine by **Fred Astaire**, George Burns, and Gracie Allen. Years later, when **Ira Gershwin** was slated to write the lyrics for Kern's music in *Cover Girl*, he resurrected the clever lyric that listed things a lover would do to prove his love, from going over Niagara Falls in a barrel to getting tickets to the latest Noel Coward play. Kern wrote an original melody (which, ironically, was very Gershwinesque in flavor), and by request the lyric was toned down to less daunting exploits, such as swimming in the Radio City fountain and doing kitchen chores. A very distinctive recording of the song was made by Bobby Short in the 1970s, and on Broadway it was sung by Noah Racey in the musical *Never Gonna Dance* (2003).

R

THE RED PETTICOAT. A musical comedy by Rida Johnson Young, Paul West (book and lyrics); Jerome Kern (music). [13 November 1912, Daly's Theatre, 61 performances] Produced by the Shubert Brothers, directed by Joseph W. Herbert, musical direction by Clarence West, orchestrations by **Frank Saddler**. Playwright Young's comedy *Next* had been produced in 1911 by the Shuberts and quickly closed. But the star Helen Lowell was applauded and the plot seemed to be a good possibility for a musical so the Shuberts hired Kern to write one of his first full scores for the project. In the mining town of Lost River, Nevada, small-time entrepreneur Otto Schmaltz (James B. Carson) advertises back East for a barber so he can open a tonsorial parlor in his emporium. The job is given to one S. Brush who arrives in Lost River and surprises everyone because she is Sophie Brush, a homely, gangling tomboy. Sophie (Lowell) not only proves herself an expert barber but also tames the local madam Stage Brush Kate (Frances Kennedy) and her girls and manages to clear Jack Warner (Joseph Phillips) of a theft charge and match him up with the town schoolteacher, Phyllis Oldham (Louise Mink). Sophie pretties herself up and wins the heart of Phyllis's brother Brick (Donald MacDonald). The Nevada setting was unique for a musical and the plotting was solid. Lowell shone as Sophie and there were compliments for the whole cast, including Katherine Belknap who played a parrot. Kern's music was noticed and approved of by the press (the number "Since the Days of Grandmamma" was particularly praised), and the cheerful musical comedy entertained audiences for two months.

"Remind Me" is a vintage Kern–**Dorothy Fields** song that was, according to film historian Roy Hemming, "virtually thrown away in an early scene" of the first Abbott and Costello movie *One Night in the Tropics* (1940). The Latin-flavored number was introduced by the predatory Mickey Fitzgerald (Peggy Moran dubbed by an uncredited singer) in a New York nightclub scene as she tried to make trouble for her boyfriend Steve Harper (**Robert Cummings**) who is out with another girl. The lyric is about two lovers who reminded each other not to fall in love with each other again unless, of course, they should forget. Kern's music is insistent and rhythmic with the pulse of a rumba. (The music had been written years before and not used, so Kern reworked it with a Latin beat as the scene required.) Fields's lyric "is not only perfect," according to biographer Deborah Grace Winer, who sees it as "probably the best argument for the case that Dorothy Fields's popular songs are essentially feminine in viewpoint." The song was ignored until nightclub singer Mabel Mercer rescued it from obscurity by recording it in the late 1940s and singing it in clubs, and today it is a standard. In the stage revue *Jerome Kern Goes to Hollywood*, David Kernan and Elaine Delmar sang it in London in 1985 and Scott Holmes performed it with Delmar on Broadway the next year. "Remind Me" was also sung by Nancy Lemenager and Noah Racey in the Broadway musical *Never Gonna Dance* (2003). Among the notable recordings of the number are those by June Christy, Liza Minnelli, Barbara Carroll, Sandy Stewart, Andrea Marcovicci, Sylvia McNair, Margaret Whiting, Rebecca Kilgore, Helen Merrill, Ella Fitzgerald, Jeri Southern, and Peggy Lee, whose recording was used in the film *Cafe Society* (1995).

REVIVALS and REMAKES of Kern musicals. Broadway revivals of classic musicals are so common today that it is difficult to imagine a time when they were virtually unknown. A successful musical would run its course on Broadway, then tour major cities, possibly returning to New York at the end of the tour for a brief "return engagement," then was heard of no more. Sometimes a popular favorite would tour for years, stopping on Broadway for a limited run when it was nearby, but a new production in which an old musical was rethought, redesigned, redirected, and rechoreographed was far from usual. Because they have been around so long, the comic operettas by Gilbert and Sullivan hold the record for most revivals. *H.M.S. Pinafore* has returned to New York over sixty times. Other European works to be frequently revived include *Die Fledermaus*, *The Grand Duchess of Gerolstein*, and *The Merry Widow*. *The Black Crook* (1866), considered the first American musical, returned to New York seventeen times, though often it was the same production just passing through, but by 1900 it was no longer an audience pleaser. Kern's *Show Boat* (1927) is perhaps the most durable of American musicals, being revived on Broadway across the decades; New

York saw major revivals in 1932, 1946, 1948, 1954, 1961, 1966, 1983, and 1994. Other Kern works to return successfully to Manhattan include *Music in the Air* (1951), *Leave It to Jane* (1959), *Very Good Eddie* (1975), and *Oh, Boy!* (1979). London stage revivals of Kern musicals include *Show Boat* (premiered in 1929) in 1943, 1971, 1990, and 2006; *Very Good Eddie* in 1976; and *Sally*, which first played in the West End, was revived in 1942 as *Wild Rose*. In Hollywood, a new production of an existing film is called a remake. *Show Boat* was first filmed in 1929 then remade in 1936 and 1951. Kern's *Sunny* was first filmed in 1930 and remade in 1941. The 1935 screen version of *Roberta* was remade in 1952 as *Lovely to Look At.*

REYNOLDS, Herbert [né Michael Elder Rourke]. (1867–1933) Stage lyricist. A British-born writer who was active on Broadway for twenty-three years, he wrote the lyric for Kern's landmark ballad **"They Didn't Believe Me."** He was born in Manchester, England, but emigrated to the States around the turn of the century and worked as a press agent in New York. Reynolds started writing lyrics in 1902, and using the name M. E. Rourke, some of his songs with Kern and others were interpolated into Broadway shows. His first full score was for *The Knickerbocker Girl* (1903), and for the next ten years he contributed to seventeen musicals, including Kern's *The Red Petticoat* (1912). During World War I, he adopted the pen name Herbert Reynolds, and when he and Kern were asked to contribute some new songs for the London import *The Girl from Utah* (1915), one of the them was the innovative "They Didn't Believe Me." Reynolds also collaborated with Kern on the **Princess Theatre Musicals** *Nobody Home* (1915) and *Very Good Eddie* (1915), as well as Kern's *Miss Springtime* (1916) and *Rock-a-Bye Baby* (1918). His other Broadway credits include *The Blue Paradise* (1915), *Ziegfeld Follies* (1922), and *Honeymoon Lane* (1926). The cigar-chomping Irish-American was a colorful figure on Broadway, and although he lacked the sophistication of some of Kern's later lyricists, he was able to come up with playful and even moving lyrics that sat on Kern's music beautifully.

ROBERTA. A musical comedy by **Otto Harbach** (book and lyrics), Jerome Kern (music). [18 November 1933, New Amsterdam Theatre, 295 performances] Produced by **Max Gordon**, directed by **Hassard Short**,

VERY GOOD EDDIE. Kern had his first bona fide Broadway hit with this daffy 1915 Princess Theatre musical. The show ushered in an era of bright American musical comedy that flourished until the Depression. The Goodspeed Opera House in Connecticut revived *Very Good Eddie* sixty years later, and it was popular enough to transfer to Broadway. Pictured from that revival, left to right, are Percy (Nicholas Wyman), Elsie (Virginia Seidel), Eddie (Charles Repole), and Georgina (Spring Fairbank). *Photofest*

choreographed by José Limón, musical direction by Victor Baravalle, orchestrations by **Robert Russell Bennett**.

Plot: All-American football player John Kent inherits a Paris dress shop called Roberta from his Aunt Minnie so he goes to France with his pal Huckleberry Haines, where he falls in love with his aunt's able assistant Stephanie. John's old flame Sophie arrives to complicate matters but he ends up with Stephanie, who turns out to be a Russian princess in disguise. In the subplot Haines is swept off his feet by the Polish beauty Clementina Scharwenka, one of Roberta's most prized customers.

A lackluster musical comedy with a superior score, the show was saved by a hit song. Harbach adapted Alice Duer Miller's novel *Gowns by Roberta* into an operetta, right down to the old-fashioned device of the princess in disguise. It was a labored libretto, but the cast was sparkling and the score included modern swing as well as operatic pieces. The reviews were mixed, and business for the expensive production was spotty. Then the song "Smoke Gets in Your Eyes" became a huge hit on the radio and the shrewd producer Gordon advertised *Roberta* as "the 'Smoke Gets in Your Eyes' show." Business picked up and the musical ran a profitable nine months. Also in the score were the flowing ballads "Yesterdays" and "The Touch of Your Hand," the adoring "You're Devastating," the sassy "I'll Be Hard to Handle" (lyric by Bernard Dougall), and the jazzy "Let's Begin." Hassard Short directed the splendid cast (and designed the dramatic lighting), Clark

CASTS FOR *ROBERTA* AND *LOVELY TO LOOK AT*

Character	*Roberta* 1934 Broadway	*Roberta* 1935 film	*Lovely to Look At* 1952 film
Stephanie	**Tamara**	**Irene Dunne**	**Kathryn Grayson**
John Kent/Tony	Ray Middleton	**Randolph Scott**	**Howard Keel**
Huckleberry Haines/ Al Marsh	**Bob Hope**	**Fred Astaire**	**Red Skelton**
Scharwenka/Bubbles	**Lyda Roberti**	**Ginger Rogers**	**Ann Miller**
Aunt Minnie	**Fay Templeton**	**Helen Westley**	
Jerry			**Gower Champion**
Clarisse			**Marge Champion**

Robinson designed the lavish sets, Kiviette did the stylish costumes (there was a stunning fashion show), and José Limon choreographed the production numbers. *Roberta* was Kern's last Broadway hit, and while much of the show was a throwback to an earlier era, there was also evidence that Kern had lost none of his innovative powers. Although there was no London production, *Roberta* toured successfully and there was an applauded production in Australia.

Film version: Roberta. A movie musical by Jane Murfin, Sam Mintz, Glen Tryon, Allan Scott (screenplay); Otto Harbach, **Dorothy Fields** (lyrics); Jerome Kern (music). [1935, RKO] Produced by **Pandro S. Berman**; directed by William A. Seiter; choreographed by Hermes Pan, **Fred Astaire**; musical arrangements by Max Steiner. Although *Roberta* has rarely been revived on stage, Hollywood saw fit to make two screen versions of it.

In the 1935 version, the musical lost much its terrific score on screen, but the musical gained Fred Astaire and Ginger Rogers in the secondary roles of bandleader Huckleberry Haines and a phony Russian countess, and they were much more fun than the leading roles played by Irene Dunne and Randolph Scott. The screenplay was somewhat contrived but an improvement over the stage libretto, and much of the movie is top-flight entertainment. Dorothy Fields collaborated with Kern on two splendid new songs, "Lovely to Look At" and "I Won't Dance" (based on an **Oscar Hammerstein** lyric), and the movie was directed with pizzazz by William A. Seiter with choreography by

---

ROBERTA/LOVELY TO LOOK AT SONGS

"Let's Begin"
"Alpha Beta Pi"
"You're Devastating"
"Yesterdays"
"Something's Got to Happen"
"The Touch of Your Hand"
"I'll Be Hard to Handle"
"Hot Spot"
"Smoke Gets in Your Eyes"

Added to 1935 film version:

"Indiana" (not by Kern)
"I Won't Dance"
"Lovely to Look At"

Added to 1952 remake, Lovely to Look At:

"Lafayette"
"The Most Exciting Night"

Astaire and Hermes Pan. The film was very popular and decades later was remade using one of the new songs as the title.

Film version: Lovely to Look At. A movie musical by George Wells, Harry Ruby (screenplay); Otto Harbach, Dorothy Fields (lyrics); Jerome Kern (music). [1952, MGM] Produced by Jack Cummings; directed by **Mervyn LeRoy**, Vincente Minnelli; choreographed by Hermes Pan; musical direction by Saul Chaplin, Carmen Dragon; orchestrations by Leo Arnaud. The 1952 remake went back to the source material and told of American comic Al Marsh who inherits the Paris dress shop and goes to France with his buddies Tony and Jerry to find the store run by sisters Stephanie and Clarisse, who are facing bankruptcy. The boys help put on a big fashion show, save the shop, and win the hearts of the sisters and the provocative Bubbles Cassidy. It was not as solid as the earlier film but there was still much to enjoy, including Kern-Harbach songs from the original stage score not used in the 1935 film and a daffy new number called "Lafayette." Mervyn LeRoy directed the lush production, which was filled with talented players and forty-two gowns by Adrian for the fashion show finale (directed by Vincente Minnelli). Pan again was the choreographer and the MGM production was a hit at the box office. Bob Hope and Howard Keel reprised their roles in a 1958 TV version of *Roberta* that also featured Anna Maria Alberghetti and Janis Paige. Hope played Huckleberry again in a much-abridged and updated 1969 television version on NBC. Michele Lee, John Davidson, and Paige were also featured in the ninety-minute broadcast.

Recordings: After *Show Boat*, there are more recordings of *Roberta* than any other Kern musical. All the same, there is no original cast recording and only Tamara made a record of some of the songs. The 1935 film soundtrack is fairly complete but not available on CD; yet one can see the whole film on DVD. Much of the cast did a radio broadcast of *Roberta* in 1935 and it was recorded but not easy to find today. The soundtrack for the movie remake *Lovely to Look At* is available on CD and the film itself on DVD. Medley versions of the score were made by the New Mayfair Orchestra and by the Victor Light Opera Company in the 1930s. There are at least five studio recordings of the *Roberta* score, two of them available on CD. A 1944 recording with Kitty Carlisle and Alfred Drake is very good, but more fun is a 1952 disc with Stephen Douglass, Joan Roberts, Kaye Ballard, and Jack Cassidy. Difficult to find are the three LP recordings made in the 1950s. Ray Charles is featured in a 1950 record, opera star Anna Moffo in another, and a third has lesser-known artists such as Marion Grimaldi and Andy Cole.

ROBERTI, Lyda. (1906–1938) Stage and screen performer. A platinum blonde who excelled at playing man-hungry females, she made some memorable appearances in 1930s musicals before her premature death, and she originated the role of the Parisian Clementina Scharwenka in the Broadway version of Kern's *Roberta* (1933). Roberti was born in Warsaw, Poland, the daughter of a circus clown, and grew up traveling with him around the world. Arriving in the States, she went into vaudeville where her thick but sexy accent was a novelty, and by 1931 she was on Broadway in the musical revue *You Said It*, followed by *Pardon My English* (1933) and *Roberta*. Roberti made her screen debut in 1932 and completed only eleven features before her fatal heart attack at the age of thirty-two. Her musicals were *Dancers in the Dark* (1932), *The Kid from Spain* (1932), *Torch Singer* (1933), *College Rhythm* (1934), *George White's Scandals* (1935), *Big Broadcast of 1936* (1935), and *Nobody's Baby* (1937). Roberti was much imitated by other performers, including **Ginger Rogers** who used a Roberti accent when she played the Polish actress's role in the 1935 film version of *Roberta*.

ROBESON, Paul [né Paul Leroy Bustill Robeson]. (1898–1976) Stage, screen, and concert singer, actor. One of the greatest of all African American performers, he was long associated with *Show Boat* and sang **"Ol' Man River"** throughout his life as a kind of identity for himself and his race. Robeson was born in Princeton, New Jersey, the son of a Presbyterian minister, and was educated in law at Rutgers University (where he was a top athlete) and Columbia University (during which he played professional football for a time). About the time he was admitted to the bar he started performing professionally, appearing in the chorus of the landmark all-black musical *Shuffle Along* (1921) on Broadway. Robeson's first success as a dramatic actor was as the lawyer Jim Harris married to a white woman in *All God's Chillun Got Wings* (1924), followed by his towering performance as Brutus Jones in the expressionistic *The Emperor Jones* (1925), which he reprised in a 1933 film. The role of the dockhand Joe in *Show Boat* was written for him by Kern and **Oscar Hammerstein**, but Robeson was engaged to perform in

SWING TIME. Although they don't dance one step, Ginger Rogers and Fred Astaire had one of their best duets with the beguiling song "A Fine Romance" in this 1936 movie classic. Kern's music and Dorothy Fields's lyric create a complete musical scene set in a snowy wood. The scene and the couple's relationship are as deliciously ambiguous as the song. *RKO Radio Pictures/Photofest ©RKO Radio Pictures*

ROYCE, Edward [né James William Reddall]. (1870–1964) Stage director and choreographer. He staged many American and British musicals in the 1910s and 1920s, including early landmark efforts by Kern. Royce was born in Bath, England, the son of musical comedy star E. W. Royce, and began his career as a scenic designer, but he soon followed in his father's footsteps and took up dancing. Eventually he became more interested in choreography and started to stage dances in West End musicals at the turn of the century. By 1905 Royce was directing as well as choreographing British musicals. He was brought to America by his friend Kern, making his Broadway debut in 1913 and going on to direct and choreograph Kern's *Have a Heart* (1917), *Oh, Boy!* (1917), *Leave It to Jane* (1917), *Oh, Lady! Lady!!* (1918), *Rock-a-Bye Baby* (1918), *She's a Good Fellow* (1919), *Sally* (1920), and *Good Morning, Dearie* (1921). Royce also staged such hits as *Going Up!* (1917), *Irene* (1919), *Kid Boots* (1923), *Billie* (1928), and a few editions of the *Ziegfeld Follies*. In 1929 he choreographed a few early movie musicals then returned to England for the rest of his declining career. As a creative member of the team who put together the **Princess Theatre Musicals** in the 1910s, Royce was instrumental in the American musical's development from large, dazzling extravaganzas to smaller, more intimate and intelligent works. His choreography was sprightly and contagious and his staging of those early literate book musicals was effective enough to be noticed at the time.

SADDLER, Frank. (1864–1921). Stage orchestrator. An early and important theatre orchestrator who rethought the pit orchestra and made lively arrangements that attempted to fit each show, he orchestrated Kern's first full score, *The Red Petticoat* (1912), and collaborated with the composer on a dozen other musicals. Saddler was born in Franklin, Pennsylvania, and studied music in Munich, Germany. He began his career as a conductor of a pit band in burlesque then started arranging other composers' work. Because orchestrators were not always credited in the playbill program, it is difficult to say just how many Broadway musicals Saddler worked on. At least fifty shows bear his name, but in actuality he probably arranged music for twice that number. His first credited Broadway show was *Broadway to Tokio* (1900), and by 1904 he was arranging the music for a handful of shows each season. Saddler was music publisher Max Dreyfuss's top orchestrator by the 1910s, and it was Dreyfuss who first matched him with Kern. The two men got along very well and Saddler was soon Kern's favorite orchestrator. Their other collaborations include *Nobody Home* (1915), *Very Good Eddie* (1915), *Have a Heart* (1917), *Love o' Mike* (1917), *Oh, Boy!* (1917), *Leave It to Jane* (1917), *Oh, Lady! Lady!!* (1918), *She's a Good Fellow* (1919), *The Night Boat* (1920), and *Hitchy-Koo* (1920). Saddler's many other New York credits include *The Jolly Bachelors* (1910), *The Passing Show* (1912 and 1913), *Ziegfeld Follies* (1912), *The Honeymoon Express* (1913), *Stop! Look! Listen!* (1915), *Robinson Crusoe, Jr.* (1916), *Going Up!* (1917), and *George White's Scandals* (1920). After Saddler's death, Kern worked with some other orchestrators until he began a long and fruitful collaboration with **Robert Russell Bennett**. Many of Saddler's orchestrations are now lost, but the surviving scores illustrate what a masterful and inventive orchestrator he was. George Gershwin called him "the father of modern arranging."

SALLY. A musical comedy by **Guy Bolton** (book; Clifford Grey, B. G. De-Sylva, etc. (lyrics); Jerome Kern, Victor Herbert (music). [21 December 1920,

New Amsterdam Theatre, 561 performances] Produced by **Florenz Ziegfeld**, directed and choreographed by **Edward Royce**, musical direction by Gus Salzer.

Plot: The orphaned Sally Rhinelander works as a dishwasher at the Elm Tree Alley Inn in Greenwich Village where her friend is the exiled Duke Constantine of Czechogovinia whom everyone calls "Connie." The monied Blair Farquar comes to the restaurant to hire workers for a party he's throwing and is smitten by Sally. The day of the party he is thrilled when the dancer that theatrical agent Otis Hooper has booked doesn't show, and Sally gets to perform. Hooper is so impressed that he gets Sally into the *Ziegfeld Follies* where she becomes a star and wins the hand of Blair.

A Cinderella musical given a splashy production by producer Florenz Ziegfeld, *Sally* made Marilyn Miller the First Lady of musical comedy on Broadway. It was no accident, for the show was built around her singing-dancing-comic talents and she shone like the star everyone expected. While the simple but efficient libretto and the score were the work of several hands, *Sally* seemed to come together effortlessly and was so popular that Broadway kept up a steady supply of imitations for the rest of the decade. "Look for the Silver Lining" by Kern and DeSylva was the outstanding hit of the show yet the score was packed with memorable songs, including the charming "The Church Around the Corner," the haunting ballad "Wild Rose," the romantic "Whip-Poor-Will," the saucy "The Lorelei," and the vivacious title number. (Victor Herbert provided the music for the "Butterfly Ballet"; all of the rest

CASTS FOR *SALLY*

Character	1920 Broadway	1921 London	1929 film
Sally	**Marilyn Miller**	**Dorothy Dickson**	Marilyn Miller
Blair Farquar	Irving Fisher	Gregory Stroud	Alexander Gray
"Connie"	**Leon Errol**	Leslie Henson	**Joe E. Brown**
Otis Hooper	**Walter Catlett**		T. Roy Barnes
Mrs. Ten Broek	Dolores	Molly Ramsden	Maude Turner Gordon
Rosie	May Hay		Pert Kelton
Pops	Alfred P. James		Ford Sterling
Jimmy Spleen/ Spelvin	Stanley Ridges	Seymour Beard	

of the music was by Kern.) Ziegfeld spared no expense, hiring Joseph Urban for the lavish scenery. Notices were like valentines, and the musical ran a year and a half. Miller and much of the same cast returned to Broadway with the show in 1923, and the 1948 revival featured Bambi Linn (Sally), Willie Howard (Connie), Robert Shackleton (Blair now called Mickey), and Jack Goode (Otis). The William Berbey–Hunt Stromberg production lasted only thirty-six performances. The 1921 London production starred Dorothy Dickson and it was a hit, running 387 performances. A 1942 London revival, retitled *Wild Rose*, featured British stage-screen favorite Jessie Matthews, and it managed a run of 205 performances.

SALLY SONGS

"Way Down East"
"On with the Dance"
"This Little Girl"
"Joan of Arc"
"Look for the Silver Lining"
"Sally"
"The Social Game"
"Wild Rose"
"The Schnitza Komisski"
"Whip-Poor-Will"
"The Lorelei"
"The Church Around the Corner"

Added for 1929 film: (not by Kern)

"All I Want to Do, Do, Do Is Dance"
"Walking Off Those Balkan Blues"
"What Will I Do Without You?"

Film version: Sally. A movie musical comedy by Waldemar Young (screenplay); Al Dubin, B. G. DeSylva, etc. (lyrics); Joe Burke, Jerome Kern (music). [1929, Warner/First National] Produced by Florenz Ziegfeld; directed by John Francis Dillon; choreographed by Albertina Rasch, Larry Ceballos; musical direction by Leo F. Forbstein. Marilyn Miller made her screen debut as she reprised her Sally in this elaborate, overstuffed early talkie. Yet even surrounded by hundreds of extras, Miller's singing and dancing talents hold their own and one gets a glimpse of why she was so beloved on the stage. Most of the Kern songs were dropped and new ones by Joe Burke (music) and Al Dubin (lyrics) were added. Larry Ceballos choreographed the giant production numbers, some of which were in color, and Albertina Rasch staged the ballet numbers. *Sally* on screen is more a curiosity than a satisfying movie musical, but it has its charms.

Recordings: While there was no original Broadway cast recording of *Sally*, the original London cast headed by Dorothy Dickson recorded much of the score in 1921. It is one of the best of the 1920s theatre recordings and is available on CD. The 1929 movie soundtrack is not as complete and is very difficult to find. The 1942 London revival, titled *Wild Rose*, was recorded and it also is hard to locate today. A New Zealand studio recording is a rare find, but one can more easily find the Victor Light Opera Company's 1938 medley of highlights from the score.

SANDERSON, Julia [née Julia Sackett]. (1887–1975) Stage performer. A petite, doll-faced soprano who starred in several Broadway musicals in the 1910s and 1920s, she played the Mormon wife Una Trance in *The Girl from Utah* (1914) in which she and **Donald Brian** introduced Kern's trendsetting ballad **"They Didn't Believe Me."** Sanderson was born in Springfield, Massachusetts, the daughter of an actor, and was on the stage as a child. By the age of fifteen she had years of experience and made her Broadway bow in the chorus of *A Chinese Honeymoon* (1902). Sanderson moved up from the chorus in her next show, *Winsome Winnie* (1903), to replace the title character. The next year she was widely noticed as the exotic Mataya in *Wang* (1904) and was finally a star as the Utopian lass Eileen Cavanaugh in *The Arcadians* (1910). Her other musical credits include *Fantana* (1905), *The Tourists* (1906), *Kitty Grey* (1909), *The Sunshine Girl* (1913), *Rambler Rose* (1917), Kern's **Hitchy-Koo** (1920), and *Tangerine* (1921), as well as the leading lady in tours of such musical hits as *No, No, Nanette* and *Oh, Kay!* Sanderson usually played the secondary female lead, a lively soubrette opposite the show's comics. When she was past the age of playing such ingenues, she went into vaudeville with her husband Frank Crumit (1889–1943); the two of them became very popular together on radio from 1929 to 1943. She was also married to actor Tod Sloan (1874–1933) for a time.

SCOTT, [George] **Randolph** [Crane]. (1898–1987) Film performer, producer. One of Hollywood's favorite cowboy stars, the tall, rugged-looking actor also shone in some comedies and a few major musicals, most memorably in two Kern films: as the American footballer John Kent in Paris in *Roberta* (1935) and as the defiant pioneer Peter Cortlandt in *High, Wide and Handsome* (1937). Scott was born in Orange, Virginia, and educated for an engineering career at Georgia Tech and the University of North Carolina before and after serving in World War I. After graduation he turned to acting and, having gotten experience at the Pasadena Playhouse, went into films in 1927. By the mid-1930s Scott had established himself as a cowboy star and retained the image for twenty years. He usually played physically strong but romantically shy heroes, and he was often cast that way in musicals as well. His other musical credits include *Hello, Everybody!* (1933), *Follow the Fleet* (1936), *Rebecca of Sunnybrook Farm* (1938), *Follow the Boys* (1944), *Belle of the Yukon* (1944), and *Starlift* (1951). He served as associate producer for many of his films in the 1950s. A shrewd investor, Scott retired from Hollywood in the early 1960s as one of the richest men in California.

SEGAL, Vivienne. (1897–1992) Stage and film singer, actress. A skillfully adaptable leading lady on Broadway for many years because of her ability to perform in both operetta and musical comedy, she was featured in a Kern musical play and film: as the leading "lady" Molly Farrington in *Oh, Lady! Lady!!* (1918) and as the temperamental prima donna Mlle. Odette in *The Cat and the Fiddle* (1934). Born in Philadelphia, the daughter of a renowned physician, Segal trained for an opera career and appeared in some local productions before making an impressive Broadway debut as Mizzy in *The Blue Paradise* (1915). For the next forty years she would appear in all kinds of musicals, moving from perky ingenue to mature character player. Among her other successes were *Ziegfeld Follies* (1924), *The Desert Song* (1926), *The Three Musketeers* (1928), and the 1931 revival of *The Chocolate Soldier*. Some of her most memorable performances were in Rogers and Hart musicals, such as the wily Countess Peggy in *I Married an Angel* (1938), the devious Morgan le Fay in the 1943 revival of *A Connecticut Yankee*, and the worldly-wise Vera Simpson in the original 1940 production and the acclaimed 1951 revival of *Pal Joey*. She made only a few films, including *Golden Dawn* (1930), *Viennese Nights* (1930), and *The Cat and the Fiddle*, and only a handful of television appearances. Segal had a round baby face, dark hair, and a wide-ranged singing voice that allowed her to trill high notes as well as deliver comic lyrics.

SEITER, William A. (1891–1964) Film director. The former silent screen actor helmed over sixty movies during a forty-year career, including some two dozen musicals, among which are the Kern films *Sunny* (1930), *Roberta* (1935), and *You Were Never Lovelier* (1942). Seiter was born in

New York City and worked as a writer and an artist before appearing in silents as one of the Keystone Kops. By 1918 he was directing two-reelers, then graduated to features in 1920. Seiter helmed all genres but was most accomplished with lightweight or romantic pictures. Among his other musicals were *Smiling Irish Eyes* (1929), *Girl Crazy* (1932), *Hello, Everybody!* (1933), *Dimples* (1936), *Stowaway* (1936), *Life of the Party* (1937), *Sally, Irene and Mary* (1938), *Four Jills in a Jeep* (1944), *That Night with You* (1945), *I'll Be Yours* (1947), *Up in Central Park* (1948), and *One Touch of Venus* (1948).

SHAW, Oscar [né Oscar Schwartz]. (1889–1967) Stage and film performer. A boyishly handsome leading man in Broadway musicals, his toothy grin, slicked-back dark hair, and jovial style were as consistent as the juvenile roles he played for twenty years, among them four Kern musicals: as the amorous Dick Rivers in ***Very Good Eddie*** (1915), the college student Stub Talmadge in ***Leave It to Jane*** (1917), the millionaire Billy Van Cortlandt in ***Good Morning, Dearie*** (1921), and the playboy Laddie Munn in ***Dear Sir*** (1924). The Philadelphia native was educated at the University of Pennsylvania before going on the Broadway stage as a singer in the chorus of *The Mimic* (1908). After playing second leads in the landmark musicals *Very Good Eddie* and *Leave It to Jane*, he rose to primary roles in such musicals as *Two Little Girls in Blue* (1920), *Good Morning, Dearie* (1921), *Dear Sir* (1924), *Oh, Kay!* (1926), *The Five O'Clock Girl* (1927), *Flying High* (1930), and *Everybody's Welcome* (1931), as well as some London musicals. Shaw was also given featured spots in the revues *The Passing Show* (1912), *Ziegfeld's Midnight Frolic* (1916), *Ziegfeld's Nine O'Clock Frolic* (1921), and *Music Box Revue* (1924). He made a few silent films and was in the screen musicals *The Cocoanuts* (1929) and *Rhythm on the River* (1940). Shaw was a solid song-and-dance man but not a very flexible actor, so his career faded once he grew too old to play juveniles.

"She Didn't Say 'Yes' (She Didn't Say 'No')" is the lighthearted (and a little bit naughty) hit song from ***The Cat and the Fiddle*** (1931), Kern's "modern" operetta. The American composer Shirley Sheridan (**Bettina Hall**), who lives in Brussels and is trying to get discovered, sang the ballad of indecision about a gal who is tempted to sin. The wry lyric by **Otto**

Harbach does not state what the heroine actually did but slyly concludes that she did what "you would do." Kern's music is a series of an ascending and descending pattern of eighth notes that gives the song a very swinging, American sound that contrasts with the rest of the score's operatic flavor. In the 1931 screen version of *The Cat and the Fiddle*, the number was sung by **Jeanette MacDonald** while she accompanied herself on the piano. In the Kern biopic *Till the Clouds Roll By* (1945), the song was sung by the Wilde Twins. Elisabeth Welch sang "She Didn't Say 'Yes'" in the revue *Jerome Kern Goes to Hollywood*, which played London in 1985 and on Broadway in 1986. Also on stage, a duet version was performed by Deidre Goodwin and Eugene Fleming in the Broadway musical *Never Gonna Dance* (2003). Welch recorded it, as did Ella Fitzgerald, Jeanne Lehman, Margaret Whiting, Peggy Lee, George Feyer, Frank Chacksfield, the Robert Shaw Chorale, Jane Pickens, and the orchestras of Paul Weston, Leo Reisman, and Carroll Gibbons.

SHEAN, Al [né Albert Schonberg]. (1868–1949) Stage and film performer. As half of the team of "Gallagher and Shean," one of the most famous of all vaudeville comedy duos, the "Dutch comic" had a long career that climaxed with one of his most touching performances, as the elderly music teacher Dr. Walther Lessing in Kern's *Music in the Air* (1932). Shean was born in Dornum, Germany, but grew up in New York City where he went into vaudeville as a member of the Manhattan Comedy Four. In 1919 he teamed up with Ed Gallagher (1873?–1949) who was a skinny, bespectacled straight man who began his career doing comic military sketches. Shean was short and stocky with a thick German accent, and the two men were hilarious foils for each other. Their most famous routine was singing "Mr. Gallagher and Mr. Shean" in which they asked each other a series of silly questions. Gallagher and Shean stopped the show when they performed it in the *Ziegfeld Follies* (1922) and later recorded it. The team's other Broadway musicals were *Rose Maid* (1912), *Greenwich Village Follies* (1923), and the 1924 edition of *Ziegfeld Follies*. The partners quarreled and split up on occasion, finally parting for good in 1925. Gallagher suffered a nervous breakdown and retired, but Shean continued on and had success as a character actor in plays and musicals, most memorably in *Music in the Air*. He reprised the role of Dr. Lessing in the 1934 film version and appeared in many other films, including *Ziegfeld Girl* (1941) in which he sang "Mr. Gallagher and Mr. Shean" with **Charles Winninger** as Gallagher. Shean's other screen musicals include *Sweet Music* (1935), *San Francisco* (1936), *Rosalie* (1937), *The Great Waltz* (1938), *Broadway Serenade* (1939), and *The Daughter of Rosie O'Grady* (1942). Shean was the uncle of the Marx Brothers.

SHE'S A GOOD FELLOW. A musical comedy by **Anne Caldwell** (book and lyrics), Jerome Kern (music). [5 May 1919, Globe Theatre, 120 performances] Produced by **Charles Dillingham**; directed and choreographed by Fred G. Latham, **Edward Royce**; musical direction by William Daly; orchestrations by **Frank Saddler**. A silly but endearing musical that relied on its leading man to be disguised as a woman for a good part of the evening, *She's a Good Fellow* was one of the many shows that season that suffered from a major actors' strike. Caldwell's book concerned Robert McLane (Joseph Santley) who has married the girls seminary student Jacqueline Fay (Ivy Sawyer) without getting her guardian's consent. Jacqueline is not of age so when the guardian finds out, he attempts to annul the marriage and has her confined to the school grounds. Robert has to dress like one of the coeds to get into the school and then must continue to impersonate a girl to remain there until the happy ending. The score was filled with delightful numbers, some of which had little bearing on the plot. At one point, Robert in drag and the country hick Chester (Olin Howland) did a comic duet together titled "Oh, You Beautiful Person!" and the vaudeville favorites the Duncan Sisters did a specialty that included some of their past hits. Kern and Caldwell's best song was "The First Rose of Summer," which enjoyed some popularity when Irish tenor John McCormack recorded it. (With a rewritten lyric by **P. G. Wodehouse**, the sentimental ballad was used in Kern's 1922 London musical *The Cabaret Girl*.) The Duncan Sisters recorded a few songs from *She's a Good Fellow*, and the Victor Light Opera Company made a disc with a medley of highlights from the Kern score.

SHORT, [Hubert Edward] **Hassard**. (1877–1956) Stage director. One of the most prolific and innovative directors of musicals from the 1920s through the 1940s, he excelled at revues but staged some memorable book musicals as well, including Kern's *Sunny* (1925), *Lucky* (1927), *Roberta* (1933), *Very Warm for May* (1939), and the 1946 revival of *Show Boat*.

He was born in rural Lincolnshire, England, and ran away from home at the age of fifteen to become an actor. Short made his London debut in 1895 and six years later emigrated to New York where he appeared in a number of Broadway productions, most memorably *Peg o' My Heart* (1912). His first New York directing assignment was the hit play *The Man from Home* in 1908, but he was not noticed until his staging of sketches for the Lambs' Club annual benefit revues called *Gambols* (1911 to 1913). Directing his first Broadway musical in 1920, Short's mastery of visuals and the use of lighting stood out, and he changed the way musicals looked. He replaced footlights with lighting instruments hung in the auditorium, used elevator and revolving stages, added color to light, used mirrors on stage effectively, and even had whiffs of perfume sent out into the house for certain numbers. Perhaps the high points of this kind of visual magic was seen in his direction of the landmark revues *The Band Wagon* (1931), with its twin turntables and the use of moving platforms to introduce and conclude scenes, and *As Thousands Cheer* (1933), with the scenery ablaze with newspaper headlines that introduced each scene. In addition to many popular revues, Short also staged such book musicals as *Face the Music* (1932), *The Great Waltz* (1934), *Jubilee* (1935), *Between the Devil* (1937), *Lady in the Dark* (1941), *Something for the Boys* (1943), *Carmen Jones* (1943), *Mexican Hayride* (1944), and *Seventeen* (1951).

SHOW BOAT. A musical play by **Oscar Hammerstein** (book and lyrics), Jerome Kern (music). [27 December 1927, Ziegfeld Theatre, 572 performances] Produced by **Florenz Ziegfeld**, directed by Zeke Colvan and Hammerstein (uncredited), choreographed by Sammy Lee, musical direction by Victor Baravalle, orchestrations by **Robert Russell Bennett**.

Plot: In the 1880s, Cap'n Andy Hawks pilots the show boat *Cotton Blossom* up and down the Mississippi River, bringing stage melodramas to the riverside towns and cities. His wife Parthy doesn't like raising her daughter Magnolia among show people so she is particularly suspicious of Gaylord Ravenal, a dashing-looking gentleman who she (rightly) suspects is a river gambler. When the local sheriff learns that Julie LaVerne, the featured actress on the *Cotton Blossom*, is a mulatto and is married to a white man, Steve, the couple is forced to flee and Gaylord and Magnolia take over the leading roles in the show boat's repertoire. The two fall in love and, with Cap'n Andy's help, elope and move to Chicago. Ravenal's gambling luck deserts him, and unable to face his failure, he abandons Magnolia and their little girl Kim. Magnolia gets a job singing in a Chicago nightclub after the star of the show quits; the star is the alcoholic Julie, and unknown to Magnolia, she hears Magnolia's audition and quits so that her friend can get the job. On New Year's Eve the Cap'n and Parthy are reunited with Magnolia at the nightclub where she is such a success that her singing career is launched. Years pass and Kim has grown up and is now a Roaring Twenties singing and dancing star. Magnolia decides to retire from performing, and joining her parents and Kim back on the *Cotton Blossom*, she is reunited with the aged Ravenal once again. Throughout the years, the African American riverboat worker Joe and his wife, the cook Queenie, remain on the *Cotton Blossom* and observe the changes that occur in the Hawks family. As much as life on the Mississippi may change, Joe knows that the river itself is unaware of the plight of humans and continues on regardless of people's fortunes or failures.

CASTS FOR *SHOW BOAT*

Characters:	Magnolia	Ravenal	Julie	Joe
1927 Broadway	**Norma Terris**	**Howard Marsh**	**Helen Morgan**	**Jules Bledsoe**
1928 London	Edith Day	Howett Worster	Marie Burke	**Paul Robeson**
1929 film	Laura La Plante	Joseph Schildkraut	Alma Rubens	Stepin Fetchit
1932 Broadway	Norma Terris	Dennis King	Helen Morgan	Paul Robeson
1936 film	**Irene Dunne**	**Allan Jones**	Helen Morgan	Paul Robeson
1946 Broadway	Jan Clayton	Charles Fredericks	Carol Bruce	Kenneth Spencer
1951 film	**Kathryn Grayson**	**Howard Keel**	**Ava Gardner**	**William Warfield**
1966 Broadway	Barbara Cook	Stephen Douglass	Constance Towers	William Warfield
1983 Broadway	Sheryl Woods	Ron Raines	Lonette McKee	Bruce Hubbard
1994 Broadway	Rebecca Luker	Mark Jacoby	Lonette McKee	Michel Bell

Characters:	Cap'n Andy	Parthy	Queenie
1927 Broadway	**Charles Winninger**	**Edna May Oliver**	**Tess Gardella**
1928 London	Cedric Hardwicke	Viola Compton	Alberta Hunter
1929 film	Otis Harlan	Emily Fitzroy	
1932 Broadway	Charles Winninger	Edna May Oliver	Tess Gardella
1936 film	Charles Winninger	**Helen Westley**	**Hattie McDaniel**
1946 Broadway	Ralph Dumke	Ethel Owen	Helen Dowdy
1951 film	**Joe E. Brown**	**Agnes Moorehead**	Frances E. Williams
1966 Broadway	David Wayne	Margaret Hamilton	Rosetta LeNoire
1983 Broadway	Donald O'Connor	Avril Gentles	Karla Burns
1994 Broadway	John McMartin	Elaine Stritch	Gretha Boston

The American musical theatre's first masterpiece and arguably still the finest musical play, *Show Boat* had a libretto and score with a larger scope and a more complex temperament than any work before it. Hammerstein's adaptation of Edna Ferber's sprawling novel was a masterwork of storytelling and character development. The Kern-Hammerstein score was richer and more varied than any other yet seen, filled with operetta numbers, folk and blues music, and bright musical comedy songs. *Show Boat* is also the first musical to hold together so well thematically, the song "Ol' Man River" linking the score just as the Mississippi ties together the plot and characters. For Kern and Hammerstein, *Show Boat* was a realization of their dream of integrating the score with the story and taking the theatre's musical form more seriously than previously thought. Their efforts finally resulted in America's first true musical play. Ziegfeld's original Broadway production boasted one of the most extraordinary casts of any Broadway production. In addition to those mentioned above, there were vibrant performances by **Sammy White** and **Eva Puck** as the show boat's comedy couple, Frank and Ellie, and thrilling choral work by the large black and white choruses, under the direction of William Vodery. Robert Russell Bennett did the famous orchestrations, which still sparkle in revival. Ziegfeld spared no expense on this, his most atypical show. Joseph Urban designed the many sets, and Hammerstein himself took over much of the direction of the mammoth production. Critical and popular responses were overwhelming, and the musical was the greatest success yet in Kern and Hammerstein's career.

The 1928 London production of *Show Boat* at the Drury Lane Theatre featured Edith Day as Magnolia, Howett Worster as Ravenal, and Paul Robeson playing Joe, the role written with him in mind. It ran 350 performances and prompted productions in Australia, Canada, and France. The musical successfully toured across America for seven months (with Irene Dunne playing Magnolia) and later returned to New York on eight occasions. Terris, Morgan, Winninger, Robeson, and Dennis King (as Ravenal) were the featured players in the 1932 return engagement on Broadway that ran 180 performances. The 1946 revival, produced by Hammerstein and Kern with the former directing with **Hassard Short**, ran a very profitable 418 performances. The New York City Center production in 1948 was far less successful, as was the New York City Light Opera mounting, which played two different engagements in 1954. The same company revived *Show Boat* in 1961 and its commendable cast included Jo Sullivan (Magnolia), Robert Rounseville (Ravenal), Andrew Frierson (Joe), and Anita Darian (Julie). One of the most fondly remembered revivals was the Music Theatre of Lincoln Center's 1966 production with Barbara Cook (Magnolia), Stephen Douglass (Ravenal), William Warfield (Joe), and Constance Towers (Julie). The Houston Grand Opera, the Kennedy Center, and other organizations pre-

SHOW BOAT SONGS

"Cotton Blossom" (Opening)
"Where's the Mate for Me?"
"Make Believe"
"Ol' Man River"
"Can't Help Lovin' Dat Man"
"Life Upon the Wicked Stage"
"Till Good Luck Comes My Way"
"I Might Fall Back on You"
"C'mon Folks (Queenie's Ballyhoo)"
"You Are Love"
"When We Tell Them All About It/ At the Fair"
"Why Do I Love You?"
"In Dahomey"
"Bill" (lyric by **P. G. Wodehouse**)
"Goodbye, My Lady Love"
"Hey, Fellah"
"After the Ball" (not by Kern)

Added for the 1928 London production:

"Dance Away the Night"

Added for 1929 film version: (not by Kern)

"The Lonesome Road"
"Deep River, Down South"
"Love Sings with a Song in My Heart"
"Here Comes the Show Boat"

Added for 1936 film version:

"Ah Still Suits Me"
"Gallivantin' Aroun'"
"I Have the Room Above Her"

Added for 1946 Broadway revival:

"Nobody Else But Me"

sented a *Show Boat* in 1983 that starred Donald O'Connor as Cap'n Andy and had lesser-known performers giving excellent performances as Magnolia (Paige O'Hara), Ravenal (Ron Raines), Joe (Bruce Hubbard), and Julie (Lonette McKee). McKee reprised her Julie in the acclaimed 1994 revival directed by Harold Prince that used dance (choreographed by Susan Stroman) to tie together the many events in the second act. The much-awarded production ran 946 performances, nearly twice as long as the original *Show Boat*. Notable London revivals of the musical include a well-remembered 1943 production that managed 264 performances during the World War II blitz, a 1971 mounting with a British-American cast that ran a surprising 910 performances, an Opera North–Royal Shakespeare Company revival at the Palladium in 1990, and the 1998 London version of the 1995 Broadway revival. Although it is an expensive and difficult musical to produce, cast, and perform, *Show Boat* has remained in the popular musical theatre repertoire for eighty years.

Film version: Show Boat. A movie musical by Charles Kenyon (screenplay), score by Kern, et al. (music) and Hammerstein, et al. (lyrics). [1929, Universal] Produced by Carl Laemmle, directed by Harry Pollard. Production of this silent film version of Ferber's book had already begun when the musical opened on Broadway. Universal added sound to some scenes, put Negro spirituals in the background, and filmed an eighteen-minute prologue in which members of the Broadway company sang some of the hits from the musical. The result is an odd, disjointed movie, but it does have those historic clips of the original players. Laura La Plante and Joseph Schildkraut are Magnolia and Ravenal in the non-musical story and they are often quite effective, but the supporting characters are mostly stereotypic and melodramatic.

Film version: Show Boat. A movie musical by Hammerstein (screenplay), score by Kern (music) and Hammerstein (lyrics). [1936, Universal] Produced by Carl Laemmle, Jr., directed by **James Whale**, choreography by LeRoy Prinz, musical direction by Victor Baravalle, orchestrations by Robert Russell Bennett. Helen Morgan, Charles Winninger, and others from the original Broadway cast were reunited for this superb sound version, beautifully filmed, acted, and sung. Irene Dunne and Allan Jones shine as Magnolia and Ravenal, Paul Robeson is a towering Joe, and every player down to the smallest role is excellent. Some songs from the stage score had to be cut and Hammerstein and Kern wrote three new ones, some of which were later incorporated into stage revivals of the show. Hammerstein's screenplay made changes in the later part of the story, and the ending is closer to a Hollywood finale rather than the bittersweet conclusion of the play. But all in all, this *Show Boat* is a film classic and is still powerful and pleasing.

The 1946 Kern biopic *Till the Clouds Roll By* opens with a fifteen-minute sequence in which the opening night of *Show Boat* is illustrated. It is a beautifully edited and sung condensation featuring **Kathryn Grayson** as Magnolia, Tony Martin as Gaylord, Lena Horne as Julie, Caleb Peterson as Joe, and Virginia O'Brien as Ellie. In some ways the sequence was a screen test by MGM in preparation for a full-length color remake of the entire musical, though only Grayson was used in the subsequent film.

Film Version: Show Boat. A movie musical by John Lee Mahin (screenplay), score by Kern (music) and Hammerstein (lyrics). [1951, MGM] Produced by **Arthur Freed**, directed by **George Sidney**, choreographed by Robert Alton, musical direction by Adolph Deutsch, orchestrations by Conrad Salinger. The use of color and location shooting distinguish the MGM remake, but, some fine performances aside, it is disappointing. Grayson and Howard Keel as Magnolia and Ravenal are in top form vocally but neither performance is totally convincing. Ava Gardner (dubbed by Annette Warren) is effective in the enlarged part of Julie, but too many of the other supporting cast are only superficially entertaining. Again there are many changes in the latter half of the plot, some of which work well. Julie, for instance, is instrumental in bringing Magnolia and Ravenal back together at the end of the film. Yet after the outstanding 1936 version, this *Show Boat* sometimes seems unnecessary.

Recordings: Perhaps no other American musical has been recorded as many times as *Show Boat*, and several outstanding discs have been made over the decades. Members of the original Broadway cast later appeared in revivals or films so there is some kind of record of that important production. The 1928 London cast recording, with Edith Day, Howett Worster, and Paul Robeson, is historically valuable and has been reissued on CD. The exhilarating 1936 film soundtrack has not, but the movie itself is available on DVD. The 1951 film version can be enjoyed on CD and DVD. (Interestingly, Ava Gardner's singing voice is not dubbed on the soundtrack recording.) Among the recorded Broadway revivals, there is much to recommend in the 1946 version with Jan Clayton, Charles Fredericks, Carol Bruce, and Kenneth Spencer; the 1966 Lincoln Center revival with Barbara Cook, Stephen Douglass, Constance Towers, and William Warfield; the 1971 London revival with Lorna Dallas, André Jobin, Cleo Laine, and Thomas Carey; and the 1994 Toronto-Broadway revival with Rebecca Luker, Mark Jacoby, Lonette McKee, and Michel Bell. Studio recordings of the *Show Boat* score range from simple song selections to complete versions with all the material written for all the film versions and revivals. Of particular note are a 1946 recording with Robert Merrill and Dorothy Kirsten; a 1949 disc with Bing Crosby, Frances Langford, Kenny Baker, and Tony Martin; a 1951 record with Martin, Louise Carlisle, Patti Page, and Sophie Tucker; a 1956 version with Merrill, Patrice Munsel, Rise Stevens, and Kevin Scott; a 1962 recording with John Raitt, Cook, Warfield, and Anita Darian; a very complete 1988 version with Jerry Hadley, Frederica von Stade, Teresa Stratas, Bruce Hubbard, and Paige O'Hara; and a 1993 collection with Janis Kelly, Jason Howard, Sally Burgess, and Willard White. Because interest in *Show Boat* has never waned, most of the above are available on CD.

SIDNEY, George. (1916–2002) Film director, producer. Specializing in movie musicals, he directed both original musicals and screen adaptations of Broadway hits, including the 1951 remake of Kern's ***Show Boat***. He was born in Long Island City, New York, into a theatrical family: his father was a Broadway producer and his mother and uncle were actors. Sidney was a child performer in vaudeville before pursuing a career in films, working his way up from messenger boy for MGM to sound technician, editor, second unit director, director of shorts, to finally a feature director in 1937. Although he directed some dramas and comedies, Sidney was most adept at musicals, including *Anchors Aweigh* (1945), *The Harvey Girls* (1946), *Annie Get Your Gun* (1950), *Kiss Me, Kate* (1953), *Pal Joey* (1957), *Bye Bye Birdie* (1963), and *Half a Sixpence* (1967).

SILVERS, Phil. (1911–1985) Television, stage, and film performer and producer. One of television's greatest clowns, the balding, bespectacled comic had a long and varied career that included vaudeville, burlesque, radio, and nightclubs, as well as Broadway and Hollywood musicals, including Kern's ***Cover Girl*** (1944) in which he played the sidekick Genius, arguably his best screen performance. The Brooklyn native sang in variety as a teenager and made some silent comedy shorts before going into burlesque, where he eventually became one of the top comics at Minsky's. Silvers was featured in the

SHOW BOAT. Few pre–World War II musicals have been revived on Broadway as often as this renowned Kern classic. In 1983, the Houston Grand Opera brought its production to New York City with Donald O'Connor (center, on barrel) featured as Cap'n Andy. Entertaining the crowd are the *Cotton Blossom's* comedy-dancing duo, Frank (Paul Keith) and Ellie (Alexandra Korey). *Photofest*

Broadway musical *Yokel Boy* (1939) then the next year started making talking films beginning with the musical *Hit Parade of 1941* (1940). In Hollywood he often played sidekicks or the friend of the leading man, as in the musicals ***Lady, Be Good!*** (1941), *Ice-Capades* (1941), *My Gal Sal* (1942), *Footlight Serenade* (1942), *Coney Island* (1943), *Cover Girl, Four Jills in a Jeep* (1944), *Something for the Boys* (1944), *Diamond Horseshoe* (1945), *If I'm Lucky* (1946), *Summer Stock* (1950), and *Lucky Me* (1954). Silvers never became a screen star, but he was roundly praised on Broadway as the con man Harrison Floy in the musical *High Button Shoes* (1947) and for his low comic Jerry Biffle in *Top Banana* (1951), which he repeated on screen in 1954. True stardom came with his Sergeant Bilko comedy series on television in the 1950s, making him one of the most familiar performers in America. Throughout the rest of his career, Silvers returned to musicals, as with the TV musicals *Keep in Step* (1959) and *Damn Yankees* (1967), in which he played the devilish Applegate, and in the film version of *A Funny Thing Happened on the Way to the Forum* (1967). On Broadway he shone as the wheeler-dealer Herbie Cram in *Do Re Mi* (1960) and as the clever Pseudolus in the 1972 revival of *A Funny Thing Happened on the Way to the Forum*. Silvers sometimes produced plays and television shows, such as the long-running *Gilligan's Island* in the 1960s, and continued acting in films and on television into the 1980s. Autobiography: *The Laugh Is on Me*, with Robert Saffron (1974).

"The Siren's Song" is an alluring number from Kern's collegiate musical ***Leave It to Jane*** (1917) with a sly lyric by **P. G. Wodehouse**. In order to recruit football halfback Billy Bolton (Robert G. Pitkin) to play for Atwater College, coeds Jane Witherspoon (Edith Hallor) and Bessie Tanner (Ann Orr) entice him with this song that tells the legend of Lorelei, the Rhine maiden whose call lured fisherman to their destruction. Wodehouse's playful lyric then warns that there are modern-day Loreleis out there and to beware. Kern's music is slow and dreamy, yet with a syncopated, swinging strain that keeps it fresh and modern. "The Siren's Song" was sung by a chorus in the Kern biopic ***Till the Clouds Roll By*** (1945). A memorable recording of the number was made by Joan Morris and William Bolcom. Three years after *Leave It to Jane*, **Anne Caldwell** wrote a new lyric for a different Kern song on the same subject and, titled **"The Lorelei,"** it was used in ***Sally*** (1920).

SITTING PRETTY. A musical comedy by **Guy Bolton**, **P. G. Wodehouse** (book and lyrics); Jerome Kern (music). [8 April 1924, Fulton Theatre, 95 performances] Produced by **F. Ray Comstock**, Morris Gest; directed by Fred G. Latham, Julian Alfred; musical direction by Max Steiner; orchestrations by **Robert Russell Bennett**.

Plot: The bumbling crook Horace and his cohort Uncle Joe attempt to rob the home of the wealthy Pennington family and seem to have the caper in the bag when the eccentric Mr. Pennington disinherits his family and decides to leave the estate to two orphans. Horace is passed off as an orphan and he falls in love with May Tolliver, a real orphan. May's sister Dixie finds out the truth about Horace and attempts to reform him. Horace's affections move from May to Dixie, and May falls in love with the Pennington's nephew Bill. Mr. Pennington gives his fortune to both Horace and May so both couples are in the money by the final curtain.

Five years after the **Princess Theatre Musical** series came to an end, the threesome of Bolton, Wodehouse, and Kern were reunited one last time and wrote *Sitting Pretty*, a frolic very much in the spirit of that famous series. Bolton's plot was filled with familiar musical comedy types, most memorably lovable crooks, but the writing was sassy and the cast was outstanding. The score is one of Kern's finest, filled with contagious tunes and clever lyrics by Wodehouse that still entertain. While the comic numbers "Tulip Time in Sing Sing" and "Bongo on the Congo" stopped the show each night, there was much to admire in the graceful lullaby "The Enchanted Train,"

CAST FOR *SITTING PRETTY*

Character	Performer
Dixie	**Queenie Smith**
May Tolliver	Gertrude Bryan
Bill Pennington	Rudolph Cameron
Horace	Dwight Frye
Joe	Frank McIntyre
Empress Eugenia	Dorothy Janice
Mr. Pennington	George E. Mack
Judson Waters	Eugene Revere

the lovely waltz "All You Need Is a Girl," and the cozy duet "A Year from Today." Perhaps the finest number was the engaging title song, which was far ahead of its time in its interesting chromatics. Ironically, the performer Frye had a slight speech impediment, turning "s" to "sh," which rendered the title phrase embarrassingly vulgar so the song was cut. The reviews for *Sitting Pretty* were very enthusiastic and audience reaction was joyous, so it is a mystery why the musical ran only twelve weeks. Equally puzzling is why this delightful gem has not played in London, on screen, or in revival.

Recordings: This lovely score went unrecorded for nearly seventy years, but the 2003 studio recording put together by John McGlinn was worth the wait. Very complete and sung by a powerhouse cast, it is one of the best of all Kern recordings.

"Sitting Pretty" is the charming title song from Kern's 1924 musical with lyrics by **P. G. Wodehouse**. Horace Peabody (Dwight Frye) turns from a life of crime to the arms of Dixie Tolliver (**Queenie Smith**) and they sing this cheery song in which all they want out of life is to sit together in a chair that "fits just two." The number has the same kind of romantic silliness as the popular "Tea for Two" with simple repeated rhymes and a jaunty melody. The merry duet was slated for the finale of *Sitting Pretty*, but during rehearsals Frye's slight lisp turned the repetitive "just sit and sit and sit" lyric into an embarrassing string of profanities. The song was cut but the show was still titled *Sitting Pretty*. Jason Graae and Judy Blazer made a recording of the reconstructed duet in 1989.

SITTING PRETTY SONGS

"Is This Not a Lovely Spot?"
"Worries"
"Bongo on the Congo"
"Mr. and Mrs. Rorer"
"There Isn't One Girl"
"A Year from Today"
"Shufflin' Sam"
"The Polka Dot"
"Days Gone By"
"All You Need Is a Girl"
"Tulip Time in Sing Sing"
"A Desert Island"
"The Enchanted Train"
"Shadow of the Moon"
"Sitting Pretty" (cut)

SKELTON, [Richard Bernard] **Red.** (1910–1997) Television and film performer. The beloved clown with a nervous chuckle, rubber face, and physical comedy, appeared in just about every form of entertainment, including the Kern movie musical ***Lovely to Look At*** (1952) in which he played the

Broadway producer Al Marsh who inherits a Paris dress shop. Skelton was born in Vincennes, Indiana, the son of a circus clown who died before his son was born. He quit school at a young age to beg on the streets and later toured with a medicine show even though he was not yet an adolescent. Skelton worked on show boats, in circuses, burlesque, and vaudeville before finding some recognition on radio. His comic monologues led to a movie contract and he was cast as sidekicks or childish buffoons in a number of films, including the musicals *Having Wonderful Time* (1938), ***Lady, Be Good!*** (1941), *Panama Hattie* (1942), *Ship Ahoy* (1942), *DuBarry Was a Lady* (1943), *I Dood It* (1943), *Thousands Cheer* (1943), *Bathing Beauty* (1944), *Ziegfeld Follies* (1946), *Neptune's Daughter* (1949), *The Duchess of Idaho* (1950), *Three Little Words* (1950), *Excuse My Dust* (1951), *Texas Carnival* (1951), and *Lovely to Look At*. Skelton also had a popular radio show in the 1940s. Rarely was he cast in leading roles on screen, but he became familiar enough to audiences that he was given his own television show in 1951 and it was a hit for twenty years. Television was the best medium for Skelton to demonstrate his versatility, letting him play a variety of characters that ranged from the farcical to the whimsical. He returned to Hollywood in the 1960s to make some non-musicals, then spent the rest of his career doing concerts and personal appearances. Biographies: *Red Skelton*, Arthur Marx (1979); *Seeing Red: The Skelton in Hollywood's Closet*, Wes D. Gehring (2001).

SLEZAK, Walter [Leo]. (1902–1983). Stage and film actor, singer. A leading man on Broadway and later a character actor in films, he originated the role of the young music student Karl Reder in Kern's *Music in the Air* (1932). Born in Vienna, Austria, the son of opera tenor Leo Slezak, he worked as a bank clerk to finance his medical studies and then was discovered by film director Michael Curtiz. Slezak appeared in several German and Austrian silents even as he started to sing on the Berlin stage. American producer Lee Shubert brought Slezak to New York where he made his Broadway debut in 1930. (Legend has it that Shubert had a different singer than Slezak in mind, but the producer's emissary mistakenly engaged the wrong man.) He made his Broadway debut in *Meet My Sister* (1930) then received recognition for his performance in the operetta *Music in the Air*. His other New York musicals were *May Wine* (1935) and *I Married an Angel* (1938). Slezak put on weight in the late 1930s, so when he made his first Hollywood film in 1942 he was cast in a comic character role. He appeared in similar roles in dozens of movies, yet returned to Broadway in 1954 to play the elderly wooer Panisse in the musical *Fanny*. Slezak retired in 1976 and lived in Switzerland for the rest of his life. Autobiography: *What Time's the Next Swan?* (1962).

SMITH, Harry B[ache]. (1860–1936) Stage lyricist and writer. The American theatre's most prolific writer of lyrics and librettos, he collaborated with Kern on *Oh, I Say!* (1913), *The Girl from Utah* (1914), *90 in the Shade* (1915), and *Love o' Mike* (1917). Smith was born in Buffalo and was working as drama and music critic for Chicago's *Evening Journal* when he started writing scripts and lyrics for touring companies coming through town. Soon he was in such demand that he gave up journalism and concentrated on theatre, writing quickly but intelligently to order. Before he retired in 1932 he had penned 123 musicals for Broadway and is believed to have written some six thousand lyrics. Smith's first New York entry was *The Begum* (1887) with composer Reginald DeKoven. The two collaborated on many other shows, none more popular than *Robin Hood* (1891), the most produced American operetta of the nineteenth century. Throughout his career, Smith worked with such renowned composers as A. Baldwin Sloane, Victor Herbert, John Stromberg, John Philip Sousa, Ivan Caryll, Sigmund Romberg, Irving Berlin, and Kern, and adapted musicals by such European composers as Gustave Kerker, Emmerich Kalman, Franz Lehar, Oscar Straus, and Jacques Offenbach. A list of his most notable works include *The Serenade* (1897), *The Fortune Teller* (1898), *The Singing Girl* (1899), *The Casino Girl* (1900), *The Little Duchess* (1901), *Babette* (1903), *The Rich Mr. Hoggenheimer* (1906), *Ziegfeld Follies* (1907 through 1910 and 1912), *The Spring Maid* (1910), *Gypsy Love* (1911), *A Winsome Widow* (1912), *Sweethearts* (1913), *Watch Your Step* (1914), *Stop! Look! Listen!* (1915), *Angel Face* (1919), *Princess Flavia* (1925), *Countess Maritza* (1926), *Cherry Blossoms* (1927), *Three Little Girls* (1930), and *Marching By* (1932). While Smith's work may appear clichéd and routine by later standards, he was an intelligent, dedicated writer who was highly respected by his colleagues and by the audiences of his day. His brother was librettist and lyricist Robert B. Smith. Autobiography: *First Nights and First Editions* (1931); biography: *Harry B. Smith: Dean of American Librettists*, John Franceschina (2003).

SMITH, Queenie. (1898–1978) Stage, film, and television performer. A small, round-faced, energetic singer-dancer who usually stopped the show playing supporting roles, she portrayed the spunky Dixie trying to reform a crook in Kern's *Sitting Pretty* (1924) on Broadway and the chipper show boat performer Ellie May in the 1936 screen version of *Show Boat*. The native New Yorker began dance training when she was just a child at the Metropolitan Opera Ballet School where she later performed as an adult. In 1919 she left ballet for the musical stage where she played second leads in *Roly-Boly Eyes* (1919), *Just Because* (1922), *Orange Blossoms* (1922), and *Helen of Troy, New York* (1923). Smith epitomized the Roaring Twenties flapper, as when she played the down-and-out vaudevillian Tip-Toes Kaye looking for a rich husband in *Tip-Toes* (1925). Her later stage musicals include *Be Yourself* (1924), *Judy* (1927), *Street Singer* (1929), and *A Little Racketeer* (1932), as well as replacing the starring part of Loulou in *Hit the Deck* (1927). During the Depression, Smith turned to Hollywood where she made many films, including the musicals *Mississippi* (1935), *Show Boat*, *On Your Toes* (1939), and *My Sister Eileen* (1955). For many years she was a drama teacher at Hollywood Professional School, training many future stars, and she acted in dozens of television programs up until the year of her death.

"Smoke Gets in Your Eyes" is the haunting ballad from the Broadway musical *Roberta* (1933) that saved the show and went on to become one of Kern's most popular and beloved ballads. He wrote it with lyricist **Otto Harbach** for the expatriate Russian princess Stephanie (**Tamara**) to sing as she accompanied herself on the guitar. The number so impressed audiences that soon it was heard on national radio and the fumbling *Roberta* was a hit. Kern wrote the melody as a soft-shoe number for *Show Boat* (1927), but it was never used. The music was then used as the theme song for an NBC Radio series that never got on the air. For *Roberta*, he gave the song a brisk, march-like beat in keeping with the rest of the swinging 1930s musical, but in rehearsals it was a failure. Harbach suggested that it be played at a more leisurely tempo and wrote the enchanting lyric, which was based on an ancient Russian proverb. It is Harbach's finest lyric, a mysterious piece with the unforgettable image of lost love being like a dying fire with smoke that stings your eyes. As for Kern's music, musicologist David Ewen described it best when he wrote "the diatonic skips in the broad upsweep of the melody and the seductive change of key in the release that follows never seem to lose their capacity to win the heart and ear." The song has no verse so it resembles a folk song in some ways.

Tamara recorded the ballad in 1933, followed by dozens of others ranging from the haunting interpretation by Sarah Vaughan to a rock and roll version by the Platters in 1958 that sold a million records to a 1972 best-selling disc by the English group Blue Haze. Other memorable recordings were made by Jeri Southern, Louis Armstrong, Andrea Marcovicci, Billie Holiday, jazz pianist Beegie Adair, Billy Eckstine, Oscar Peterson, Joan Roberts, Peggy Lee, Sonny Rollins, Judy Garland, Benny Goodman, Eartha Kitt, Cher, Kiri Te Kanawa, The Four Preps, Edith Piaf, Jeanne Lehman, Johnny Mathis, Harry Belafonte, Elaine Paige, Dinah Shore, and Thelonious Monk. "Smoke Gets in Your Eyes" was heard during the opening credits of the 1935 screen version of *Roberta,* then was sung by **Irene Dunne**, then reprised as a dance by **Fred Astaire** and **Ginger Rogers**. In the 1952 remake titled *Lovely to Look At*, the ballad was first heard when **Marge** and **Gower Champion** danced an elegant *pas de deux* to the music, then later in the movie **Kathryn Grayson** sang it as a solo. "Smoke Gets in Your Eyes" was sung by a chorus and danced to by Cyd Charisse and Gower Champion in the Kern biopic *Till the Clouds Roll By* (1945). The popular ballad has also been heard on the soundtrack of over thirty movies, including *American Graffiti* (1973), *Night of the Creeps* (1986), *La Bamba* (1987), *Someone to Watch Over Me* (1987), *Good Morning, Vietnam* (1987), *How to Get Ahead in Advertising* (1989), *Catch Me If You Can* (1989), *Always* (1989), *Anita* (1992), *Chaplin* (1992), *Four Weddings and a Funeral* (1994), *Smoke* (1995), *Why Do Fools Fall in Love* (1998), *October Sky* (1999), *Tea with Mussolini* (1999), *Being Julia* (2004), *Breakfast on Pluto* (2005), *Blue Valentine* (2010), and *Somewhere* (2010). On stage, Elisabeth Welch performed the number in the revue *Jerome Kern Goes to Hollywood* in London in 1985 and on Broadway in 1986.

"Some Sort of Somebody" is a lilting song with a feet-on-the-ground lyric from the groundbreaking **Princess Theatre Musical *Very Good Eddie*** (1915). When the dashing Dick Rivers (**Oscar Shaw**) tries to woo Elsie Lilly (Ann Orr), she is not easily persuaded, for she knows Dick only too well, and it seems he always has "some sort of somebody" with whom he is in love. Kern wrote the playful duet with lyricist Elsie Janis who sang it in Kern's *Miss Information* (1915). Neither the song nor Janis's performance made much impression in the short-lived show, but when the number was added to the *Very Good Eddie* score with no changes, it became an audience favorite. While the lyric is not exceptional, Kern's music has a catchy counter melody that gives the duet sparkle. "Some Sort of Somebody" was sung by Walter Williams (Dick) and Veronica Brady (Elsie) in the 1918 London production of *Very Good Eddie*, and the duet was performed by David Christmas and Cynthia Wells in the 1975 Broadway revival. Nancy Andrews and Harold Lang recorded a playful duet version of the song.

"The Song Is You" is the ardent, operatic song from the Broadway musical *Music in the Air* (1932) by Kern and lyricist **Oscar Hammerstein**. In Munich, the opera librettist Bruno Mahler (Tullio Carminati) sings the elegant aria to his mistress, the prima donna Frieda Hatzfeld (**Natalie Hall**), as she is being fitted for a new dress by her dyspeptic maid. The scene is farcical but the song is entrancing. Hammerstein's lyric is expansive but sincere, and Kern's music moves higher and higher to an overwhelming climax. The song became very popular, and among its many recordings were best-sellers by Tommy Dorsey and His Orchestra and by Frank Sinatra. Other discs were made by Bing Crosby, Jane Pickins, Mary Ellis, Jane Powell, Earl Wrightson and Lois Hunt, Vic Damone, Oscar Peterson, Keely Smith, Terry Gibbs, Thomas Hampson, Shirley Bassey, Nancy Wilson, Kiri Te Kanawa, Marilyn Maye, Barbara Cook, Beegie Adair, Marni Nixon, Lawrence Tibbett, Benny Carter, and Gordon MacRae. Surprisingly, "The Song Is You" was not used in the 1934 movie version of *Music in the Air*, but it was heard in the film *Husbands and Wives* (1992). It was also sung by the ensemble of the 1985 London revue and the 1986 Broadway revue *Jerome Kern Goes to Hollywood*, and by Karen Ziemba, Peter Gerety, and the female chorus in the Broadway musical *Never Gonna Dance* (2003).

STEPPING STONES. A musical comedy fantasy by **Anne Caldwell** (book and lyrics), R. H. Burnside (book), Jerome Kern (music). [6 November 1923, Globe Theatre, 241 performances] Produced by **Charles Dillingham**; directed and choreographed by R. H. Burnside, John Tiller, Mary Read; musical direction by Victor Baravalle; orchestrations by **Robert Russell Bennett**.

CAST FOR *STEPPING STONES*

Character	Performer
Peter Plug	**Fred Stone**
Rougette Hood	Dorothy Stone
Otto DeWolfe	Oscar Ragland
Widow Hood	Allene Stone
Prince Silvio	Roy Hoyer
Remus	John Lambert
Lupina	Evelyn Herbert
Captain Paul	**Jack Whiting**

Plot: In a fanciful version of Little Red Riding Hood, the singing-dancing shop-girl Rougette Hood is hunted by the bandit Otto DeWolfe but finds a rescuer in the ingenious plumber Peter Plug and a sweetheart in the handsome Prince Silvio.

This loose adaptation of the fairy tale was a vehicle for the Stone family, in particular the beloved comic Fred and his daughter Dorothy. Producer Dillingham gave Dorothy top billing with her father even though it was her first major role on Broadway. But the audience and the critics thought she deserved the recognition and she became a stage star. While the plot was a piece of unpretentious nonsense with room for specialty acts and interpolated songs, *Stepping Stones* played very well and pleased patrons for seven months, was a success on the road, and returned to Broadway in 1924 for another forty performances. While the show did not demand an exceptional score, Kern and Caldwell provided a handful of superb songs, most memorably the enchanting lullaby "Once in a Blue Moon," the carefree ballad "In Love with Love," the silly ditty "Pie," and the razzle-dazzle "Raggedy Ann." *Stepping Stones* was the first of many Kern shows that were orchestrated by the prolific Robert Russell Bennett.

STEPPING STONES SONGS

"Little Angel Cake"
"Because You Love the Singer"
"Little Red Riding Hood"
"Wonderful Dad"
"Pie"
"Babbling Babette"
"In Love with Love"
"Our Lovely Rose"
"Once in a Blue Moon"
"Raggedy Ann"
"Stepping Stones"

STEVENS, George. (1904–1975) Film director. A distinguished and versatile Hollywood director, he only helmed three musicals but one of them was the classic Kern movie *Swing Time* (1936). Stevens was born in Oakland, California, the son of two actors, and was on the stage as a child. He started in movies as a cameraman in 1921, then worked his way to directing shorts for Hal Roach and others. By 1933 Stevens was helming features and the next year found recognition with *Alice Adams*, his first of many insightful character dramas. Among his most famous pictures were *Woman of the Year* (1942), *A Place in the Sun* (1951), *Shane* (1953), and *Giant* (1956). Stevens' first musical *Nitwits* (1935) was forgettable but not his subsequent features *Swing Time* and *A Damsel in Distress* (1937). His son is film executive George Stevens, Jr. (b. 1932). Biography: *Giant: George Stevens, a Life on Film*, Marilyn Ann Moss (2004).

STONE, Fred [né Val Alfred Andrew Stone]. (1873–1959) Stage and film performer. A much-loved actor-singer-dancer who was half of a famous musical comedy team, the agile comic enjoyed a long career as a solo artist as well, as in the Kern musicals *Stepping Stones* (1923) and *Criss-Cross* (1926). Stone was born in Longmont, Colorado, and raised in Topeka, Kansas, where he first started doing acrobatic stunts with his brother Erwin. The siblings joined the circus as clowns, then Fred performed in a minstrel troupe with David Montgomery (1870–1917), with whom he later teamed up to become a very popular act in vaudeville, British music halls, circuses, burlesque, and Wild West shows. The twosome were first seen on Broadway as comic pirates in *The Girl from Up There* (1901), which they repeated in London, but the show that made them Broadway stars was *The Wizard of Oz* (1903) in which Stone played the Scarecrow to Montgomery's Tin Woodman. The team was a hit as two American tourists bumbling their way through Holland in *The Red Mill* (1906) and as two Chinese sidekicks in *Chin-Chin* (1914). Montgomery and Stone's other musical credits together were *The Old Town* (1909) and *The Lady of the Slipper* (1912). Montgomery died in 1917 and Stone continued performing solo in such musicals as *Jack o' Lantern* (1917), *Tip Top* (1920), *Stepping Stones*, *Criss Cross*, *Ripples* (1930), and *Smiling Faces* (1932). He acted in a handful of silent and talking films, none of which utilized his musical comedy talents. In 1934 Stone turned to playing character parts in non-musicals, then retired from Broadway in 1946. His daughters were actress-singer Dorothy Stone (1905–1974), actress-producer Paula Stone (1912–1997), and television actress Carol Stone (1915–2011). Autobiography: *Rolling Stone* (1945); biography: *Fred Stone: Circus Performer and Musical Comedy Star*, Armond Fields (2002).

STYLE of Kern's songwriting. It is not as easy to define or describe *style* in music as it is for literature, because music is by nature abstract while written work utilizes words that can be discussed by using words. As composer-lyricist Stephen Sondheim has noted, "If music could be described in language, there would be no need for it." Yet certain American songwriters have a distinct style and some attempt must be made to illustrate Kern's musical style without getting too deep into music theory and composition.

Because Kern predates Richard Rodgers, George Gershwin, Cole Porter, Harold Arlen, and most other major American theatre composers, the innovations and fresh ideas that Kern introduced were utilized by these later songwriters and there is a great deal of overlap. For example, Rodgers was a genius at shifting harmonies in such a way that the music continually surprised and pleased. Yet it was Kern who first experimented with this technique in popular music and it inspired Rodgers and others of his generation. Porter is known for his long melodic lines, yet Kern earlier broke away from the short and snappy melodic phrases of Tin Pan Alley. Most importantly, it was Kern who moved American popular music away from European models and helped establish a distinct American sound. Rodgers described Kern as a "giant with one foot in Europe and the other in America. Before he died, he picked up the European foot and planted it squarely alongside the American one."

One might assume that the work of such a pioneer as Kern might date as later composers built on the early efforts and made them more sophisticated. Yet that is not true in the case of Kern's music. Even as he broke new ground, he often remained subtle in his innovations and found fame by almost subliminally training the ear of the American public. The simple diatonic structure in his songs was not noticeable to the untrained listener, yet one detected something fresh and exciting in the way it sounded. Kern was also a precise and diligent craftsman so his musical efforts are rarely sloppy, predictable, or trite. As Sondheim has observed, "The melody has an enduring freshness. The harmony is usually simple and not very inventive or eventful, yet graceful and clear and full of air. The melodic rhythm is perhaps the strongest point—a direct and simple motif developed through tiny variations into a long and never boring line."

Growing up hearing nineteenth-century ballads and European operetta, Kern was not quick to pick up on the more American forms of ragtime, blues, jazz, and swing. Yet he later wrote works in those styles very successfully. There is little syncopation in Kern's melodic line, but he incorporates these new sounds into his work by subtly referencing them within his tight composition. The result is a truly American composer who absorbs the distinct sounds of his homeland even as he builds on the traditional European forms of music composition. As for the Kern style, a straightforward definition is still elusive. It might best be described as intricate craftsmanship disguised as simplicity. Nothing is forced yet everything is surprising. This aspect of Kern's music might explain why his work remains fresh and bears hearing over and over again.

SUNNY. A musical comedy by **Otto Harbach**, **Oscar Hammerstein** (book and lyrics); Jerome Kern (music). [22 September 1925, New Amsterdam Theatre, 517 performances] Produced by **Charles Dillingham**; directed by **Hassard Short**; choreographed by Julian Mitchell, David Bennett, etc.; musical direction by Gus Salzer; orchestrations by **Robert Russell Bennett**.

Plot: The American circus performer Sunny Peters is doing her bareback riding act in a British circus when she falls in love with the American tourist Tom Warren. When Tom returns to America, Sunny stows aboard the ocean liner to follow him. She is caught and is to be thrown into the brig, but Tom's friend Jim Denning marries Sunny to keep her legal. Once in America, she divorces Jim and marries Tom.

An illogical libretto and a disastrous rehearsal period foreshadowed doom for *Sunny,* but the show was pulled together on the road and turned into one of the biggest hits of the season. Marilyn Miller was the established star and did not disappoint, but producer Dillingham surrounded her with circus acts, a hunting scene in the English countryside, and Ukulele Ike's specialty act to ensure the musical's success. *Sunny* was the first of many collaborations between Hammerstein and Kern, and their unique chemistry was seen in such popular numbers as the entrancing "Who?," the slangy

CASTS FOR *SUNNY*

Character	1925 Broadway	1926 London	1930 film	1941 film
Sunny Peters	**Marilyn Miller**	Binnie Hale	Marilyn Miller	Anna Neagle
Jim Deering	**Jack Donahue**	Jack Buchanan	Joe Donahue	
Tom/Larry Warren	Paul Frawley	Jack Hobbs	Lawrence Gray	John Carroll
Marcia Manners	Elsa Peterson		Barbara Bedford	
Sue/Elizabeth Warren	Esther Howard	Maidie Hope	Judith Vosselli	Freida Inescort
Harold/Henry	**Clifton Webb**	Claude Hulbert	Mackenzie Ward	Edward Everett Horton
Weenie	Mary Hay	Elsie Randolph	Inez Courtney	
Siegfried Peters	Frank Doane	Nicholas Adams	O. P. Heggie	
Bunny Billings				Ray Bolger

"D'Ye Love Me?," and the zippy title song. Critics applauded the score as much as they adulated Miller, and *Sunny* was a rousing hit, running over fifteen months on Broadway, six months on tour, followed by popular productions in Great Britain and Australia. For the 1926 London version, Sunny (Binnie Hale) ended up with Jim (Jack Buchanan) rather than Tom (Jack Hobbs); it says something about the logic of the libretto that the change was made by the alteration of only a few lines of dialogue.

Film version: Sunny. A movie musical by Humphrey Pearson, Henry McCarthy (screenplay), Kern (music), Hammerstein, Harbach (lyrics). [1930, Warner Brothers/First National] Directed by **William A. Seiter**, choreographed by Theodore Kosloff, musical direction by Erno Rapee. Miller got to reprise her stage performance in the first film version of *Sunny*, and despite her limited movie experience, she still managed to sparkle on the screen. Joe Donahue and Lawrence Gray were the two men in Sunny's life, and again they were pretty much interchangeable. Most of the stage score was deleted and only one new song ("I Was Alone"—Kern and Hammerstein's first film song) was added so this is musically a pretty thin movie.

> ### *SUNNY* SONGS
>
> ---
>
> **"Sunny"**
> **"Who?"**
> "So's Your Old Man"
> "Let's Say Good Night Till It's Morning"
> **"D'Ye Love Me?"**
> "The Wedding Knell"
> "Two Little Blue Birds"
> "When We Get Our Divorce"
> "Sunshine"
> "Strolling, or What Have You"
> "Magnolia in the Woods"
>
> ---
>
> *Added to 1930 film:*
>
> **"I Was Alone"**
> "Oh! Didn't He Ramble" (not by Kern)
>
> ---
>
> *Added to the 1941 film* (not by Kern):
>
> "The Lady Must Be Kissed"
> "Jack Tar and Sam Gar"

Film version: Sunny. A movie musical by Sig Herzig (screenplay), Kern, etc. (music), Hammerstein, Harbach, etc. (lyrics). [1941, RKO] Produced and directed by Herbert Wilcox; choreographed by Aida Broadbent, Leon Leonidoff; music arrangements by Anthony Collins, Gene Rose. This remake, a vehicle for British star Anna Neagle as Sunny, kept only three songs from the stage score and reduced the silly plot to something less silly and more boring. The English circus performer Sunny wants to marry a New Orleans aristocrat (John Carroll), but his family objects until enough musical numbers have passed that a happy ending is required. There was little singing but plenty of dance, in particular some very agile hoofing by Ray Bolger. The British film was more popular in its native country than in the States.

Recordings: The 1926 London cast recording is the only disc that comes close to covering this wonderful score. Binnie Hale, Jack Buchanan, and company deliver the best songs with panache. The two film versions had so few songs that neither produced soundtrack recordings. The Victor Light Opera Company recorded a medley of *Sunny*'s hits in 1938.

"Sunny" is the catchy title song from the 1925 Broadway musical, the first collaboration between Kern and **Oscar Hammerstein**. The American tourist Tom Warren (Paul Frawley) and the male chorus sang the lilting number about the beautiful circus bareback rider Sunny Peters (**Marilyn Miller**) and gave her such bohemian advice as "Never comb your hair, Sunny!" **Otto Harbach** worked on the sassy, colloquial lyric with Hammerstein, and it sits nicely on Kern's bombastic music. Jack Hobbs and the chorus sang "Sunny"

SUNNY. Marilyn Miller got to reprise two of her best stage roles when Hollywood let her star in the screen versions of *Sally (1929)* and *Sunny (1930)*. How well the camera took to Miller is debatable, but both films give a glimpse into why the dancing star was so beloved. Some of her charm is evident in this shot with O. P. Heggie from *Sunny*. *First National Pictures/Photofest ©First National Pictures*

in the 1926 London production about Binnie Hale's Sunny Peters. Joe Donahue and the chorus sang the number on the soundtrack of the 1930 screen
version of *Sunny*, and John Carroll led the ensemble in singing it about Anna
Neagle in the 1941 remake. The song was also heard in the Marilyn Miller
biopic *Look for the Silver Lining* (1949) and was sung by the chorus in the
Kern biopic *Till the Clouds Roll By* (1945). Jack Buchanan of the original
London cast was among the first to record "Sunny."

"Sure Thing" is a beguiling ballad by Kern and lyricist **Ira Gershwin** that
insists that one found a sure thing when one found a certain sweetheart. In
a flashback sequence in the movie *Cover Girl* (1944), entertainer Maribelle
Hicks (**Rita Hayworth** dubbed by Martha Mears) sang the song with the
chorus at Tony Pastor's in what Gershwin described as a "pre–World War
I music hall number with a racetrack background." Kern and Gershwin had
written the song back in 1939, but Gershwin penned a new lyric for *Cover
Girl*. Kern could not locate the original sheet music nor could he remember
the melody until his daughter, who did recall it, hummed it for him. The
music is unusual in its length (an atypical twenty-eight measures) and in the
way the refrain moves out of its key of E-flat for four measures, creating an
effective diversion. Musicologist Alec Wilder considers it "one of the most
American-sounding of Kern's later ballads." Glen Gray and the Casa Loma
Orchestra made a notable disc of the song, and more recently there have
been recordings by Andre Previn, Barry Tuckwell, Carole Simpson, Danny
Carroll, Sylvia McNair, Sally Kellerman, Rebecca Kilgore, Andrea Marcovicci, Blue Mitchell, David Allyn, and Mary Clare Haran. Dave Frishberg
sang "Sure Thing" on the soundtrack of the film *Someone to Love* (1987).

SWANSON, Gloria [neé Gloria Josephine Mae Swenson]. (1897–1983)
Film and television actress. Perhaps the most glamorous of the silent screen
stars, she became a favorite character actress in the talkies, giving one of her
funniest performances as the predatory prima donna Frieda Hatzfeld in Kern's
Music in the Air (1934). Swanson was born in Chicago but, being the daughter of an Army officer, grew up in various places before making her first films
in her native city. She married actor Wallace Beery and the two relocated to
Hollywood in 1916, he finding roles in Mack Sennett comedies and she in
weepy melodramas. Under the direction of Cecil B. DeMille, Swanson be-

COVER GIRL. Even the milkman in Brooklyn is taken up with the enthusiasm shown by pals Genius (Phil Silvers, left), Rusty Parker (Rita Hayworth), and Danny McGuire (Gene Kelly) as they dance down the street in this 1944 movie. *Cover Girl* was the only collaboration between Kern and lyricist Ira Gershwin. *Columbia Pictures/Photofest ©Columbia Pictures*

came a major movie star, whose clothes and mannerisms were copied by fans as a sign of romantic allure. Among her many silent film hits were *Male and Female* (1919), *The Great Moment* (1921), *Zaza* (1923), and *Sadie Thompson* (1928). The oft-married Swanson made the transition to talkies, though no longer as an ingenue. Her most famous role was the crazed movie star Norma Desmond in *Sunset Blvd.* (1950), but she also shone in *Queen Kelly* (1929), *The Trespasser* (1929), *Music in the Air, Father Takes a Wife* (1941), and others. Swanson appeared in many television shows in the 1960s and even took up the stage late in her career. Autobiography: *Swanson on Swanson* (1981); biography: *Gloria Swanson*, Richard M. Hudson and Raymond Lee (1970).

SWEET ADELINE. A musical play by **Oscar Hammerstein** (book and lyrics), Jerome Kern (music). [3 September 1929, Hammerstein's Theatre, 234 performances] Produced by Arthur Hammerstein, directed by Reginald Hammerstein, choreographed by Danny Dare, musical direction by Gus Salzer, orchestrations by **Robert Russell Bennett.**

Plot: Addie Schmidt sings in her father's beer garden in Hoboken, New Jersey, during the days of the Spanish-American War and falls in love with the sailor Tom Martin. Addie's sister Nellie steals Tom away from her, so Addie goes to New York to sing in the big time, only to get stuck in burlesque. There she is discovered by the high-society gent James Day who gets her the right connections and she ends up on Broadway. Addie believes she loves James but is not sure until she meets the composer Sid Barnett and discovers true love at last.

CASTS FOR *SWEET ADELINE*

Character	1929 Broadway	1935 film
Addie	**Helen Morgan**	**Irene Dunne**
James Day	Robert Chisholm	Louis Calhern
Tom Martin	Max Hoffman, Jr.	
Sid Barnett	John Seymour	Donald Woods
Nellie	Caryl Bergman	Nydia Westman
Dot	Violet Carson	Dorothy Dare
Rupert	**Charles Butterworth**	Hugh Herbert
Elysia		Winifred Shaw

SWEET ADELINE SONGS
"Play Us a Polka Dot"
"'Twas Not So Long Ago"
"My Husband's First Wife" (lyric by Irene Franklin)
"Here Am I"
"First Mate Martin"
"Spring Is Here"
"Out of the Blue"
"Naughty, Naughty Boy"
"Oriental Moon"
"Molly O'Donahue"
"Why Was I Born?"
"Adeline Belmont/The Sun About to Rise"
"A Girl Is on Your Mind"
"Don't Ever Leave Me"
Added to 1934 film version:
"We Were So Young"
"Lonely Feet"

Sweet Adeline was a careful blending of nostalgia for the Gay Nineties, a tearful operetta, and a slick musical comedy, and it succeeded beautifully on all three accounts. The overture was comprised of period favorites and the many stage sets conjured up the past. Morgan gave a touching performance as the vulnerable Addie and sang some lovely ballads in the operetta mode; yet comic performances by Charles Butterworth, Irene Franklin, and old-time vaudevillian Jim Thornton kept the show from getting too ponderous. The Kern-Hammerstein score was one of their richest, with the torchy "Why Was I Born?," and folk-like "'Twas Not So Long Ago," the joyous "Here Am I," the heartrending "Don't Ever Leave Me," and the thrilling choral number "A Girl Is on Your Mind." Morgan's portrayal of Addie was as accomplished as her *Show Boat* (1927) performance of Julie LaVerne, and "Why Was I Born?" became one of her signature songs. Notices were laudatory and business was strong until the stock market crash a month after the show opened; the musical closed five months later. A 1930 tour lasted five months. *Sweet Adeline* is a major achievement because Kern's music echoes the 1890s period, and Hammerstein's libretto mixed comedy and pathos effectively as he would in his musicals with Richard Rodgers. It is also a neglected classic in its own right; there have been no Broadway revivals, though a 1997 concert version in Manhattan revealed how strong and involving the piece still was.

Film version: Sweet Adeline. A movie musical by Erwin Gelsey (screenplay), score by Kern (music) and Hammerstein (lyrics). [1935, Warner Brothers] Produced by Edward Chodorov, directed by **Mervyn LeRoy**, choreographed by Bobby Connolly, musical direction by Leo F. Forbstein, orchestrations by Ray Heindorf. Eight of the stage score's seventeen songs were retained (Hammerstein and Kern provided two new ones), and the libretto at least resembled the stage script. One of Addie's romances was cut and a backstage triangle was added involving composer Sid and Elysia, a temperamental star who is a spy for Spain. Morgan was not considered a big enough film star so Addie was played on screen by Irene Dunne. She gives a touching performance and delivers the songs beautifully, but without Morgan's sense of desperation, the heart of the picture is missing. Louis Calhern and Donald Woods, as the two men in Addie's life, were competent (the loss of "A Girl Is on Your Mind" robbed them of their characters' best moments) but not memorable. *Sweet Adeline* is a mild and dull movie and not a fair representation of the splendid stage work.

Recordings: Morgan recorded her major songs from the Broadway score, but that is all that was put on disc. The film soundtrack is more complete but far from exciting. Medleys of highlights from the score were recorded by the Victor Light Opera Company and the New Mayfair Orchestra in the 1930s. One of Broadway's great scores has yet to be completely recorded and preserved.

SWING TIME. A movie musical by Howard Lindsay, Allan Scott (screenplay); **Dorothy Fields** (lyrics); Jerome Kern (music). [1936, RKO] Produced by **Pandro S. Berman**, directed by **George Stevens**, choreographed by Hermes Pan, musical direction by Nathaniel Shilkret, orchestrations by Fletcher Henderson, **Robert Russell Bennett** (uncredited).

Plot: After the irresponsible gambler "Lucky" Garnett leaves his fiancée Margaret Watson at the altar while he's partying with his pal Pop Cardetti, Judge Watson tells Lucky he has to raise $25,000 in order to marry his daughter. Lucky and Pop go to New York to try and raise the cash, but he is sidetracked by the beautiful dance instructor Penny Carroll. He takes lessons just to be near her, but she's engaged to bandleader Ricardo Romero. Before you know it the quarreling Lucky and Penny have a successful dance act and are falling in love, though Ricardo and Margaret present a major obstacle until the final reel.

Even with its convoluted plot twists and turns, *Swing Time* still ranks as a strong candidate for the best of the Fred Astaire and Ginger Rogers musicals and boasts one of Kern's best film scores. The contrived screenplay at least had some sparkling dialogue for the lovers and comic bits for the secondary

CASTS FOR *SWING TIME* AND *NEVER GONNA DANCE*

Character	Swing Time (1936 film)	Never Gonna Dance (Broadway 2004)
John "Lucky" Garnett	**Fred Astaire**	Noah Racey
Penny Carroll	**Ginger Rogers**	Nancy Lemenager
Pop Cardetti	Victor Moore	
Mabel	Helen Broderick	Karen Ziemba
Mr. Pangborn		Peter Bartlett
Alfred J. Morganthal		Peter Gerety
Gordon	**Eric Blore**	
Margaret Watson/Chalfont	Betty Furness	Deborah Leamy
Ricardo Romero	Georges Metaxa	David Pittu
Judge Watson/Mr. Chalfont	Landers Stevens	Philip LeStrange

couple, made up of Victor Moore and Helen Broderick. It also left plenty of room for dance and all of it was superb: the couple's effervescent "Waltz in Swing Time," Astaire's rhythmic "Bojangles of Harlem," the seductive *pas de deux* "Never Gonna Dance," and the clever "Pick Yourself Up," in which Astaire pretends he cannot dance very well in order to keep getting lessons from Rogers. Astaire and Hermes Pan devised the choreography and it was quintessential Astaire and Rogers magic. The Pandro S. Berman production was originally titled *I Won't Dance* and then *Never Gonna Dance* until the studio, worried that the public would not come and see a Fred Astaire picture where no one danced, changed it to *Swing Time* (though there is only one swing number in the film). Although the movie is remembered as one of the great dance musicals, its song score is one of the best of the 1930s. In addition to the dance numbers already mentioned, two outstanding numbers were presented to perfection: "A Fine Romance" was a wry musical conversation with the lovers quarreling in a snow-covered wood, the song itself becoming a complete musical scene; and Astaire sang the Oscar-winning "The Way You Look Tonight" to Rogers as she lathered her head with shampoo. The offbeat way of setting the number made it all the more romantic. Although Kern was resistant to swing when it came upon the scene in the 1930s, he proved in *Swing Time* that he could provide music that was fresh and up-to-date as the hits of the day.

SWING TIME SONGS

"It's Not in the Cards"
"Pick Yourself Up"
"The Way You Look Tonight"
"Waltz in Swing Time"
"A Fine Romance"
"Bojangles of Harlem"
"Never Gonna Dance"

Stage version: Never Gonna Dance. A musical comedy by Jeffrey Hatcher (book), Dorothy Fields, etc. (lyrics), Jerome Kern (music). [4 December 2003, Broadhurst Theatre, 84 performances] Produced by Harvey Weinstein, etc., directed by Michael Greif, choreographed by Jerry Mitchell, musical direction by Robert Billig, orchestrations by Harold Wheeler. The Broadway version of *Swing Time* used the title that was once considered for the film and made other efforts not to copy the famous screen musical. Jeffrey Hatcher's libretto stuck to the movie plot somewhat, though Pop Cardetti was dropped and some of the details changed. Most of the screen songs were used plus others by Kern, such as **"Dearly Beloved," "Who?," "The Song Is You," "I'm Old-Fashioned,"** and **"I'll Be Hard to Handle."** The production boasted some inventive choreography by Mitchell, but the charming leads lacked star charisma and critics found the musical more pleasant than exhilarating, so it struggled to run ten weeks.

Recording: The film soundtrack is not easy to find but the movie itself is available on DVD. Sadly, *Never Gonna Dance* was not recorded. It would have been a delightful collection of Kern standards and the show might have been picked up later by theatre companies and summer stock.

TAMARA [née Tamara Drasin]. (1907–1943) Stage, concert, and film performer. The dark, exotic singer with a captivating throaty voice, her most famous performance was as the Russian princess Stephanie in Kern's *Roberta* (1933) where she introduced **"Smoke Gets in Your Eyes."** Tamara was born in Odessa, Russia, and was educated in the Ukraine and in New York City before she started singing professionally in nightclubs. She made her Broadway bow in the revue *Innocent Eyes* (1924) and was featured in *The New Yorkers* (1927), *Crazy Quilt* (1931), *Free for All* (1931), and *New Americana* (1932) before getting the plum role of Stephanie in *Roberta*. Tamara was also lauded for her phony wife Mimi in the short-lived *Right This Way* (1938), where she got to introduce another standard, "I'll Be Seeing You." Her final Broadway musical, *Leave It to Me!* (1938), was more successful, and as the sassy Colette she sang "Get Out of Town." Tamara appeared in two Hollywood musicals, *Sweet Surrender* (1935) and *No, No, Nanette* (1940), was popular on the radio during the Depression years, and was a favorite in swank supper clubs before her untimely death in the same plane crash in Portugal that crippled singer Jane Froman.

TAMIROFF, Akim. (1899–1972) Stage, film, and television performer. A heavy-set character actor who often played heavies on screen, the thick-accented performer was often cast as silly foreigners in musicals, such as the con man Joe Varese in Kern's *High, Wide and Handsome* (1937) and the fortune hunter Prince Gregory in *Can't Help Singing* (1944). Tamiroff was born in Tiflis, Georgia, to Armenian parents and eventually became a member of the distinguished Moscow Art Theatre. When the troupe toured America in 1923, he remained in New York and enjoyed a productive career on Broadway acting in dramas. Tamiroff headed to Hollywood in 1931 and was soon cast in supporting roles. As the years passed the parts got better but rarely any bigger as he was cast as foreign villains, eccentric immigrants, corrupt authority figures, and sidekicks. His other film musicals include

Here Is My Heart (1934), *The Merry Widow* (1934), *Naughty Marietta* (1935), *Go Into Your Dance* (1935), *Big Broadcast of 1936* (1935), *Paris Honeymoon* (1939), and *Fiesta* (1947). Tamiroff made many television appearances in both series and specials, such as the original TV musical *Aladdin* (1958).

TEMPLETON, Fay. (1865–1939) Stage performer. The beloved Broadway singing-acting star enjoyed a career of sixty-four years during which she was an ingenue in early developmental musicals, a mature comedienne in Weber and Fields's burlesques, a leading lady in George M. Cohan's new form of book musical, and a featured character actress in a modern Kern musical, **Roberta** (1933). Templeton was born in Little Rock, Arkansas, the daughter of a singer and a theatre manager, and was on stage as a youngster. After working in vaudeville she made her Broadway debut at the age of eight as Puck in *A Midsummer Night's Dream* (1873). She appeared in the musicals *The Mascot* (1881) and *Billee Taylor* (1883), then attracted attention in the "pants" role of Gabriel in a revival of *Evangeline* (1885). Templeton was also featured in *Hendrik Hudson* (1890), *Madame Favart* (1893), and *Excelsior, Jr.* (1895), as well as the London show *Monte Cristo, Jr.* (1886). Her career moved in a new direction in 1898 when she joined with comics Weber and Fields and played saucy characters in a famed series of musical spoofs such as *Hurly Burly* (1898), *Fiddle-Dee-Dee* (1900), *Broadway to Tokio* (1900), *Hoity Toity* (1901), and *Twirly Whirly* (1902). She also shone in book musicals, most memorably as the housekeeper-heiress Mary Jane Jenkins in Cohan's *Forty-Five Minutes from Broadway* (1906). Templeton retired from the stage in 1910 but returned for the Weber and Fields reunion *Hokey Pokey* (1912) and to play Little Buttercup in the operetta *H.M.S. Pinafore* in 1911, 1924, 1926, and 1931. She made a final and memorable appearance as the aging dress salon owner Minnie in *Roberta* (1933). Irene Manning played Templeton in the Cohan movie bio-musical *Yankee Doodle Dandy* (1942).

TERRIS, Norma [née Norma Allison]. (1904–1989) Stage singer, actress. An accomplished performer who played several leading roles on Broadway before retiring early in life, she originated the part of Magnolia Hawks in the first stage version of **Show Boat** (1927). A native of Columbus, Kansas, she was educated locally and in Chicago before going into the theatre to be a dramatic actress. Terris began working professionally as a singer in vaudeville, and her first New York job was in a Broadway chorus when she was only sixteen years old. Her subsequent career was mostly in musicals, getting her first major part in **Oscar Hammerstein**'s *Queen o' Hearts* (1922). The songwriter hired her again five years later for *Show Boat* where she introduced **"Make Believe," "You Are Love,"** and other standards from the musical. Terris reprised her performance in the 1932 revival of *Show Boat*, but most of her other musicals failed to run so, realizing she would never get a role as satisfying as Magnolia, she retired to Connecticut in 1939 and lived there quietly for the next fifty years. The Goodspeed Opera House in nearby Chester named its second performance space the Terris Theatre in honor of the local actress.

"There's a Hill Beyond a Hill" is a bright and cheerful marching song from Kern's operetta *Music in the Air* (1932) with a lyric by **Oscar Hammerstein**. In the Bavarian hills and dales, Hans (Edward Hayes) and members of the Edendorf Walking Club sing the lively number as they travel to Munich. Kern's music is a merry march and Hammerstein's lyric uses repetition to accentuate the cadence of rhythmic number. A chorus of hikers sang "There's a Hill Beyond a Hill" in the 1934 screen version of *Music in the Air*. The number is sometimes listed as "Edendorf Walking Club Song."

"They Didn't Believe Me" is the Kern masterwork that, perhaps more than any other song, pointed out the direction that the American musical theatre would take as it broke away from European operetta. When the British musical *The Girl from Utah* was presented on Broadway in 1914, producer **Charles Frohman** hired Kern to write a handful of new numbers. "They Didn't Believe Me" had a conversational lyric by **Herbert Reynolds** and was sung by Una Trance (**Julia Sanderson**), who has fled from her Mormon husband, and Londoner Sandy Blair (**Donald Brian**), resulting in a tender and resolute duet. Although few critics pointed out the song in their praise for the show, "They Didn't Believe Me" was not lost on audiences and over two million copies of music were sold. The song is one of the most beloved of theatre pieces and much has been written analyzing its unique accomplishments: the unusual harmonic influence on the melody, the use of quarter notes in the refrain to build up to the climax that is a key change, and a melody line that is, as musicologist Alec Wilder stated, "as natural as walking." The lyric is also bold in its use of the casual phrase "and I'm cert'n'ly going to tell them" that also breaks away from operetta. All analysis aside, "They Didn't Believe Me" was Kern's first standard and is one of the few theatre songs that sounds unique and fresh no matter what decade it is sung. The ballad was first sung on the London stage by **George Grossmith** and Haidee de Rance in *Tonight's the Night* (1915). On screen, the ballad was sung by Connie Griffith in *Back Pay* (1930), by Dorothy Patrick (vocal by Ruth Clark) and reprised by Dinah Shore in the Kern biopic *Till the Clouds Roll By* (1945), and by Mario Lanza and **Kathryn Grayson** in *That Midnight Kiss* (1949). "They Didn't Believe Me" was also heard in the films *Oh! What a Lovely War* (1969), *Agatha* (1979), and *Being Julia* (2010). The cast of the revue *Jerome Kern Goes to Hollywood* sang it in London in 1985 and on Broadway the next year. Among the many recordings are duet versions by Grace Kearns and Reed Miller in 1915 and by Kate Baldwin and Matthew Scott in 2012, and solo renditions by Shore, Barbra Streisand, Frank Sinatra, **Jeanette MacDonald**, Leontyne Price, Harry Belafonte, Andrea Marcovicci, Ella Fitzgerald, Beegie Adair, Marian McPartland, Steve Lawrence, Bill Frisell, Dinah Washington, Dean Martin, Stan Kenton, Elvis Costello, Charlie Parker, and **Johnny Mercer**.

"The Things I Want" is a superb music hall number that riverboat chanteuse Molly Fuller (**Dorothy Lamour**) sang to farmers Peter Cortlandt (**Randolph Scott**), Walt Brennan (Alan Hale), and other saloon patrons in Kern's frontier movie musical *High, Wide and Handsome* (1937). Kern's music is very bluesy and **Oscar Hammerstein**'s lyric is very self-mocking, the gal lamenting that the things she gets are not what she wants and true love seems to elude her.

"Thirteen Collar" is a show-stopping comic number from Kern's **Princess Theatre Musical** *Very Good Eddie* (1915) that still has a charm even though detachable collars are long gone. Henpecked Eddie Kettle (**Ernest Truex**) is a man small in stature and in courage and he sings regretfully that he wears only a size thirteen collar and a number three shoe. The risible lyric by Schuyler Greene is a lament by an overlooked and bullied man seeking recognition. Kern's music is busy with a series of alternating dotted eighths and sixteenths, yet has a melancholy flavor as well. Nelson Keys played Eddie in the

1918 London production of *Very Good Eddie* and sang "Thirteen Collar," and it was performed by Charles Repole in the successful 1975 Broadway revival. The number is sometimes listed as "When You Wear a 13 Collar."

THREE SISTERS. A musical play by **Oscar Hammerstein**, **Otto Harbach** (book and lyrics); Jerome Kern (music). [19 April 1934, Theatre Royal, Drury Lane, London, 72 performances] Produced by H. M. Tennent, directed by Hammerstein and Kern, choreographed by Ralph Reader, music direction by Charles Prentice, orchestrations by **Robert Russell Bennett**.

Plot: The struggling English photographer Will Babour has three daughters, each one caught up in a romance. The eldest (and tallest) sister, Tiny, is the most down to earth and has selected a policeman, Eustace Titherley, as her love interest. The second and most ambitious sister, Dorrie, has her eye on a peer of the realm. The youngest, Mary, falls for an unfaithful gypsy groom. World War I breaks out and all three men bid farewell to their sweethearts when they are called to the front. A happy ending does not come until after the war when all are reunited back in England.

This highly anticipated London musical was a major disappointment for Kern and Hammerstein; the reviews were not only negative but resentful that two Americans would try to write a musical about England for an English audience. Lost in the patriotic snobbery was one of the team's finest scores, filled with variety and lyricism. The only number to find wide popularity later on was "I Won't Dance" when it was given an altered lyric by **Dorothy Fields** and used in the film version of

---

CAST FOR *THREE SISTERS*

Character	Performer
Tiny Babour	Charlotte Greenwood
Dorrie Babour	Adele Dixon
Mary Babour	Victoria Hopper
Eustace Titherley	Stanley Holloway
John	Richard Dolman
Gypsy	Esmond Knight
Will Babour	Eliot Makeham
George	Albert Burdon

THREE SISTERS SONGS
"Roll on Rolling Road"
"Now I Have a Spring Time"
"My Beautiful Circus Girl"
"What's in the Air Tonight?"
"There's a Joy That Steals upon You"
"Hand in Hand"
"Somebody Wants to Go to Sleep"
"While Mary Sleeps"
"You Are Doing Very Well"
"Lonely Feet"
"What Good Are Words?"
"There's a Funny Old House"
"Welcome to the Bride"
"Keep Smiling"
"I Won't Dance"

Kern's *Roberta* (1935). "Lonely Feet" was interpolated into the score for the Kern-Hammerstein movie *Sweet Adeline* (1935), but the rest of the songs were pretty much forgotten. Only years later did biographers and music critics realize how accomplished this neglected score was. *Three Sisters* was not produced professionally in the States until 2011 when the San Francisco troupe called 42nd Street Moon mounted a production for a limited run.

Recording: Surprisingly, five songs from the show were recorded with some original London cast members. Kern himself supervised the recording so it is accurate as well as revealing, but very difficult to locate.

TILL THE CLOUDS ROLL BY. A movie musical biography by Myles Connolly, Jean Holloway (screenplay); **Oscar Hammerstein, Dorothy Fields, Otto Harbach**, etc. (lyrics); Jerome Kern (music). [MGM 1946] Produced by **Arthur Freed**; directed by Richard Whorf, Vincente Minnelli, **George Sidney** (uncredited); choreographed by Robert Alton; musical direction by Lennie Hayton; orchestrations by Conrad Salinger, Robert Franklyn, etc.

Plot: On the opening night of his Broadway masterpiece *Show Boat* (1927), Jerome Kern thinks back to the days when he was a struggling composer and was encouraged by his mentor James Hessler to expand the boundaries of American popular music. In England, Kern finds some recognition in the musical theatre and he also finds his future wife Eva. Success in New York comes with the popular **Princess Theatre Musicals**, then he meets up with Oscar Hammerstein for a series of more demanding musical plays, climaxing with *Show Boat*. Over the years Kern watches Hessler's daughter Sally grow from an adoring child to a difficult actress to a mature performer.

TILL THE CLOUDS ROLL BY

CAST FOR *TILL THE CLOUDS ROLL BY*

Character	Performer
Jerome Kern	Robert Walker
James I. Hessler	Van Heflin
Eva Kern	Dorothy Patrick
Sally Hessler	Lucille Bremer
Charles Frohman	Harry Hayden
Oscar Hammerstein	Paul Langton
Marilyn Miller	Judy Garland
Victor Herbert	Paul Maxey
Joe Hennessey	William Phillips
Mrs. Muller	Mary Nash

Specialties by June Allyson, **Gower Champion**, Cyd Charisse, **Kathryn Grayson**, Lena Horne, Van Johnson, Angela Lansbury, Tony Martin, Ray McDonald, Virginia O'Brien, Caleb Peterson, Dinah Shore, Frank Sinatra, the Wilde Twins.

The true story of Kern's life was hardly a page-turner, and this musical biopic made no effort to jazz up a dull tale. Yet with nearly two dozen Kern songs, most of them done with taste, talent, and panache, the movie was far from dull. MGM enlisted just about every musical star on the lot and the result was a series of stunning musical numbers that, while rarely making an effort to re-create the original stage situation, were correct in spirit. Having Frank Sinatra sing "Ol' Man River" in a tuxedo may not have been an apt representation of *Show Boat*, but in the 1940s it was high-class entertainment. Among the many memorable numbers: a glorious fifteen-minute condensation of *Show Boat* with Kathryn Grayson, Tony Martin, Lena Horne, Caleb Peterson, and Virginia O'Brien; a young and very English Angela Lansbury singing (in her own voice) "How'd You Like to Spoon with Me?"; June Allyson leading a medley of tunes from ***Leave It to Jane***; Judy Garland as Marilyn Miller singing "Look for the Silver Lining" and being serenaded as ***Sunny***; and the movie's title number given a lively staging by Alton with Allyson and Ray McDonald dancing in the rain. Kern agreed to a movie about his life under the stipulation that the plot not invade his privacy. So a fictional mentor and friend James I. Hessler (Van Heflin) and his troubled

SONGS AND PERFORMERS FOR *TILL THE CLOUDS ROLL BY*

"All the Things You Are"	Tony Martin
"Can't Help Lovin' Dat Man"	Lena Horne
"Cleopatterer"	June Allyson
"Cotton Blossom"	Chorus
"A Fine Romance"	Virginia O'Brien
"How'd You Like to Spoon with Me?"	Angela Lansbury, Chorus
"I Won't Dance"	Van Johnson, Lucille Bremer (vocal by Trudy Erwin)
"Ka-lu-a"	Orchestra
"The Land Where the Good Songs Go"	Lucille Bremer (vocal by Trudy Erwin), Chorus
"The Last Time I Saw Paris"	Dinah Shore
"Leave It to Jane"	June Allyson, Ray McDonald, Chorus
"Life Upon the Wicked Stage"	Virginia O'Brien, Chorus
"Long Ago and Far Away"	Kathryn Grayson
"Look for the Silver Lining"	Judy Garland
"Make Believe"	Kathryn Grayson, Tony Martin
"Ol' Man River"	Caleb Peterson, Chorus; reprised by Frank Sinatra
"One More Dance"	Lucille Bremer (vocal by Trudy Erwin)
"She Didn't Say 'Yes'"	The Wilde Twins
"The Siren's Song"	Chorus
"Smoke Gets in Your Eyes"	Chorus; danced by Cyd Charisse, Gower Champion
"Sunny"	Chorus
"They Didn't Believe Me"	Dorothy Patrick (vocal by Ruth Clark); reprised by Dinah Shore
"Till the Clouds Roll By"	Ray McDonald, Chorus
"The Touch of Your Hand"	Orchestra
"Where's the Mate for Me?"	Tony Martin
"Who?"	Lucille Bremer (vocal by Trudy Erwin); reprised by Judy Garland, Chorus
"Why Was I Born?"	Lena Horne
"Yesterdays"	Chorus

Filmed but cut from the final print:

"D'Ye Love Me?"	Judy Garland
"I've Told Every Little Star"	Kathryn Grayson
"The Song Is You"	Kathryn Grayson, Bill Phillips

daughter-performer Sally (Lucille Bremer) were created and figured largely in the story, adding little but lifeless scenes that slowed up the movie. *Till the Clouds Roll By* was written and filmed before Kern's untimely death in 1945 but securing all the copyrights and clearing up legal complications delayed its release until 1946. As a Hollywood biography, the film is no better or worse than the standard 1940s product, but as an entertaining movie musical it is one of the finest of the decade.

Recording: The film soundtrack is far from complete but what is there is excellent. More satisfying is the DVD of the film itself. It even includes musical numbers cut from the final print.

"Till the Clouds Roll By" is the jubilant song by Kern and lyricist **P. G. Wodehouse** that was the hit of the **Princess Theatre Musical *Oh, Boy!*** (1917) and perhaps captures more than any other song the vibrant style of that landmark series. The number was sung as a duet by George Budd (Tom Powers) and the daffy Jackie (Anna Wheaton) as their plans for a walk are spoiled by a sudden rainstorm. Yet the two happily take shelter together and wait for the rain clouds to roll by. The music is melodically very simple (Kern said it was suggested by an old German hymn), with a minimal number of notes and no key changes in the refrain. Yet it is totally captivating and is one of those rare early songs that do not seem to date at all. Surprisingly, none of the critics singled out the number in the original production, but audiences knew better and it became very popular. Two early recordings are of interest: Wheaton recorded it with James Harrod a month after the opening, and original London cast members Powers and Beatrice Lillie made a recording the next year. (The 1919 West End production, for some unknown reason, was retitled *Oh, Joy!*) "Till the Clouds Roll By" was a particular favorite of Kern's, and when Hollywood wanted to make a musical about his life and work, he asked that the movie use the song's title. In that 1945 film the number was sung by Ray McDonald to June Allyson as a rain-coated chorus joined in. The cast of the revue ***Jerome Kern Goes to Hollywood*** sang it in London in 1985 and on Broadway the next year. Other recordings of note include those by Bing Crosby, Helen Merrill, and duet versions by Rebecca Luker and George Dvorsky, and Graham Bickley and Katherine Evans.

TIN PAN ALLEY and Kern. While some theatre songwriters, such as Irving Berlin, spent much of their careers writing songs for Tin Pan Alley, Kern was like the majority of Broadway writers who concentrated on theatre scores rather than single songs. Tin Pan Alley was the term used to describe the music business during the first half of the twentieth century. Journalist Monroe Rosenfeld is credited with coining the phrase "tin pan alley." While writing a series of articles for the *New York Herald* in the 1910s, he wrote about the pianos hammering out tunes and the noise coming from the windows on 28th Street where most of the music publishers had their offices, saying the pounding on the cheap uprights sounded like the clanging of tin pans. The term stuck and the sale of piano rolls, sheet music, and, later, records was big business that demanded a constant flow of new songs. While most theatre songwriters hoped that one or two of the numbers from their score might cross over to be a Tin Pan Alley hit, many of them did not write directly for music publishers. They wrote for the stage, and publications, if any, came later. Kern's only notable Tin Pan Alley song is **"The Last Time I Saw Paris."** **Oscar Hammerstein** was so upset when the Nazis marched into Paris in 1940 that he wrote a lyric about his memories of the city. He asked Kern to set the lyric to music, which was not their usual way of working, but Kern composed the music and the song became a big hit without appearing in a Broadway show. It was interpolated into the film *Lady, Be Good* (1941) and won the Oscar for Best Song.

TOOT-TOOT! A musical comedy by Edgar Allan Woolf (book), Berton Braley (lyrics), Jerome Kern (music). [11 March 1918, George M. Cohan Theatre, 40 performances] Produced by Henry W. Savage; directed by Edgar Allan Woolf, Edward Rose; choreographed by Robert Marks; musical direction by Anton Heindl. A forgettable musical with a forgettable score, *Toot-Toot!* had a wartime setting but was still a light comedy (based as it was on Rupert Hughes' farce *Excuse Me*). Before he is shipped off to France, Lt. Harry Malloy (Donald MacDonald) wants to marry his beloved Marjorie Newton (Louise Allen), but they cannot find a minister before they board the train to his embarkation point. Luckily they find a young preacher Walter Colt (Earl Benham) in disguise traveling on the train, but a series of contrived complications and an attempted train robbery stall the wedding until the finale. Also aboard are a couple heading to Reno, a classical dance troupe, and a Native American (Oskenonton). The cast sparkled and newcomers **Louise Groody** and William Kent launched their careers when they performed the spirited duet "If (Only You Cared for Me)." It was the only notable Kern song in the score. The interpolated march number "The Long Last Mile" by Lt. Emil Breitenfeld was the only song to enjoy any popularity and that only during the war. Despite applause for the cast, *Toot-Toot!* was not well received by the press and folded in five weeks.

TORCH SONGS by Kern. Songs of lost or unrequited love, or torch songs, have been popular in both operetta and musical comedy since the earliest days. Charles K. Harris's "After the Ball" (1892), one of the earliest and biggest song hits to come from Broadway, is a torch song about an old man lamenting the girl he lost in his youth. Since the song told its own narrative tale of woe, it was easily interpolated into *A Trip to Chinatown* (1891), a lighthearted musical farce. It seemed all that was necessary for placing a torch song in a show was to have the boy and girl quarrel and separate temporarily, giving one of them the chance to sing of lost love. With the advent of Kern's *Show Boat* (1927) and a new kind of musical play, unmotivated torch numbers seemed more artificial than ever. There must truly be a sense of loss and a heartfelt sincerity in order to set a torchy piece in an integrated score. Perhaps Kern's most famous torch songs are **"Bill," "A Girl Is on Your Mind," "Can't Help Lovin' Dat Man,"** and **"Why Was I Born?"**

"The Touch of Your Hand" is a compassionate song of farewell from the Kern musical *Roberta* (1933) that is perhaps a bit old-fashioned for the swinging show but is still an entrancing ballad. Expatriate Russian princess Stephanie (**Tamara**) and her countryman Ladislaw (William Hain) sang the number as a heartfelt duet then, later in the musical, reprised it as a Russian peasant and an officer in the entertainment put on by the employees of the dress shop Roberta. **Otto Harbach** wrote the flowing lyric that compares a flower thirsty for water to the ache of wanting to touch a beloved's hand. Kern's waltz music is enthralling, yet it ignores traditional structure and says what it has to say in only twenty-three bars. There are also two distinct melodies in the refrain. Kern's wife Eva stated that this was her favorite of all her husband's works.

"The Touch of Your Hand" was heard only in an orchestral version in the films *Roberta* (1935) and ***Till the Clouds Roll By*** (1945), but it was sung by **Howard Keel** and **Kathryn Grayson** in the remake ***Lovely to Look At*** (1952), first with a new lyric by **Dorothy Fields** and then later in the movie with Harbach's original lyric. Among the recordings of the song are those by Mario Lanza, Andrea Marcovicci, Margaret Whiting, Sarah Vaughan, the Paul Weston and Leo Reisman orchestras, and duet versions by Alfred Drake and Kitty Carlisle, and Frank Rogier and Joan Roberts.

TRUEX, Ernest. (1889–1973) Stage, film, and television performer. A durable little comic with boyish looks and a raspy voice, he had a busy sixty-year career in all media, but he first found recognition on Broadway playing the title role in Kern's ***Very Good Eddie*** (1915). Born in Kansas City, Missouri, the son of a physician, and raised in nearby Rich Hill, Truex was on the stage at the age of five, and was soon considered a prodigy for his singing and acting talents. While still a boy he played such diverse roles as Little Lord Fauntleroy and Hamlet on tour and in stock, then made his Broadway debut in 1908 still playing children even though he was twenty years old, as in the musicals *Girlies* (1910) and *Dr. De Luxe* (1911). Truex had no trouble moving into adult roles and he was usually cast as naive dreamers or henpecked husbands, as with his touching performance as put-upon Eddie Kettle in the landmark **Princess Theatre Musical** *Very Good Eddie*. He appeared in nearly fifty Broadway productions before retiring in the mid-1960s, including the musicals *Annie Dear* (1924), *The Third Little Show* (1931), *Frederika* (1937), *Helen Goes to Troy* (1944), and *Flahooley* (1951). Truex also enjoyed a long film career, from 1913 to 1965, appearing as an impish boy in silents opposite Mary Pickford to adult character parts in many comedies and musicals, including *Everybody Dance* (1936), *Start Cheering* (1938), *Freshman Year* (1938), *Swing That Cheer* (1938), *Swing, Sister, Swing* (1938), *Lillian Russell* (1940), *Private Buckaroo* (1942), *Star Spangled Rhythm* (1942), *Rhythm of the Islands* (1943), *This Is the Army* (1943), and *Pan-Americana* (1945). He also found time for an extensive television career starting in the 1950s, appearing as a regular in four comedy series and performing in specials, such as the TV musical *Our Town* (1955). Truex was married to actress Sylvia Field (1901–1998).

"Try to Forget" is a tearful ballad of farewell from Kern's modern operetta *The Cat and the Fiddle* (1931) and an inventive number with musical surprises throughout. Three Americans in Brussels—composer Shirley Sheridan (**Bettina Hall**), her brother Alec (Eddie Foy, Jr.), and her sister-in-law Angie (Doris Carson)—sang the trio about ignoring the past, but not succeeding. **Otto Harbach** wrote the heartfelt lyric. In the London production of *The Cat and the Fiddle* the song was sung by Peggy Wood, Fred Conyngham, and Gina Malo. In the 1931 screen version, "Try to Forget" was sung by **Jeanette MacDonald** while **Charles Butterworth** accompanied her on the piano, the two of them going up and down on a freight elevator. Al Bowlly and Elisabeth Welch each made a notable solo recording of the song.

"Tulip Time in Sing Sing" is a wry comic number from Kern's Broadway musical *Sitting Pretty* (1924) that stopped the show each night with its pious, tearful salute to prison as if it were an old college alma mater. Jewel thief Uncle Jo (Frank McIntyre) and his nephew Horace (Dwight Frye) sang the tongue-in-cheek number about missing the fraternity of Sing Sing now that spring has come. **P. G. Wodehouse**'s lyric is a triumph of comic understatement. He had first explored the idea of prison being like a college in the song "Put Me in My Little Cell," the first lyric he ever wrote. Set to music by Frederick Rosse, it was heard in the London musical *Sergeant Brue*, which transferred to Broadway in 1905. The song was published, enjoyed some popularity, and was given a risible recording by Billy Murray. Wodehouse reworked the lyric in 1918, and with new music by Kern, it was heard in *Oh, Lady! Lady!!* as "Dear Old Prison Days." The revised version was listed as "Dear Old-Fashioned Prison of Mine" when it was performed in *Sitting Pretty* but was published and better known as "Tulip Time in Sing Sing." Merwin Goldsmith recorded the song in the 1989 reconstruction of *Sitting Pretty*, and Arthur Seigel recorded the ditty in 1992.

"'Twas Not So Long Ago" is a simple but effective number from the period musical *Sweet Adeline* (1929) that Kern went so far as to label a "folk song" because it was suggested by an old Viennese song. **Oscar Hammerstein** wrote a straightforward lyric about time changing many things, but not love. Saloon singer Addie Schmidt (**Helen Morgan**) sang the number three times during the show, and it was reprised also by the chorus, the song becoming a leitmotif for the musical. In the 1934 screen version of *Sweet Adeline* it was sung by **Irene Dunne**, Joseph Cawthorn, Phil Regan, Hugh Herbert, and Nydia Westman while they rode to McGowan's Tavern in different carriages. "'Twas Not So Long Ago" was published with both an English and German lyric and was subtitled "Es War Schon Damals So."

"Up with the Lark" is the exhilarating waltz that Kern and lyricist Leo Robin wrote for the period movie musical *Centennial Summer* (1946). The chipper "good morning" song was sung at the beginning of the film and at various points later on by various members of a Philadelphia household played by Kathleen Howard, **Jeanne Crain** (dubbed by Louanne Hogan), Constance Bennett, Dorothy Gish, Buddy Swan, Linda Darnell (dubbed by Kay St. Germaine), and Walter Brennan. At the end of the movie the song was reprised by the Frenchman Phillippe Lascalles (**Cornel Wilde**) and Philadelphian Julia Rogers (Crain/Hogan). Kern's music uses rests after the initial notes in each musical phrase, giving the waltz a lovely flavor. Barbara Carroll, June Ericson, Bill Evans, and Barry Tuckwell are among the handful who recorded "Up with the Lark."

VERY GOOD EDDIE. A musical comedy by Philip Bartholomae, **Guy Bolton** (book); Schulyer Greene, **Herbert Reynolds**, etc. (lyrics); Jerome Kern (music). [23 December 1915, Princess Theatre, 341 performances] Produced by **F. Ray Comstock**, **Elisabeth Marbury**; directed by Frank McCormick; choreographed by David Bennett; musical direction by Max Hirschfield; orchestrations by **Frank Saddler**.

Plot: Diminutive and weak-willed Eddie Kettle has married the bossy harridan Georgina and they are off on their honeymoon, a boat ride up the Hudson River. Also on the steamer are the newlyweds Percy and Elsie Darling. After the boat makes a stop for touristing, Georgina and Percy are accidentally left behind and Eddie and Elsie are left with each other, spending time on the steamer. That night at an inn a storm frightens Elsie and she goes to Eddie's room for protection. The experience makes a new man out of Eddie, and when Percy and Georgina catch up with their spouses, Eddie learns he can put Georgina in her place.

Very Good Eddie is the landmark **Princess Theatre Musical** that did more to establish the intimate, contemporary American musical comedy than any other. Producers Comstock and Marbury conceived the idea of presenting small-scale, modern musicals in the intimate Princess Theatre.

	CASTS FOR *VERY GOOD EDDIE*		
Character	*1915 Broadway*	*1918 London*	*1975 Broadway*
Eddie Kettle	**Ernest Truex**	Nelson Keys	Charles Repole
Elsie Darling	Alice Dovey	Nellie Briarcliffe	Virginia Seidel
Georgina Kettle	Helen Raymond	Helen Temple	Spring Fairbank
Percy Darling	John Willard	Stanley Turnbull	Nicholas Wyman
Dick Rivers	**Oscar Shaw**	Walter Williams	David Christmas
Mme. Matroppo	Ada Lewis	Veronica Brady	Travis Hudson

VERY GOOD EDDIE SONGS

"We're on Our Way"
"The Same Old Game"
"Some Sort of Somebody"
"Isn't It Great to Be Married?"
"Wedding Bells Are Calling Me"
"On the Shore at the Le Lei Wi"
"If I Find the Girl"
"Thirteen Collar"
"Old Boy Neutral"
"Babes in the Wood"
"Nodding Roses"

Added to the 1975 Broadway revival:

"Bungalow in Quogue"
"Left All Alone Blues"
"Hot Dog!"
"If You're a Friend of Mine"
"Honeymoon Inn"
"I've Got to Dance"
"Moon of Love"
"Katy-Did"

Very Good Eddie was their first major success in the venture, running over ten months (in different theatres), and the impact the show had was considerable. There were no long chorus lines, lavish sets, or period costumes. Instead audiences were treated to a witty, up-to-date musical comedy with a bright and sassy score. Bolton and Bartholomae's libretto was lively and funny; Green, Reynolds, and others wrote modern, conversational lyrics; and Kern composed inventive, zesty music for the lighthearted show. Not only did some of the songs become popular, but the score as a whole was admired and seemed to be all of one spirited frame of mind. It wasn't an integrated score, but several of the songs seemed to grow out of the situation and the blending of story and music was noticed by audiences and critics. The next generation of theatre songwriters (Richard Rodgers, Lorenz Hart, George and **Ira Gershwin**, and Cole Porter) also noticed and *Very Good Eddie*, and the subsequent Princess Musicals would serve as their inspiration. Among the memorable songs were the comic character number "Thirteen Collar," the enticing duet "Babes in the Wood," the cheerful "Isn't It Great to Be Married?," the wry "Some Sort of Somebody," and the waltzing "Nodding Roses."

Very Good Eddie was very successful on tour, and there was even a forty-five-minute version of the musical that played in vaudeville houses for years. An Australian mounting of the show in 1917 played fifteen weeks in Sydney and Melbourne but the 1918 London version was a disappointment, closing after forty-six performances. Decades later, a production of *Very Good Eddie* at the Goodspeed Opera House in Connecticut was so well received that producer David Merrick brought it to Broadway in 1975 and the show ran 304 performances without benefit of star names in the cast. It was not a very authentic revival, adding several Kern songs from other shows and rewriting the script, particularly the ending in which the two honeymooning couples find out their marriage certificates are invalid and Eddie goes off with Elsie. Yet the production, directed by Bill Gile and choreographed by Dan Siretta, was definitely in the spirit of the original, and presenting the musical in the small, intimate Booth Theatre gave audiences a taste of the Princess Musical experience. This revival inspired a London West End production in 1976 that ran 411 performances.

Recordings: The cast recording of the 1975 Broadway revival added Kern numbers from other shows, so it is not accurate. Yet all the numbers are performed with zest and it is a delicious recording. Luckily the Comic Light Opera recorded the complete score in 2010. A 1938 Victor Light Opera recording has a medley of songs from the show, but the sound quality is poor.

***VERY WARM FOR MAY*.** A musical comedy by **Oscar Hammerstein** (book and lyrics), Jerome Kern (music). [17 November 1939, Alvin Theatre, 59 performances] Produced by **Max Gordon**; directed by Vincente Minnelli, Oscar Hammerstein; choreographed by Albertina Rasch, Harry Losee; musical direction by Robert Emmett Dolan; orchestrations by **Robert Russell Bennett**.

CAST FOR *VERY WARM FOR MAY*

Character	Performer
May Graham	Grace McDonald
Winnie Spofford	Eve Arden
Ogden Quiller	Hiram Sherman
Sonny Spofford	Richard Quine
Johnny Graham	**Jack Whiting**
Liz Spofford	Frances Mercer
William Graham	**Donald Brian**
Carroll	Hollace Shaw
Kenny	Ray Mayer

Plot: May Graham doesn't want to go to summer school, as her father insists; she'd rather further her stage career. So she runs away to a summer theatre managed by Winnie Spofford where the temperamental director Ogden Quiller does "progressive" theatre productions. May falls for Winnie's son Sonny and when May's brother Johnny comes looking for her, he falls for Sonny's sister Liz. When May and Johnny's father comes to fetch them, he gets entangled with his old flame Winnie. By the end, all the couples are properly matched and the summer theatre is a big success.

One of Kern and Hammerstein's finest scores was upstaged by this terribly uneventful musical in which not much of anything happened. Critics were surprised that Hammerstein could write such a shallow and uninteresting libretto, but few of them knew that what Broadway saw was not what he had originally written. The plot Hammerstein concocted was a gangster musical comedy using backstage eccentrics in the complications. May's father was being shaken down by the mob for his gambling bets, so the hoods try to kidnap May for ransom. The plucky May escapes and hides out in a summer theatre in which the flamboyantly gay director Quiller is doing avant-garde pieces. May's family and the gangsters converge on the stock company and musical comedy mayhem ensues. It was lighter than the usual Hammerstein-Kern shows and one of the most satiric pieces the librettist ever devised. *Very Warm for May* played like gangbusters during its out-of-town tryouts, but producer Gordon and director Minnelli wanted to make the show more commercial and, ultimately, destroyed it. The gangsters were cut (and consequently the backbone of the plot was gone), the highly mannered Quiller was toned down to an annoying bore, the satire on pretentious theatre disappeared, and all that was left was a dull boys-meet-girls summer romance. The only thing that survived from the dismally short Broadway run was the marvelous song classic "All the Things You Are," and even that became famous as a solo ballad and not the choral version Kern had envisioned. The rest of the score is top drawer as well but only years later was it deemed so by musicologists. Among the other highlights in the score are the haunting "In the Heart of the Dark," the lighthearted "All in Fun," and the enchanting ballad "Heaven in My Arms." A restored revival of the original script (as closely as it could be put together) was presented Off-Off-Broadway in 1985 by the Equity Library Theatre and it was clear what a prankish and entertaining musical it was. Sadly, *Very Warm for May* was Kern's last original Broadway musical.

Film version: Broadway Rhythm. A movie musical by Dorothy Kingsley, Henry Clark (screenplay); Kern, etc. (music); Hammerstein, etc. (lyrics). [1944, MGM] Produced by Jack Cummings; directed by Roy Del Ruth; choreographed by Robert Alton, Jack Donohue; musical direction by Johnny Green; orchestrations by Phil Moore, Sy Oliver, Lewis Raymond.

VERY WARM FOR MAY SONGS

"In Other Words, Seventeen"
"All the Things You Are"
"Heaven in My Arms"
"That Lucky Fellow/That Lucky Lady"
"In the Heart of the Dark"
"All in Fun"

Added to 1944 film Broadway Rhythm (not by Kern):

"Milkman, Keep Those Bottles Quiet"
"Brazilian Boogie"
"Who's Who in Your Love Life?"
"What Do You Think I Am?"
"Solid Potato Salad"
"I Love Corny Music"
"Irresistible You"

Hollywood jettisoned the weak Broadway plot and came up with its own forgettable story. Broadway producer Johnny Demming (George Murphy) is having trouble getting his latest project afloat and tries to land big-name talent for his show when there is plenty of talent in his own family, namely, his father Sam **(Charles Winninger)** and his sister Patsy (Gloria DeHaven). But Johnny is blind to them and concentrates on getting the Hollywood star Helen Hoyt (Ginny Simms) for his show. He gets her, and Pa and Sis nearly go off and do their own show before Helen opens Johnny's eyes to their abilities. All that Hollywood retained from Broadway's *Very Warm for May* was "All the Things You Are" and the backstage setting. Three of the other Hammerstein-Kern songs were heard briefly in a medley, but the rest of the screen score was by Hugh Martin, Ralph Blane, Gene de Paul, Don Raye, and others. The thin plot allowed for specialty numbers and some of the performers were indeed special, such as Lena Horne, Nancy Walker, Ben Blue, and Tommy Dorsey and His Orchestra. The studio was correct in changing the name; this was not *Very Warm for May*.

Recordings: The original Broadway cast recording of *Very Warm for May* is surprisingly complete ("All the Things You Are" is heard four times) and there are even bits of dialogue. Yet the album is curiously unsatisfying, much like the show itself. Most of these songs were better served in later single recordings. The film soundtrack for *Broadway Rhythm* is very incomplete, with only Nancy Walker and Ginny Simms allowed to shine.

VIDOR, Charles. (1900–1959) Film director. The Hungarian-born director helmed a half-dozen Hollywood musicals, beginning with Kern's ***Cover Girl*** (1944). Vidor was born in Budapest, and after serving in World War I and performing in opera for a time, he trained at the UFA studios in Berlin before emigrating to the United States in 1924. He served as an editor and scriptwriter before directing his first feature in 1932, then went on to do a variety of movies that were popular, such as the sultry *Gilda* (1946). Vidor's other musicals include *A Song to Remember* (1945), *Hans Christian Andersen* (1952), *Love Me or Leave Me* (1955), and *Song Without End* (1960), which was completed by George Cukor after Vidor's premature death.

"Waltz in Swing Time" is the captivating dance piece that Kern composed for **Fred Astaire** and **Ginger Rogers** in the film *Swing Time* (1936), a number that dance critic Arlene Croce describes as "all in one tempo, seemingly one breath—a wide, white stream flowing in agile cross-rhythms, flowing without pause through so many intricacies and surprises." **Dorothy Fields** wrote a lyric for the piece, but it was only briefly sung by a chorus during the opening credits. Astaire and Rogers did not sing the song but performed it as a dance number at the ritzy Club Raymond. Prolific orchestrator **Robert Russell Bennett** is credited on the sheet music for "Waltz in Swingtime" as "constructed and arranged" by him, but in reality he composed much of the music. Kern gave him some basic musical themes and instructed Bennett to put together a piece that would please Astaire. The number was sung and danced by the company in the Broadway musical *Never Gonna Dance* (2003).

WARFIELD, William. (1920–2002) Stage, film, and concert singer, actor. An acclaimed African American baritone who sang internationally, he played the river worker Joe in the 1951 screen version of Kern's *Show Boat* and again in the 1966 Broadway revival. He was born in West Helena, Arkansas, the son of a preacher, and grew up in Rochester, New York, where he trained at the Eastman School of Music. Because of his mastery of German, he was trained as a spy during World War II, but the government was fearful of using a black American undercover in Germany. Warfield acted in the Broadway play *Set My People Free* (1948) and sang in the opera *Regina* (1949) before making his concert debut at Town Hall in 1950. After making the film of *Show Boat*, he embarked on an international tour and much of the rest of his career was singing in concert halls around the world. Warfield was adulated for his performance of Porgy opposite his then-wife Leontyne Price's Bess in *Porgy and Bess*, a production that toured internationally and then had a long run in New York. He played De Lawd in two different TV productions of *The Green Pastures* (1957 and 1959), appeared in several television concerts, and made many recordings. Warfield also taught voice at Northwestern University and the University of Illinois at Urbana-Champaign. A scholarship for African American classical singers is awarded at the Eastman School of music in his name. Autobiography: *My Music & My Life* (1991).

"The Way You Look Tonight" is the indelible Oscar-winning ballad and perhaps the finest collaboration by the team of Kern and lyricist **Dorothy Fields**. In the film *Swing Time* (1936), gambler Lucky Garnett (**Fred Astaire**) sat at the piano and accompanied himself as he sang the penetrating number about how in future and bleak times he will be comforted by the memory of Penny (**Ginger Rogers**) that night. Penny, who is in the next room shampooing her hair, is so moved by the song that she joins Lucky, her head still in lather. Later in the film, the ballad was reprised by bandleader Ricky Romero (Georges Metaxa) as he sang it in a nightclub, and at the end of the movie Astaire and Rogers reprised it contrapuntally with **"A Fine Romance."** The entrancing song, high on everybody's list of all-time favorites, has been described by musicologist Alec Wilder as "a lovely, warm song [that] flows with elegance and grace. It has none of the spastic, interrupted quality to be found in some ballads, but might be the opening statement of the slow movement of a cello concerto." Just as superb is Fields's effortless lyric that is romantically haunting with its picture of "when the world is cold" and how the memory of her laugh "touches my foolish heart." (With this song, Fields became the first woman to win a songwriting Oscar.) Of the hundreds of recordings over the years, those by Astaire, Billie Holiday, Skitch Henderson, the Lettermen, Eddie Duchin, and Barbara Cook are perhaps the finest. Recordings of note were also made by Arthur Tracy, Tony Bennett, Mel Tormé, Rod Stewart, Steve Tyrell, Andrea Marcovicci, James Darren, Beegie Adair, Tommy Tune, Ella Fitzgerald, Chad and Jeremy, Perry Como, the Coasters, Oscar Peterson, Kiri Te Kanawa, the Dinning Sisters, Doris Day, Michael Bublé, Roy Eldridge, Lynda Carter, Olivia Newton-John, and duet versions by Bing Crosby and Dixie Lee, and Kate Baldwin and Matthew Scott. "The Way You Look Tonight" has been heard in over two dozen films, including *Chinatown* (1974), *Hannah and Her Sisters* (1986), *Alice* (1990), *Father of the Bride* (1991), *Peter's Friends* (1992), *Son in Law* (1993), *Cobb* (1994), *Mrs. Winterbourne* (1996), *Vegas*

Vacation (1997), *My Best Friend's Wedding* (1997), *Deconstructing Harry* (1997), *Love's Labors Lost* (2000), *The Family Man* (2000), *Catch Me If You Can* (2002), *What a Girl Wants* (2003), *Anything Else* (2003), *First Daughter* (2004), *Ice Age: The Meltdown* (2006), *Mr. Fix It* (2006), *The Other End of the Line* (2008), *New York, I Love You* (2009), and *Valentine's Day* (2010). In the revue **Jerome Kern Goes to Hollywood**, David Kernan sang it in London in 1985 and Scott Holmes performed it on Broadway the next year, and Noah Racey and Nancy Lemenager sang it in the Broadway musical version of *Swing Time* titled **Never Gonna Dance** (2003).

WEBB, Clifton [né Webb Parmallee]. (1893–1966) Stage and film performer. The agile, dapper, sophisticated actor-singer-dancer whom many mistakenly thought was British because of his precise, affected manner, he played the effete dancer Harold Harcourt Wendell-Wendell in Kern's **Sunny** (1925) on Broadway. Webb was born in Indianapolis and, pushed by his legendary stage mother, was singing and dancing in public by the age of ten. As a teenager he gave up show business to study painting and music, then he pursued an opera career for a while, performing with the Boston Opera Company. After appearing in a few silent films, Webb became somewhat known in New York as a ballroom dancer and at the age of nineteen was on Broadway in supporting roles in plays and musicals. Of his many Broadway credits, he shone brightest in revues such as *The Little Show* (1929), *Three's a Crowd* (1930), *Flying Colors* (1932), and *As Thousands Cheer* (1933). His other musicals include *Dancing Around* (1914), *Town Topics* (1915), *Sunny*, *She's My Baby* (1928), *Treasure Girl* (1928), and *You Never Know* (1938). After this last musical, Webb retired from musicals and concentrated on comedies where he played witty, urban characters on Broadway as in *The Importance of Being Earnest* (1939), *Blithe Spirit* (1941), and *Present Laughter* (1946). He left the stage in the mid-1940s to concentrate on films, playing similarly waspish, pedantic characters in such films as *Laura* (1944), *Sitting Pretty* (1948), *Cheaper by the Dozen* (1950), *Three Coins in the Fountain* (1954), and *Boy on a Dolphin* (1957). Biography: *Sitting Pretty: The Life and Times of Clifton Webb*, David L. Smith (2011).

WESTLEY, Helen [née Henrietta Remsen Meserole Manney]. (1875–1942) Stage and film performer. A very busy character actress with a severe pinched face that made her ideal for spinsters and villainesses, she played three very different women in three Kern films: the disapproving Parthy Hawks in the 1936 version of *Show Boat*, the aging dress shop owner Minnie in *Roberta* (1935), and the meddling Aunt Barbara in *Sunny* (1941). Westley was born in Brooklyn and studied at the American Academy of Dramatic Arts before making her Broadway bow in 1897. She then left New York and spent years in stock companies across the country, returning to Manhattan in 1915 to cofound the Washington Players, which later developed into the Theatre Guild where she was a principal player for twenty years. Westley acted in a variety of new and revived works but not musicals until her film career was launched in 1934. Her other screen musicals include *The Melody Lingers On* (1935), *Stowaway* (1936), *Dimples* (1936), *I'll Take Romance* (1937), *Rebecca of Sunnybrook Farm* (1938), *Alexander's Ragtime Band* (1938), *Lillian Russell* (1940), and *My Favorite Spy* (1942).

WHALE, James. (1896–1957) Film and stage director. The British-born director of *Frankenstein* (1931) and other horror movies in Hollywood, his only musical was the acclaimed 1936 screen version of Kern's *Show Boat*. He was born in Dudley, England, one of seven children of a furnace man and a nurse, and showed promise as an artist. While serving in World War I, he was captured and spent time in a German prison camp where he got involved in theatre. After the war he worked in London as an actor, designer, and director, gaining recognition for his staging of the war drama *Journey's End*. His direction of the 1929 Broadway version brought Whale to the attention of Hollywood, and his screen direction debut was the 1930 film version of *Journey's End*. Although he was adept at directing different kinds of melodrama, it was Whale's expert handling of horror films that made him famous. He soon tired of the genre and looked for opportunities to direct other kinds of projects. His most successful non-horror credit was *Show Boat*, which he directed with style and visual finesse. It is considered the best film treatment of the musical, if not the best Kern movie musical. Whale retired from moviemaking in 1949 and later committed suicide at the age of sixty-seven. Whale was portrayed by Ian McKellen in the semi-biographic film *Gods and Monsters* (1998). Biographies: *James Whale: A Biography of the Would-Be Gentleman*, Mark Gatiss (1995); *James Whale: A New World of Gods and Monsters*, James Curtis (2003).

"What's Good About Good Night?" is the parting ballad written by Kern and lyricist **Dorothy Fields** that was used in an interesting manner in the film *Joy of Living* (1938). The song was performed by a chorus in a production number near the beginning of the movie; it was then reprised by Broadway star Maggie Garret (**Irene Dunne**) in a radio studio later in the film. Because she is anxious to retreat, Maggie hurried the temperamental Conductor (Franklin Pangborn) and the performance sped up to a comic climax. The song has no verse, and Kern's music ingeniously hangs on to a repeated short musical phrase as it leads into the next section. Rod McKuen is among the very few to record the song, which is sometimes listed as "Tell Me What's Good About Goodnight?"

"Where's the Mate for Me?" is the arresting "I am" song for the riverboat gambler Gaylord Ravenal in the Kern classic *Show Boat* (1927) with a knowing lyric by **Oscar Hammerstein**. Gaylord (**Howard Marsh**) relishes his freedom and independence as he drifts through life, but once in a while he has to stop and ask himself if there will ever be a true love for him. The smooth and carefree number was sung by Howett Worster in the 1928 London production, and it was performed on screen by **Allan Jones** in the 1936 version of *Show Boat*, by Tony Martin in the Kern biopic *Till the Clouds Roll By* (1945), and by **Howard Keel** in the 1951 remake of *Show Boat*. Jerry Hadley sang the number in John McGlinn's comprehensive 1988 recording of *Show Boat*, and other recordings were made by Worster, Keel, David Kernan, and Jason Howard. Barbara Cook is one of the very few women to record it.

"Whip-Poor-Will" is the melodic romantic duet that was one of the hits from Kern's *Sally* (1920). Humble dishwasher Sally (**Marilyn Miller**) and wealthy Blair Farquar (Irving Fisher) sing this airy recollection of their first meeting, set to the sounds of birds singing. B. G. DeSylva wrote the charming lyric, and the number was originally heard in Kern's *Zip Goes a Million,* which closed out of town in 1919; but the number was a showstopper in *Sally* the next year. Kern's music is unique in its unexpected harmonies and sudden octave jumps that subtly suggest the calling of birds. When asked why he didn't utilize the three-note call of the true Whip-Poor-Will, bird lover Kern replied that the song would sound very much like George M. Cohan's "Over There." "Whip-Poor-Will" was sung by **Dorothy Dickson**

and Gregory Stroud in the 1921 London production of *Sally*. The song was not used in the 1929 screen version of *Sally* but was sung by June Haver in the Marilyn Miller biopic *Look for the Silver Lining* (1949). Glenn Miller's Orchestra and Jesse Matthews each had a successful recording of the song, years later. Andre Previn also recorded it, and there is also a pleasing duet version by Jeanne Lehman and George Dvorsky.

WHITE, Sammy. See **Eva Puck**.

WHITING, Jack. (1901–1961) Stage and film performer. A smiling, blond leading man in Broadway comedies and musicals, he played juvenile roles far into his middle age and appeared in three Kern musicals: as Captain Paul in the fantasy musical ***Stepping Stones*** (1923), airplane pilot Jack Ames in the film *Men of the Sky* (1931), and vengeful Johnny Graham in Kern's last Broadway show, ***Very Warm for May*** (1939). Whiting was born and educated in Philadelphia and worked as a stenographer before going on the vaudeville stage as a song-and-dance man. His Broadway bow was in the 1922 edition of *Ziegfeld Follies*, followed by many musicals in which he played the all-American boy who gets the all-American girl: *Orange Blossoms* (1922), *Cinders* (1923), *When You Smile* (1926), *The Ramblers* (1926), *She's My Baby* (1928), *Hold Everything* (1928), *Heads Up!* (1929), *America's Sweetheart* (1931), *Take a Chance* (1932), *Hooray for What!* (1937), *Walk with Music* (1940), *Of Thee I Sing* (1952), and others, as well as such popular London productions as *Anything Goes* (1935), *Rise and Shine* (1936), and *On Your Toes* (1937). While few of these characters were very substantial, Whiting got to introduce such song hits as "You're the Cream in My Coffee," "I've Got Five Dollars," "All Alone Monday," and "Down with Love." Some of his more interesting characterizations came near the end of his career, such the jaunty Mayor of New York in *Hazel Flagg* (1953) and the mythical Hector and the soft-shoe dancing stockbroker Charybdis in *The Golden Apple* (1954). Whiting acted in a handful of films in the 1930s, including the musicals *Top Speed* (1930); Kern's *Men of the Sky* (1931), which had all its songs cut; *Sailing Along* (1938); and *Give Me a Sailor* (1938), and in a few television programs in the 1950s. His last New York stage appearance was as agent Charlie Davenport in the 1958 revival of *Annie Get Your Gun*.

"**Who?**" is the rhythmic romantic ballad from the musical *Sunny* (1925), the first Broadway collaboration between Kern and lyricist **Oscar Hammerstein**. The number is one of the most unique songs to come from the American theatre. As was his way, Kern composed the melody before any title or lyric was written. For two lovers he wrote a surging, spirited melody whose refrain starts with a single note sustained for two and a quarter measures (nine beats), then repeats the same long musical phrase five times later in the song. Hammerstein, given the music and realizing that no phrase could be effectively sung on one note for nine beats, looked for a single word that would be singable, understandable, and appropriate. The result was the famous "Whoooooo . . . stole my heart away?" that is so distinctive and so right. The song became very popular, and Kern attributed its success to that magic word "who." The number was sung in *Sunny* as a duet between circus performer Sunny Peters (**Marilyn Miller**) and the American tourist in London, Tom Warren (Paul Frawley). Miller reprised "Who?" with Joe Donahue in the 1930 movie version of *Sunny,* and in the 1941 remake it was performed by Anna Neagle and John Carroll. Judy Garland sang it in the Kern biopic ***Till the Clouds Roll By*** (1946), and Ray Bolger sang it in the Marilyn Miller biopic *Look for the Silver Lining* (1949). The song can also be heard on the soundtrack of several films, including *Cain and Mabel* (1936), *The Male Animal* (1952), *The Great Gatsby* (1974), *September* (1987), *Billy Bathgate* (1991), and *Bullets Over Broadway* (1994). Jack Buchanan and Binnie Hale of the 1926 London production of *Sunny* were the first of many to record "Who?," and the most unique disc was a trio version with George Olsen's band that sold over a million copies and started a vogue for trio arrangements of popular songs. Other recordings of note include those by Tommy Dorsey and His Orchestra, the Pied Pipers, jazz violinist Joe Venuti, Rebecca Kilgore, Billy Ternent and his Band, Erroll Garner, Ralph Sharon Trio, and duet versions by Brent Barrett and Rebecca Luker, and Jessica Boevers and Matt Bogart. The cast of the revue ***Jerome Kern Goes to Hollywood*** sang it in London in 1985 and on Broadway the next year.

"**Why Do I Love You?**" is the sparkling romantic duet from the Kern–**Oscar Hammerstein** classic ***Show Boat*** (1927), sung by the two lovers once they have matured and the blush of young love is gone. Magnolia (**Norma**

Terris) and Gaylord (**Howard Marsh**), married and living in Chicago, are in debt and their marriage is being tested. Yet the two still love each other and sing this straightforward duet that uses none of the romanticized embellishments of their earlier **"You Are Love."** The song is also sung by Magnolia's parents, Andy (**Charles Winninger**) and Parthy (**Edna May Oliver**), with the chorus and later is reprised by Magnolia's daughter Kim (also played by Terris) and some 1920s flappers. Kern's music is entrancing, effectively repeating its initial five-note phrase throughout the song, and Hammerstein's lyric is direct and questioning. "Why Do I love You?" was heard only as background music in the 1936 screen version of *Show Boat* and it was sung by **Kathryn Grayson** and **Howard Keel** in the 1951 remake. Liz Robertson sang "Why Do I Love You?" as a solo in the Broadway revue *Jerome Kern Goes to Hollywood* (1986), and in the 1994 Broadway revival of *Show Boat*, it was sung as a solo by Parthy (Elaine Stritch) to the infant Kim. Many superb duet versions of the song have been recorded over the years, beginning with Edith Day and Howett Worster from the 1928 London production. Others include Frances Langford and Tony Martin, Dorothy Kirsten and Robert Merrill, Patrice Munsel with Merrill, Anna Moffo and Richard Fredericks, Frederica von Stade and Jerry Hadley, June Bronhill and Freddie Williams, Jan Clayton with Charles Fredericks, Barbara Cook and John Raitt, and Cook with Stephen Douglass. Other recordings were made by Margaret Whiting, Frances Langford, Dizzy Gillespie with Johnny Richards, Paul Weston, Andre Previn, Tony Martin, Jessica Williams, Percy Faith, New York Swing, Barry Tuckwell, Andre Kostelanetz, Stephane Grappelli, and Barbara Carroll.

"Why Was I Born?" is the famous torch song by Kern and lyricist **Oscar Hammerstein** that **Helen Morgan** introduced in the Broadway musical *Sweet Adeline* (1929); the song was forever after associated with her. Saloon singer Addie Schmidt (Morgan) sings the song of utter devotion about the sailor Tom (Max Hoffman, Jr.) who loves Addie's sister instead of her. Hammerstein's lyric consists of a series of terse questions ending with "Why was I born to love you?" Kern's music, which ingeniously uses a series of repeated notes without becoming predictable, has a delicate blues flavor in the harmony that makes the number very beguiling. In the 1935 film version of *Sweet Adeline*, "Why Was I Born?" was sung by **Irene Dunne** and

Winifred Shaw. Ida Lupino sang it in *The Man I Love* (1946), Lena Horne in the Kern biopic ***Till the Clouds Roll By*** (1946), Ann Blyth (dubbed by Gogi Grant) performed it in the biopic *The Helen Morgan Story* (1957), and it was heard in the film *Going All the Way* (1997). Morgan recorded the number and sang it in nightclubs throughout her tragically short career. Among the other artists to record it were Dunne, Horne, Billie Holiday, Art Tatum, Etta Jones, Margaret Whiting, Ella Fitzgerald, Vic Damone, Sonny Rollins, Judy Garland, Georgia Brown, Dinah Washington, Cher, Andrea Marcovicci, John Coltrane and Kenny Burrell, Judy Kaye, jazz violinist Joe Venuti, Steve Tyrell, Aretha Franklin, Joni James, Dorothy Lamour, Sarah Vaughan, and Karen Akers. The seventy-seven-year-old African American singer Elisabeth Welch performed the number in the Broadway revue ***Jerome Kern Goes to Hollywood*** (1986).

"Wild Rose" is the frenzied self-description of the low-born, life-affirming heroine of Kern's Cinderella musical ***Sally*** (1920). Sally Green (**Marilyn Miller**) from Greenwich Village explains to the guests at a ritzy party that she's as unpedigreed as a wild rose. Clifford Grey wrote the eager lyrics, but it is Kern's music that makes the number unique. The song starts with a whole note at C, the sixth interval of the scale. Very few songs, particularly ballads, begin in such a way, and Kern's melody returns to that C and even jumps to the C an octave above to bring home his startling innovation. Also, the melody is so simple and fulfilling that no harmony is really needed; instead, only four chords are used in the entire song's harmony. **Dorothy Dickson** played *Sally* in the 1921 London production and sang "Wild Rose," as did Jessie Matthews in the 1942 West End revival, which was retitled *Wild Rose*. On screen it was performed by Alexander Gray and the chorus in the 1929 version of *Sally* while Miller and the chorus danced to the number. June Haver also sang it in the Marilyn Miller biopic *Look for the Silver Lining* (1949).

WILDE, Cornel [né Kornel Lajor Weisz]. (1912–1989) Film, television, and stage actor, director, producer. A dashing leading man who usually played romantic European types, he portrayed the Frenchman Phillippe Lascalles who is loved by two sisters in Kern's movie musical ***Centennial Summer*** (1946). Born to Hungarian-Czech parents in Prievidza in present-day Slovakia, Wilde and his family emigrated to New York City. Under the Americanized name Cornelius Louis Wilde, he grew up traveling the world with his father who was a salesman for a cosmetics firm. As a youth he learned several languages, studied medicine at Columbia University, and was a promising fencing athlete, but he gave up the opportunity to compete in the 1936 Olympics in Berlin to pursue an acting career on the New York stage. Wilde made his Broadway debut in 1933 and attracted the attention of Hollywood. By 1940 he made his first of many movies, often playing foreign characters because of his knowledge of so many languages. He is perhaps best remembered as Frederic Chopin in *A Song to Remember* (1945), but Wilde also shone in such films as *High Sierra* (1941), *Wintertime* (1943), *Leave Her to Heaven* (1945), *Centennial Summer*, *Forever Amber* (1947), *The Greatest Show on Earth* (1952), *Omar Khayyam* (1957), and *Edge of Eternity* (1959). Wilde appeared on television in the 1960s and 1970s while he directed and produced a handful of films, most memorably *The Naked Prey* (1966).

WINNINGER, Charles [né Karl Winninger]. (1884–1969) Film and stage performer. A rotund, blustering character actor who often played fathers, he originated the role of Cap'n Andy Hawke in the original Broadway production of Kern's ***Show Boat*** (1927) and reprised his performance in the 1932 revival and the 1936 screen version. Born into a show business family in Athens, Wisconsin, he quit school at the age of nine to tour the variety circuits with the Five Winninger Brothers. He also worked as a trapeze artist in the circus and in 1900 was employed on a show boat named (prophetically) *Cotton Blossom*. Winninger made his New York legit bow in 1910 and became a familiar face on Broadway by the time he created the role of the Bible salesman Jimmy Smith in *No, No, Nanette* (1925), stopping the show with his rendition of "I Want to Be Happy." Winninger's other notable Broadway performance was as the heroine's father, Dr. Walther Lessing, in the 1951 revival of Kern's ***Music in the Air***. He made over thirty movies in Hollywood, including the musicals *Children of Dreams* (1931), *Three Smart Girls* (1937), *Babes in Arms* (1939), *Little Nellie Kelly* (1941), *Coney Island* (1943), ***Broadway Rhythm*** (1944), *State Fair* (1945), and *Give My Regards to Broadway* (1948). Winninger was married to actress-singer Blanche Ring (1876?–1961).

WODEHOUSE, P[elham]. **G**[ranville]. (1881–1975) Stage lyricist and writer. A prolific writer who only spent a small portion of his long career in the theatre, the British humorist greatly influenced the sound and shape of the Broadway musical, particularly with his work with Kern for the **Princess Theatre Musicals**. Born in Guildford, England, Wodehouse was educated at Dulwich College and worked in banking before turning to writing short stories in magazines for boys. He first made a name for himself as the author of comic short pieces and novels featuring such memorable characters as Bertie Wooster, Jeeves, Psmith, and Mr. Mulliner. Wodehouse came to America in 1915 and served as drama critic for *Vanity Fair*, writing lyrics for Kern's *Miss Springtime* (1916) before meeting writer Guy Bolton and contributing lyrics to the trio's Princess Musicals *Have a Heart* (1917), *Oh, Boy!* (1917), and *Oh, Lady! Lady!!* (1918). His lyrics were sophisticated yet colloquial, witty but highly accessible. The flowing words and deft rhymes were noticed by the critics and inspired a generation of young lyricists such as **Ira Gershwin**, Cole Porter, and Lorenz Hart, the three men later publicly acknowledging Wodehouse as their idol and inspiration. Wodehouse also collaborated with Kern on *Leave It to Jane* (1917), *Miss 1917* (1917), *Sitting Pretty* (1924), and with other composers he wrote *The Riviera Girl* (1917), *Kitty Darlin'* (1917), *The Girl Behind the Gun* (1918), *The Canary* (1918), *Oh, My Dear* (1918), *The Rose of China* (1919), *The Nightingale* (1927), and *Rosalie* (1928), as well as the books for *Oh, Kay!* (1926) and *Anything Goes* (1934). Wodehouse also contributed to a half-dozen London musicals in the early 1920s, including Kern's *The Cabaret Girl* (1922) and *The Beauty Prize* (1923). By 1935 he had become disillusioned with the lack of control writers had in the musical theatre so he concentrated on non-musical plays and novels, writing a total of ninety-six of the latter by the time he died. He also cowrote the screenplay for the film musical *Damsel in Distress* (1937), which was based on one of his stories, as was the Broadway musical *By Jeeves* (2001). Autobiography: *Bring on the Girls! The Improbable Story of Our Life in Musical Comedy*, with Guy Bolton (1953); biography: *P. G. Wodehouse*, Francis Donaldson (2001).

WORKING METHODS of Kern. The age-old question about writing songs for musicals is: Which comes first, music or lyrics? Stephen Sondheim once gave the best answer; he said, "The book." Since both Kern and lyricist-librettist **Oscar Hammerstein** made efforts in the 1920s to create a more cohesive kind of musical, both men discussed the situation of the song, how it fit into the plot, what characters were involved, and what the song hoped to accomplish. Neither man was much interested in writing for **Tin Pan Alley**; that is, songs that stood outside of the context of a story. They both saw theatre music as plot songs. To an extent, librettist Guy Bolton did this with Kern in the **Princess Theatre Musicals** of the 1910s. From the start Kern was a theatre composer, not a song composer.

The music always came first in the creation of a Kern song. (The notable exception is the ballad **"The Last Time I Saw Paris"** with lyricist Hammerstein.) While some songwriters claimed to come up with a melody quickly, Kern was a slow and meticulous worker. He did not create music in his head but had to work at a piano. Even when a musical phrase came to him somewhere, he had to rush to a piano and notate the phrase, otherwise he would lose it. Richard Rodgers, for example, thought about music in his head for several days without writing it down. When he sat down at the piano to notate it, the music poured forth. Kern, on the other hand, sat at a piano and worked out melody and harmony as if by trial and error, experimenting with musical phrases and altering them by as little as one sharp or an additional beat. Not until the music was exactly as he wanted it did Kern then turn over the song to a lyricist. Kern was not at all flexible about his work, polishing the music so tightly that when the lyricist asked for an extra note or rest, the composer refused. Also, being an innovative composer, Kern often gave his collaborators music that posed major lyric problems, such as the long sustained notes in the song **"Who?"** These challenges sometimes led to superior lyric writing, such as the way Hammerstein turned "Who?" into a jazzy question. Kern had his own idiosyncrasies regarding songwriting and musical notation. For example, he insisted that the main body of a song, usually referred to as the *chorus* or the *refrain*, be called the *burthen*. The word is a variation on the German word *burden*. Not only did Kern want his collaborators to use the expression (which no one else used) but he insisted "burthen" be used in the published sheet music of his work.

Kern was not adverse to reusing parts or all of one of his songs. If a show was not successful or the song was not noticed or published, he often returned to it, using a verse or a whole refrain in another show with a new lyric by a different collaborator. On a few occasions he even reused a published or fairly popular song in a later project. If a song was written for one production but cut before opening, Kern saw that it did not go to waste. Many of his most memorable songs were cases of a rejected number finding new life in a different musical. The most famous example is probably **"Bill,"** which had a lyric by **P. G. Wodehouse** and had been cut from *Oh, Lady! Lady!!* (1918) and *Sally* (1920). Needing a torch song for *Show Boat* (1927), Kern handed the song to Hammerstein who made some minor changes in the lyric and "Bill" became popular. Because of such recycling of music, tracing the origins of the music for a Kern song is a complicated and frustrating process. There are some Kern songs that have two or more titles and sets of lyrics. Sometimes a song that was a hit on Broadway is discovered to have come from a London musical years before.

Kern worked alone. Some composers like to have the lyricist and/or book writer at hand as they write the music. Kern had to be secluded in a quiet place away from others in order to work. The collaboration with others was done before the writing or later in rehearsals, not during the composing process. In fact, Kern's first songs with lyricist **Dorothy Fields** were written before the two even met each other. She had only his sheet music to come up with the lyrical idea. Even after the two met and discussed songs before writing them, Fields found herself working with completed and polished material that could not be altered. One of the reasons Kern worked so well with Hammerstein is that the lyricist worked in a similar fashion. Hammerstein labored over a lyric in private and for a long time before showing it to his collaborator. Each working in their own personal and deliberate way, the two men wrote dozens of songs together that seem to have come from one distinctive voice.

"Yesterdays" is the tender, evocative ballad from Kern's *Roberta* (1933) that the beloved **Fay Templeton** sang near the end of her long career. The aging Aunt Minnie (Templeton), who owns the Paris dress shop called Roberta, recalls times past in this simple but captivating song that has the flavor of a lullaby. **Otto Harbach** wrote the heartfelt lyric and Kern provided entrancing music that requires no verse and is narrow in range but rich in satisfaction. The sixty-eight-year-old Templeton, who had been on the stage since the age of five, got to cap her stage career singing the lovely number. "Yesterdays" was sung by **Irene Dunne** in the 1935 screen version of *Roberta*, it was performed by a chorus in the Kern biopic *Till the Clouds Roll By* (1945), and **Kathryn Grayson** sang it in *Lovely to Look At* (1952). In the revue *Jerome Kern Goes to Hollywood*, David Kernan and Elisabeth Welch sang it in London in 1985, and Scott Holmes performed it with Welch on Broadway the next year. Among the many recordings over the years were those by such varied artists as jazz pianist Beegie Adair, Barbra Streisand, Billie Holiday, Helen Merrill and Stan Getz, Sonny Rollins and Coleman Hawkins, Oscar Peterson, Jeri Southern, Ella Fitzgerald, Kiri Te Kanawa, Jo Stafford, Miles Davis, Stephane Grappelli, Art Tatum, Joan Ryan, Margaret Whiting, Ray Charles, Hampton Hawes, Carmen McRae, and Portia Nelson. Holiday's recording was heard in the animated film *Fritz the Cat* (1972), and Johnny O'Neil sang it on the soundtrack of the movie *Ray* (2004).

"You and Your Kiss" is the adoring ballad that Kern and lyricist **Dorothy Fields** wrote for the movie *One Night in the Tropics* (1940), which is most remembered today for introducing the comedy team of Abbott and Costello to movie audiences. Amorous Jim Moore (**Allan Jones**) serenaded Cynthia Merrick (Nancy Kelly) with the pleasing song on board a cruise ship. Kern's flowing melody was also heard under the opening credits and as background at various times throughout the movie.

"You Are Love" is the most operatic number in the Kern–**Oscar Hammerstein** landmark musical *Show Boat* (1927), an expansive duet with a waltzing tempo and a passionate lyric. It was sung by Magnolia (**Norma Terris**) and Gaylord (**Howard Marsh**) near the end of the first act when they decide to wed. The duet is later reprised at the musical's poignant finale when the aged Gaylord and the estranged Magnolia are reunited. **Irene Dunne** and **Allan Jones** sang "You Are Love" in the 1936 film version of *Show Boat*, and it was performed by **Kathryn Grayson** and **Howard Keel** in the 1951 remake. Edith Day and Howett Worster of the 1928 London production made one of the earliest recordings of the song, and of the many fine duet discs to follow were those by Patrice Munsel and Robert Merrill, Dorothy Kirsten with Merrill, Bing Crosby and Frances Langford, Frederica von Stade and Jerry Hadley, Barbara Cook and John Raitt, Cook with Stephen Douglass, Anna Moffo and Richard Fredericks, Jan Clayton and Charles Fredericks, and Mark Jacoby with Rebecca Luker, Grace Moore, Mario Lanza, Lorna Dallas, Paul Weston, Andre Kostelanetz, and Marni Nixon also made noteworthy recordings of "You Are Love."

"You Couldn't Be Cuter" is that rare thing: an all-out swing number by Kern who usually disdained the new sound. **Dorothy Fields** wrote the slangy lyric ("the well-known goose is cooked"), and the number was heard in the film *Joy of Living* (1938) where Broadway star Maggie Garret (**Irene Dunne**) sang the song and played it on a toy piano in her two nieces' bedroom to lull them to sleep. The ploy did not work, for Maggie fell asleep singing it and the two young girls (Dorothy and Estelle Steiner) had to finish the number. At other points in the movie, "You Couldn't Be Cuter" was reprised by Douglas Fairbanks, Jr., James Burke, and John Qualen. Kern's music not only atypically swings, building up to a rousing conclusion, but as presented on screen it is muted and comes across as more a rhythm lullaby. Interesting recordings of the number were made by Ella Fitzgerald, Joan Morris and William Bolcom, Al Bowlly, Yo-Yo Ma with Diana Krall, Margaret Whiting, Sylvia McNair, Rebecca Kilgore, Lew Stone, Sandy Stewart, Edythe Wright, and Robert Clary.

"You Never Knew About Me" is a warm comic duet from the **Princess Theatre Musical** *Oh, Boy!* (1917) in which two newlyweds wryly imagine the fun they would have had making mud pies, raising rabbits, and other activities if they had known each other as children. **P. G. Wodehouse** wrote the bright lyric, and Kern came up with the particularly rich music in which only one musical sentence is ever repeated in all the refrain's eighteen measures. It was performed by George (Tom Powers) and his bride Lou Ellen (Marie Cahill) in the Broadway production and by Powers and Dot Temple in the 1919 London version, which was retitled *Oh, Joy!* Andrea Marcovicci and Hal Cazalet are among the very few to record the refreshing ditty, and there is a playful duet recording by Barbara Cook and Cy Young.

"You Said Something" is a sprightly but touching ballad from Kern's *Have a Heart* (1917) that happily gushes over a proclamation of love. Kern not only wrote the intoxicating music but collaborated with **P. G. Wodehouse** on the lyric. The number was sung by sweethearts Lizzie (Marjorie Gateson) and Ted (Donald MacDonald) at a seaside hotel and it became the hit of the show. Soon after opening night, the song was recorded by Alice Green and Harry MacDonough. Five decades later a fine duet version was recorded by Kaye Ballard and Arthur Seigel.

YOU WERE NEVER LOVELIER. A movie musical by Michael Fessier, Ernest Pagano, Delmer Daves (screenplay); **Johnny Mercer** (lyrics); Jerome

CAST FOR *YOU WERE NEVER LOVELIER*

Character	Performer
Robert Davis	**Fred Astaire**
Maria Acuña	**Rita Hayworth**
Eduardo Acuña	**Adolphe Menjou**
Mrs. Maria Castro	Isobel Elsom
Cecy Acuña	Leslie Brooks
Lita Acuña	Adele Mara
Fernando	Gus Schilling
Mrs. Acuña	Barbara Brown
Juan Castro	Douglas Leavitt
Cugie	Xavier Cugat

Kern (music). [1942, Columbia] Produced by Louis F. Edelman; directed by **William A. Seiter**; choreographed by Val Raset, Fred Astaire, Nicanor Molinare; musical direction by Leigh Harline; orchestrations by Sidney Cutner, Gil Grau, etc.

Plot: Manhattan nightclub hoofer Robert Davis goes to Argentina to gamble on the horses, loses all his money, and seeks a job at a ritzy hotel, only to have the owner Eduardo Acuña hire him because he thinks the young man is a good match for his daughter Maria. Acuña even goes so far as to write love letters to his daughter, signing Robert's name. To no one's surprise, Robert and Maria are wed in the final reel.

Although this musical was set in Bueno Aires, Argentina, the characters, music, and plot seemed to have nothing to do with its location. The scriptwriters based their tale on a story by Carlos Oliveri and Sixto Pondal Rios, so they kept the Latin American setting and filled it with Americans. Kern and Mercer (in their only film collaboration) wrote a set of memorable songs to entertain audiences until the plot came to its inevitable conclusion, and Astaire and Hayworth had some sensational dance duets to fill in the dull stretches. "I'm Old Fashioned" was sung (Hayworth dubbed by Nan Wynn) and danced in a moonlit garden in one of the era's most romantic sequences. Also in the score were the snappy wedding number "Dearly Beloved" and the delectable title song. Xavier Cugat and his orchestra provided the only Hispanic touch, unless you count fifteen-year-old Fidel Castro who was one of the extras in the film.

YOU WERE NEVER LOVELIER SONGS

"Chiu, Chiu" (not by Kern)
"Dearly Beloved"
"I'm Old Fashioned"
"Shorty George"
"Wedding in the Spring"
"You Were Never Lovelier"
"These Orchids"

Recording: The film soundtrack is available on CD with Kern's *Cover Girl*. The movie *You Were Never Lovelier* is also available on DVD.

"You Were Never Lovelier" is the scintillating title song by Kern and lyricist **Johnny Mercer** from the 1942 movie musical starring **Fred Astaire** and **Rita Hayworth** in a South American setting. Nightclub hoofer Bob Davis

(Astaire) sang it to the rich Argentine Maria Acuña (Hayworth), and then the two of them danced to the tingling number. The song was also played by Xavier Cugat's Orchestra and was heard throughout the movie, including the opening credits and the finale. Kern's music is slightly swinging with some dazzling chromatics, and Mercer's adoring lyric asks pardon for staring but her beauty was never as dazzling at it was tonight. Astaire recorded the song, as did Vaughn Monroe, Steve Ross, Andrea Marcovicci, Paul Whiteman and his Orchestra, and Danny Carroll. John Pizzarelli sang "You Were Never Lovelier" in the Broadway revue of Mercer songs titled *Dream* (1997).

"Your Dream (Is the Same as My Dream)" is the enticing romantic ballad by Kern and lyricists **Oscar Hammerstein** and **Otto Harbach** that, because it was presented in such an awkward manner in the film *One Night in the Tropics* (1940), never caught on as it should have. Originally written for the stage musical *Gentlemen Unafraid* (1938) that never made it to Broadway, the song was refitted for the movie. On a tropical veranda, tourist Cynthia Merrick (Nancy Kelly dubbed by an uncredited singer) sang the ardent ballad to a bullfighter in order to make sweetheart Jim Moore (**Allan Jones**) jealous. Jim then sang it to Mickey Fitzgerald (Peggy Moran) to make Cynthia jealous. In both cases the song was sacrificed to the contrived situation, and only in a handful of later recordings did it get noticed at all. A lovely duet recording of "Your Dream (Is the Same as My Dream)" was made by Susan Watson and Reid Shelton.

"You're Devastating" is the haunting, if hyperbolic, song of affection from Kern's Broadway musical *Roberta* (1933) that was sung by bandleader Huckleberry Haines (**Bob Hope**) and later reprised by the princess-in-disguise Stephanie (**Tamara**). Kern's music for the number was previously heard on stage in the song "Do I Do Wrong?" (with a lyric by Graham John), which was sung by Evelyn Herbert and Geoffrey Gwyther in Kern's London musical *Blue Eyes* (1928). The number enjoyed some popularity so it is surprising Kern used it again, this time with a lyric by **Otto Harbach**, as "You're Devastating" in *Roberta*. Regardless, the reworked song was one of the hits of the show. Although the number was used only for background music in the 1935 screen version of *Roberta*, it was sung by **Howard Keel** in the 1952 remake titled *Lovely to Look At*. Stephen Douglass made a full-voiced recording of the haunting number, and there were also discs by Eric Parkin, George Feyer, the Morris Nanton Trio, and Alfred Drake.

"You're Here and I'm Here" is an early hit song by Kern that sold thousands of copies of sheet music and was a popular favorite with dance bands in its day. **Harry B. Smith** provided the lyric about finding cozy contentment just being near one's beloved, and the music for the rhythmic number points to Kern's early break from the European operetta model. Musicologists point out its unique use of syncopation, the way the words sit so casually on the notes, and the dance tempo that was very modern. The sheet music was advertised as being the hit song from six different shows, and it was no exaggeration. Kern and Smith wrote it for *The Marriage Market* (1913), but it didn't get noticed until it was interpolated into *The Laughing Husband* (1914), which led to its placement in other Broadway and London shows. Legend has it that when the young George Gershwin heard "You're Here and I'm Here," it showed him the direction he wanted to go with his own composing. The song can be heard on the soundtrack of the film *The Story of Vernon and Irene Castle* (1939). Arthur Seigel is among the very few to record the number.

ZIEGFELD, Florenz, Jr. (1867–1932) Stage producer. Perhaps the most famous of all American theatrical showmen, he produced two of Kern's greatest hits: *Sally* (1920) and *Show Boat* (1927), as well as the 1932 Broadway revival of the latter. He was born in Chicago, where his father ran a music conservatory, and was sent by his father to Europe to secure talent for the 1893 Colombian Exposition. It was the beginning of a life of searching out and promoting stage attractions, from the strongman Eugene Sandow to the provocative French coquette Anna Held. Ziegfeld's first Broadway production was in 1896, and he presented the first of his famous *Follies* in 1907, a series that he would repeat eighteen more times during his lifetime. He also presented book musicals, most memorably Kern's *Miss 1917* (1917), *Sally*, *Kid Boots* (1923), *Rio Rita* (1927), *Rosalie* (1928), *Whoopee* (1929), *Bitter Sweet* (1929), and *Simple Simon* (1930). Ziegfeld's least typical but most important Broadway production was the classic *Show Boat*. Although he was not the most innovative Broadway producer, he had the foresight to present this first American musical play. Ziegfeld was married to actresses Anna Held (1873–1918) and Billie Burke (1885–1970). Biographies: *Ziegfeld*, Charles Higham (1982); *The Ziegfeld Touch: The Life and Times of Florenz Ziegfeld, Jr.*, Richard and Paulette Ziegfeld (1993); *Ziegfeld: The Man Who Invented Show Business*, Ethan Mordden (2008).

APPENDIX A

Chronology of Kern Musicals

STAGE

All of the stage musicals in which Kern provided all or a substantial portion of the score are listed below. Shows that closed before opening on Broadway and London musicals are included. The list also contains major New York and London revivals. Musicals into which Kern interpolated only a few songs are found in appendix B.

1904   *Mr. Wix of Wickham* (Broadway)
1911   *La Belle Paree* (Broadway)
1912   *The Red Petticoat* (Broadway)
1913   *Oh, I Say!* (Broadway)
1915   *90 in the Shade* (Broadway)
            Rosy Rapture (London)
            Nobody Home (Broadway)
            Cousin Lucy (Broadway)
            Miss Information (Broadway)
            Very Good Eddie (Broadway)
1916   *Theodore & Co.* (London)
            Girls Will Be Girls (Philadelphia)
1917   *Have a Heart* (Broadway)
            Love o' Mike (Broadway)
            Oh, Boy! (Broadway)

Houp-La (Hartford, Conn.)
Leave It to Jane (Broadway)
Miss 1917 (Broadway)
1918   *Oh, Lady! Lady!!* (Broadway)
Toot-Toot! (Broadway)
Rock-a-Bye Baby (Broadway)
Very Good Eddie (London)
Telling the Tale [*Oh, I Say!*] (London)
Head Over Heels (Broadway)
1919   *She's a Good Fellow* (Broadway)
Oh, Joy! [*Oh, Boy!*] (London)
Zip Goes a Million (Worcester, Mass.)
1920   *The Night Boat* (Broadway)
Hitchy-Koo (Broadway)
Sally (Broadway)
1921   *Good Morning, Dearie* (Broadway)
Sally (London)
1922   *The Cabaret Girl* (London)
The Bunch and Judy (Broadway)
1923   *The Beauty Prize* (London)
Stepping Stones (Broadway)
1924   *Sitting Pretty* (Broadway)
Dear Sir (Broadway)
1925   *Sunny* (Broadway)
The City Chap (Broadway)
1926   *Criss Cross* (Broadway)
Sunny (London)
1927   *Lucky* (Broadway)
Show Boat (Broadway)
1928   *Blue Eyes* (London)
Show Boat (London)
1929   *Sweet Adeline* (Broadway)
1931   *The Cat and the Fiddle* (Broadway)
1932   *Music in the Air* (Broadway)
Show Boat (Broadway revival)
The Cat and the Fiddle (London)
1933   *Roberta* (Broadway)

	Music in the Air (London)
1934	*Three Sisters* (London)
1938	*Gentlemen Unafraid* (St. Louis)
1939	*Very Warm for May* (Broadway)
1942	*Wild Rose* [*Sally*] (London revival)
1943	*Show Boat* (London revival)
1946	*Show Boat* (Broadway revival)
1948	*Sally* (Broadway revival)
1954	*Music in the Air* (Broadway revival)
1959	*Leave It to Jane* (Off-Broadway revival)
1966	*Show Boat* (Broadway revival)
1971	*Show Boat* (London)
1975	*Very Good Eddie* (Broadway revival)
1976	*Very Good Eddie* (London revival)
1979	*Oh, Boy!* (Off-Broadway revival)
1985	*Jerome Kern Goes to Hollywood* (London)
1986	*Jerome Kern Goes to Hollywood* (Broadway)
1990	*Show Boat* (London revival)
1994	*Show Boat* (Broadway revival)
1998	*Show Boat* (London revival)
2004	*Never Gonna Dance* (Broadway)

FILMS

Movie musicals that utilized three or more Kern songs are listed. Films marked with * are based on Kern stage works.

1929	*Show Boat**
	*Sally**
1930	*Sunny**
1931	*Men of the Sky*
1934	*The Cat and the Fiddle**
	*Music in the Air**
1935	*Sweet Adeline**
	*Roberta**
	I Dream Too Much

1936	*Show Boat**
	Swing Time
1937	*High, Wide and Handsome*
1938	*Joy of Living*
1940	*One Night in the Tropics*
1941	*Sunny**
1942	*You Were Never Lovelier*
1944	*Cover Girl*
	Can't Help Singing
1946	*Centennial Summer*
	Till the Clouds Roll By
1951	*Show Boat**
1952	*Lovely to Look At**

APPENDIX B
Kern Interpolations

Jerome Kern began his career having his songs interpolated into Broadway and London productions scored by others, a common practice during the first half of the twentieth century. These were rarely credited in the program, so an accurate list of such songs is not possible. Even after Kern achieved recognition for writing complete scores, he often provided songs for other composers' musicals. This is a list of Broadway and London stage musicals and Hollywood films that had new Kern songs interpolated into them, as well as the song titles that are known.

STAGE

1902   *The Silver Slipper* (Broadway): "My Celia"
1904   *An English Daisy* (Broadway): "To the End of the World Together," "Wine, Wine (Champagne Song)"
       The Catch of the Season (London): "Won't You Kiss Me Once Before I Go?," "Molly O'Hallerhan (Edna May's Irish Song)"
1905   *The Catch of the Season* (Broadway): "Molly O'Hallerhan (Edna May's Irish Song)," "Raining"
       The Earl and the Girl (Broadway): "How'd You Like to Spoon with Me?"
       The Babes and the Baron (Broadway): "The March of the Toys"
1906   *The Beauty of Bath* (London): "The Frolic of a Breeze," "Mr. Chamberlain"

Venus (London): "Won't You Buy a Little Canoe?," "The Leader of the Labor Party"
The Spring Chicken (London): "Rosalie"
The Little Cherub (Broadway): "Meet Me at Twilight," "Under the Linden Tree," "Plain Rustic Ride ('Neath the Silv'ry Moon)"
My Lady's Maid (Broadway): "All I Want Is You"
The Rich Mr. Hoggenheimer (Broadway): "The Bagpipe Serenade," "Don't You Want a Paper, (Dearie)?," "Poker Love," "I've a Little Favor"

1907   *The Orchid* (Broadway): "Come Around on Our Veranda," "Recipe"
Fascinating Flora (Broadway): "Katie Was a Business Girl," "Ballooning," "The Subway Express"
The Dairymaids (Broadway): "Never Marry a Girl with Cold Feet," "I've a Million Reasons Why I Love You," "I'd Like to Meet Your Father," "The Hay Ride"
The Great White Way (Broadway): "Without the Girl—Inside"
The Morals of Marcus (Broadway play): "Eastern Moon"

1908   *A Waltz Dream* (Broadway): "Vienna"
The Girls of Gottenberg (Broadway): "Frieda," "I Can't Say That You're the Only One"
Fluffy Ruffles (Broadway): "(There's Something Rather Odd About) Augustus," "(Won't You) Let Me Carry Your Parcel," "Dining Out," "Echo of My Heart," "I Love You (Reckless Boy)"

1909   *Kitty Grey* (Broadway): "If the Girl Wants You," "Just Good Friends," "Eulalie"
The Dollar Princess (London): "A Boat Sails on Wednesday," "Red, White and Blue"
The Gay Hussars (Broadway): "Shine Out, All You Little Stars"
The Dollar Princess (Broadway): "Not Here! Not Here!," "A Boat Sails on Wednesday"
The Girl and the Wizard (Broadway): "Frantzi," "By the Blue Lagoon," "Suzette and Her Pet"

1910   *The King of Cadonia* (Broadway): "Father and Mother," "Coo-oo (Coo-oo)," "Come Along Pretty Girl," "Catamaran," "Every Girl I Meet," "The Blue Bulgarian Band," "Sparrow and Hippopotamus," "Lena"
The Echo (Broadway): "Whistle When You're Lonely"

Our Miss Gibbs (Broadway): "Eight Little Girls," "I Don't Want You to Be a Sister to Me"

1911   *The Hen-Pecks* (Broadway): "The Manicure Girl"

Little Miss Fix-It (Broadway): "Turkey Trot," "There Is a Happy Land"

Ziegfeld Follies (Broadway): "I'm a Crazy Daffydill"

The Siren (Broadway): "My Heart I Cannot Give You," "Confidential Source," "Follow Me Round," "Maid from Montbijou," "I Want to Sing in Opera"

The Kiss Waltz (Broadway): "Fan Me with a Movement Slow," "Ta-Ta, Little Girl," "Love Is Like a Little Rubber Band," "Love's Charming Art"

1912   *The Opera Ball* (Broadway): "Sergeant Philip of the Dancers," "Nurses Are We"

A Winsome Widow (Broadway): "Call Me Flo"

The Girl from Montmartre (Broadway): "I've Taken Such a Fancy to You," "Ooo, Ooo, Lena!," "I'll Be Waiting 'Neath Your Window," "Bohemia," "Hoop-la-la, Papa!," "Don't Turn My Picture to the Wall"

The "Mind-the-Paint" Girl (Broadway play): "If You Would Only Love Me," "Mind the Paint"

1913   *The Sunshine Girl* (Broadway): "Honeymoon Lane"

The Amazons (Broadway): "My Otaheitee Lady"

The Doll Girl (Broadway): "Come on Over," "On Our Honeymoon," "When Three Is Company," "I'm Going Away," "Will It All End in Smoke?"

The Marriage Market (Broadway): "A Little Bit of Silk," "I'm Looking for an Irish Husband," "I've Got Money in the Bank"

1914   *When Claudia Smiles* (Broadway): "Ssh, You'll Waken Mr. Doyle"

The Laughing Husband (Broadway): "You're Here and I'm Here," "Love Is Like a Violin," "Take a Step with Me," "Bought and Paid For"

The Girl from Utah (Broadway): "They Didn't Believe Me," "You Never Can Tell," "Land of Let's Pretend," "Same Sort of Girl," "Why Don't They Dance the Polka Anymore?"

A Girl of Today (Broadway play): "You Know and I Know"

Fad and Fancies (Broadway): "We'll Take Care of You All"

1915   *Tonight's the Night* (London): "Any Old Night," "They Didn't Believe Me"

         A Modern Eve (Broadway): "I'd Love to Dance Through Life with You," "I've Just Been Waiting for You"

1916   *Ziegfeld Follies* (Broadway): "Have a Heart," "My Lady of the Nile," "Ain't It Funny What a Difference a Few Drinks Make?," "When the Lights Are Low"

         Miss Springtime (Broadway): "My Castle in the Air," "Saturday Night," "Some One," "All Full of Talk"

         Go to It (Broadway): "When You're in Love, You'll Know," "Every Little While"

1917   *Ziegfeld Follies* (Broadway): "Just Because You're You"

         The Riviera Girl (Broadway): "Bungalow in Quogue"

1918   *The Canary* (Broadway): "Take a Chance," "Oh Promise Me You'll Write to Him Today"

1919   *The Lady in Red* (Broadway): "Where Is the Girl for Me?"

1920   *The Charm School* (Broadway play): "When I Discover My Man"

1921   *Ziegfeld Follies* (Broadway): "You Must Come Over"

1924   *Peter Pan* (Broadway play): "Won't You Have a Little Feather," "The Sweetest Thing in Life"

1928   *Lady Mary* (London): "If You're a Friend of Mine"

1930   *Ripples* (Broadway): "Anything Can Happen Any Day"

FILMS

1935   *Reckless* (MGM): "Reckless"

1937   *When You're in Love* (Columbia): "The Whistling Bob," "Our Song"

1941   *Lady Be Good* (MGM): "The Last Time I Saw Paris"

APPENDIX C
Discography

CAST RECORDINGS

The original cast recording as we know it today originated in 1943 with *Oklahoma!* Many of the recordings below were made before that date so the scores are rarely complete and the artists may differ from the performers on the stage. Only included below are recordings that attempted to give a sense of the score, rather than the many records made in which a singing star sang the hits from a particular show. Most of the recordings listed came out long before CDs, although a good number have been reissued on CD. The rest can often be found in used record stores and online services. The purpose of the listing is to let the reader know what exists, even if some recordings are not very easy to find. Yet one should keep in mind that old recordings are continually being reissued on CD, and hopefully, more of the recordings below will be in that format by the time you read this.

The listing follows a simple pattern: After each title, the source of the recording (original Broadway cast, film soundtrack, revival, etc.) is followed by the year the recording was first released. Singers on the recording are then identified, and finally, whether the recording is available on CD and (in the case of films) on DVD is indicated.

Blues Eyes
London cast (1928); with Evelyn Laye, Geoffrey Gwyther.

The Cabaret Girl
London recording (1937); with Dorothy Dickson.
Ohio Light Opera cast (2009); with Ohio Light Opera Company. CD
Comic Light Opera cast (2010); cast unidentified. CD

Can't Help Singing
Film soundtrack (1945); with Deanna Durbin, Robert Paige. CD, DVD

The Cat and the Fiddle
London cast (1932); with Peggy Wood, Francis Lederer, Henri Leoni, Alice Delysia. CD
Film soundtrack (1934); with Jeanette MacDonald, Vivienne Segal, Ramon Novarro, Earl Oxford.
Studio recording (1953); with Patricia Neway, Stephen Douglass.
Studio recording (1958); with Doreen Hume, Denis Quilley.

Centennial Summer
Film soundtrack (1946); with Louanne Hogan (for Jeanne Crain), Larry Stevens, Avon Long, Linda Darnell. CD

Cover Girl
Film soundtrack (1944); with Nan Wynn (for Rita Hayworth), Gene Kelly, Phil Silvers. CD, DVD

Have a Heart
Comic Opera Guild cast (2005); cast unidentified. CD

High, Wide and Handsome
Film soundtrack (1937); with Irene Dunne, Dorothy Lamour, William Frawley (selections only). DVD

I Dream Too Much
Film soundtrack (1935); with Lily Pons.

Jerome Kern in Hollywood
London cast (1985); with Liz Robertson, David Kernan, Elisabeth Welch, Elaine Delmar. CD

The Joy of Living
Film soundtrack (1938); with Irene Dunne. DVD

Lady Be Good
Film soundtrack (1941); with Ann Sothern, Eleanor Powell, Dan Dailey. CD

Leave It to Jane
Off-Broadway revival (1959); with Dorothy Greener, Kathleen Murray, Jeanne Allen, Angelo Mango. CD
Comic Opera Guild cast (2010); cast unidentified. CD

Lovely to Look At
Film soundtrack (1952); with Kathryn Grayson, Howard Keel, Red Skelton. CD, DVD

Music in the Air
Studio recording (1932); with Robert Simmons, Jack Parker, Conrad Thibault, James Stanley, Marjorie Horton.
Film soundtrack (1934); with John Boles, Gloria Swanson, James O'Brien, Betty Hiestand (for June Lang), James O'Brien (for Douglass Montgomery).
Radio broadcast (1949); with Jane Powell, Gordon MacRae.
Studio recording (1951?); with Marion Grimaldi, Andy Cole, Maggie Fitzgibbon.
Radio broadcast (1952); with Marion Claire, Everett Clark, Nancy Carr, Thomas L. Thomas, Lois Gentille. CD

Oh, Boy!
Comic Opera Guild cast (2005); cast unidentified. CD

One Night in the Tropics
Film soundtrack (1940); with Allan Jones, Bud Abbott, Lou Costello. DVD

Roberta

Film soundtrack (1935); with Fred Astaire, Ginger Rogers, Irene Dunne. DVD

Radio broadcast (1935); with Irene Dunne, Ginger Rogers, Fred Astaire.

Studio recording (1944); with Kitty Carlisle, Alfred Drake, Paula Lawrence. CD

Studio recording (1950); with Ray Charles, Eve Young, Jimmy Carroll, Marion Bell.

Studio recording (1952); with Stephen Douglass, Joan Roberts, Jack Cassidy, Kaye Ballard. CD

Studio recording (1956?); with Anna Moffo, Jean Sanders, Evelyn Sachs, Stanley Grover.

Studio recording (1958?); with Marion Grimaldi, Andy Cole, Maggie Fitzgibbon.

Sally

London cast (1921); with Dorothy Dickson, Gregory Stroud, Leslie Hesson.

Film soundtrack (1929); with Marilyn Miller, Alexander Gray.

London cast of *Wild Rose* (1942); with Jessie Matthews.

New Zealand studio recording (1932?)

Show Boat

London cast (1928); with Edith Day, Howett Worster, Paul Robeson, Marie Burke, Norris Smith. CD

Studio recording (1932); with Olga Albani, Frank Munn, Helen Morgan, Paul Robeson, James Melton. CD

Film soundtrack (1936); with Irene Dunne, Allan Jones, Paul Robeson, Helen Morgan, Hattie McDaniel, Sammy White, Queenie Smith. DVD

Broadway revival (1946); with Jan Clayton, Charles Fredericks, Carol Bruce, Kenneth Spencer, Colette Lyons, Helen Dowdy. CD

Studio recording (1949); with Robert Merrill, Dorothy Kirsten (selections only).

Studio recording (1949); with Bing Crosby, Frances Langford, Kenny Baker, Tony Martin, Lee Wiley.

Film soundtrack (1951); with Kathryn Grayson, Howard Keel, William Warfield, Annette Warren (for Ava Gardner), Gower and Marge Champion. CD, DVD

Studio recording (1951); with Tony Martin, Louise Carlisle, Patti Page, Sophie Tucker, Tony Fontanne, Virginia Haskins, Felix Knight.

Studio recording (1952?); with Anna Moffo, Richard Fredericks, Mary Ellen Pracht, Rosalind Elias, Valentine Pringle.

Studio recording (1953); with Helena Bliss, John Typers, Carol Bruce, William C. Smith.

Studio recording (1956); with Robert Merrill, Patrice Munsel, Rise Stevens, Janet Pavek, Kevin Scott, Katherine Graves.

Studio recording (1957?); with Lizbeth Webb, Steve Conway, Adelaide Hall, Bryan Johnson.

Studio recording (1957?); with Martin Lawrence, Isabelle Lucas, Stella Moray, Donald Scott, Janet Waters, Ian Humphries.

Studio recording (1958); with Anne Jeffreys, Howard Keel, Gogi Grant.

Studio recording (1958); with Bruce Trent, Doreen Hume (selections only).

Studio recording (1959); with Marlys Watters, Don McKay, Shirley Bassey, Inia Te Wiata, Dora Bryan, Geoffrey Webb, Isabelle Lucas.

Studio recording (1959); with Barbara Leigh, Andy Cole, Bryan Johnson, Maxine Daniels, Patricia Clark, Denis Quilley, Ivor Emmanuel.

Studio recording (1962); with John Raitt, Barbara Cook, William Warfield, Anita Darian, Fay DeWitt, Louise Parker, Jack Dabdoub. CD

Lincoln Center revival (1966); with Barbara Cook, Stephen Douglass, Constance Towers, William Warfield, Margaret Hamilton, David Wayne, Allyn McLerie, Rosetta LeNoire, Eddie Phillips. CD

Studio recording (1971); with June Bronhill, Freddie Williams, Julie Dawn, Fred Lucas, Rita Williams, Joan Brown. CD

London revival (1971); with Lorna Dallas, André Jobin, Cleo Laine, Thomas Carey, Kenneth Nelson, Jan Hunt, Ena Cabayo. CD

Studio compilation recording (1976); with Robert Merrill, Patrice Munsel, Paul Robeson, Howard Keel, Helen Morgan, Janet Pavek, Kevin Scott, Dorothy Kirsten, Rise Stevens, Gogi Grant.

Studio recording (1988); with Jerry Hadley, Frederica von Stade, Teresa Stratas, Bruce Hubbard, Paige O'Hara, Robert Nichols, David Garrison, Karla Burns. CD

Studio recording (1993); with Janis Kelly, Jason Howard, Sally Burgess, Willard White, Shezwae Powell, Caroline O'Connor. CD

Toronto/Broadway revival (1994); with Rebecca Luker, Mark Jacoby, Lonette McKee, Michel Bell, Elaine Stritch, Gretha Boston, Robert Morse. CD

Studio compilation recording (1999); with Irene Dunne, Allan Jones, Paul Robeson, Al Jolson, Bing Crosby, Elisabeth Welch, Charles Winninger, Jules Bledsoe, Todd Duncan, Kenneth Spencer, Tess Gardella. CD

Sitting Pretty

Studio recording (1992); with Judy Blazer, Davis Gaines, Richard Woods, Paige O'Hara, Jason Graae.

Sunny

London cast (1926); with Jack Buchanan, Binnie Hale, Claude Hulbert, Elsie Randolph, Jack Hobbs. CD

Sweet Adeline

Film soundtrack (1935); with Irene Dunne, Phil Regan, Joseph Cawthorn.

Swing Time

Film soundtrack (1936); with Fred Astaire, Ginger Rogers, Victor Moore. DVD

Three Sisters

Original London cast (1934); with Adele Dixon, Stanley Holloway, Esmond Knight, Victoria Hopper. CD

Till the Clouds Roll By

Film soundtrack (1946); with Judy Garland, Frank Sinatra, Kathryn Grayson, Tony Martin, June Allyson, Lena Horne, Virginia O'Brien, Dinah Shore, Caleb Peterson. CD, DVD

Very Good Eddie
Broadway revival (1975); with Charles Repole, Spring Fairbank, David Christmas, Virginia Seidel, Cynthia Wells. CD
Comic Light Opera cast (2010); cast unidentified. CD

Very Warm for May
Original Broadway cast (1939); with Jack Whiting, Grace McDonald, Frances Mercer, Eve Arden, Hiram Sherman. CD

You Were Never Lovelier
Film soundtrack (1942); with Fred Astaire, Nan Wynn (for Rita Hayworth), Lina Romay. CD, DVD

OTHER KERN RECORDINGS

The dates given for these compilation recordings are the most recent release dates, usually when the disc was brought out in the CD format.

Al Haig Plays the Music of Jerome Kern (2009); with the Al Haig Trio. CD
All the Things You Are: Music of Jerome Kern (1999); with Reid Shelton, Susan Watson, Danny Carroll. CD
Andre Kostelanetz: Music of Jerome Kern (1999). CD
Andre Previn Plays Songs by Jerome Kern (1992). CD
Andy Williams Sings Jerome Kern (1968).
Audubon Quartet: Music of Jerome Kern (2005). CD
Ben Bagley's Jerome Kern Revisited, Volume 1 (1995); with Barbara Cook, Bobby Short, Harold Lang, Nancy Andrews, Cy Young. CD
Ben Bagley's Jerome Kern Revisited, Volume 2 (1995); with Kaye Ballard, Jerry Stiller, Joanne Woodward, Anne Meara, Sheldon Harnick. CD
Ben Bagley's Jerome Kern Revisited, Volume 3 (1995); with Kaye Ballard, Ann Hampton Calloway, Dody Goodman, Armelia McQueen. CD
The Best of Jerome Kern (2005); with Bing Crosby, Artie Shaw, Frank Sinatra, Doris Day, Harry James, Allan Jones, June Christy. CD

Biography Presents Jerome Kern: Classic Movie & Broadway Show Tunes from Rare Piano Rolls (2007); with archival recordings. CD

The Complete Jerome Kern Songbooks (1997); with Dinah Washington, Ella Fitzgerald, Margaret Whiting, Anita O'Day, Billy Eckstine, Arthur Prysock, Helen Merrill, Morgana King. CD

Derek Smith Trio Plays Jerome Kern (1994). CD

Elisabeth Welch Sings Jerome Kern (1995). CD

Ella Fitzgerald Sings the Jerome Kern Songbook (1990). CD

Feyer Plays Jerome Kern (1993); with George Feyer. CD

A Fine Romance: Jerome Kern Songbook (1994); with Ella Fitzgerald, Fred Astaire, Billie Holiday, Margaret Whiting, Blossom Dearie, Billy Eckstine, Louis Armstrong. CD

The First Rose of Summer: Rare Early Theatre Songs by Jerome Kern (2004); with Craig Jessup, Susan Himes Powers, Amanda King, Stephanie Rhoads, Patrick Leveque. CD

Helen Merrill Sings Jerome Kern (1990). CD

Irene Dunne Sings Kern & Other Rarities (2011). CD

Jazz Giants Play Jerome Kern (1998); with Art Tatum, Bill Evans, Terry Gibbs, Sonny Rollins, Thelonious Monk, Art Pepper. CD

Jerome Kern in London: 1914–1923 (2008); with archival recordings. CD

Jerome Kern: Lost Treasures (1998); with archival recordings. CD

Jerome Kern Songbook (1997); with Mel Tormé, Poncho Sanchez, Monty Alexander, Art Blakey. CD

Jerome Kern Treasury (1993); with George Dvorsky, Rebecca Luker, Thomas Hampson, Jeanne Lehman, Lydia Mila. CD

Joanie Sommers & Jerome Kern: A Fine Romance (1992). CD

Kiri Sings Kern (1993); with Kiri Te Kanawa. CD

The Land Where the Good Songs Go (2012); with Rebecca Luker, Kate Baldwin, Philip Chaffin, Matthew Scott, Heidi Blickenstaff, Graham Rowat. CD

The Land Where the Good Songs Go: Lyrics By P. G. Wodehouse (2001); with Sylvia McNair, Hal Cazalet, Lara Cazalet. CD

Life Upon the Wicked Stage: Jerome Kern (2002); with Hugh Panaro, Carole Cooke, Sally Kellerman, Robert Morse, Rod McKuen. CD

Long Ago and Far Away: Kelly Harland Sings Jerome Kern. (2011). CD

Magic of Jerome Kern (2001); with the Ralph Sharon Trio. CD

Margaret Whiting Sings the Jerome Kern Song Book (2002). CD

Marni Nixon Sings Classic Kern (2006). CD

The Mike Wofford Trio and Quartet Plays the Music of Jerome Kern (1992). CD

Melodies of Jerome Kern: The 1955 Walden Sessions (1955); with Christina Lind, June Ericson, Warren Galjour, David Daniels, Jay Harnick. CD

Music of Jerome Kern: Jazz Piano Essentials (2000); with Ted Rosenthal, Dick Hyman, Walter Norris, Marian McPartland, Cedar Walton, Andy LaVerne. CD

New York Swing Plays the Music of Jerome Kern (2009); with Bucky Pizzarelli, John Bunch, Jay Leonhart, Dennis Mackrel. CD

A Night with Jerome Kern (1944); with Earl Wrightson, Lois Hunt, Percy Faith.

Oscar Peterson Plays the Jerome Kern Songbook (2009). CD

Peggy King Sings Jerome Kern (2008). CD

Sandy Stewart Sings the Songs of Jerome Kern (1995); with Sandy Stewart, Dick Hyman. CD

Silver Linings: Songs by Jerome Kern (2010); with Joan Morris, William Bolcom. CD

The Song Is You: Capitol Sings Jerome Kern (1992); with Keely Smith, Nat King Cole, Johnny Mercer, Margaret Whiting, Jo Stafford, Helen Forrest, Lena Horne, Gordon MacRae. CD

Stephane Grappelli Plays Jerome Kern (1990). CD

A Sure Thing: Music of Jerome Kern (2008); with Barry Tuckwell. CD

Sure Thing: David Allen Sings Jerome Kern (2010). CD

Sure Thing: The Jerome Kern Songbook (1994); with Sylvia McNair, Andre Previn. CD

Sure Thing: Rebecca Kilgore Sings the Music of Jerome Kern (2010). CD

Till the Clouds Roll By: The Songs of Jerome Kern (2001); with Paul Robeson, Fred Astaire, Bing Crosby, Dinah Shore, Eddy Duchin, Dick Haymes. CD

The Way You Look Tonight: The Romantic Songs of Jerome Kern (2004); with Beegie Adair. CD

Yesterdays: The Unforgettable Music of Jerome Kern (1996); with Fred Astaire, Jessie Matthews, Anne Shelton, Benny Goodman. CD

APPENDIX D

Awards

Awards and nominations for musicals by Kern are listed below. The Antoinette Perry Awards (more familiarly known as the Tonys) are given for Broadway productions. Because the Tonys did not begin until two years after Kern's death, he never won any; but revivals of his shows have. The Academy Awards (also known as the "Oscars") are given for Kern's films.

Can't Help Singing (1944 film)

Academy Award Nominations
   Best Song: "More and More" (Kern, E. Y. Harburg)
   Best Scoring of a Musical Picture: Kern, H. J. Salter

Centennial Summer (1946 film)

Academy Award Nominations
   Best Song: "All Through the Day" (Kern, Oscar Hammerstein)
   Best Scoring of a Musical Picture: Alfred Newman

Cover Girl (1944 film)

Academy Award
   Best Scoring for a Musical Picture: Carmen Dragon, Morris Stoloff

Academy Award Nominations
  Best Song: "Long Ago and Far Away" (Kern, Ira Gershwin)
  Best Cinematography (color): Rudolph Maté, Allen M. Davey
  Best Sound Recording: John Livadary
  Best Interior Decoration (color): Lionel Banks, Cary Odell, Fay Babcock

I Dream Too Much (1935 film)

Academy Award Nomination
  Best Sound Recording: Carl Dreher

Lady Be Good (1941 film)

Academy Award
  Best Song: "The Last Time I Saw Paris" (Kern, Oscar Hammerstein)

Roberta (1935 film)

Academy Award Nomination
  Best Song: "Lovely to Look At" (Kern, Dorothy Fields, Jimmy McHugh)

Show Boat

(1951 film)

Academy Award Nominations
  Best Cinematography (color): Charles Rosher
  Best Scoring of a Musical: Adolph Deutsch and Conrad Salinger

(1983 Broadway revival)

Tony Award Nominations
  Best Director: Michael Kahn
  Best Featured Actress (musical): Lonette McKee
  Best Featured Actress (musical): Karla Burns

(1994 Broadway revival)

Tony Awards
   Best Revival
   Best Director (musical): Harold Prince
   Best Choreographer: Susan Stroman
   Best Featured Actress (musical): Greta Boston
   Best Costume Designer: Florence Klotz
Tony Award Nominations
   Best Actor (musical): Mark Jacoby
   Best Actor (musical): John McMartin
   Best Actress (musical): Rebecca Luker
   Best Featured Actor (musical): Michel Bell
   Best Featured Actor (musical): Joel Blum

Sunny (1941 film)

Academy Award Nomination
   Best Musical Scoring: Anthony Collins

Swing Time (1936 film)

Academy Award
   Best Song: "The Way You Look Tonight" (Kern, Dorothy Fields)
Academy Award Nomination
   Best Dance Direction: Hermes Pan

You Were Never Lovelier (1942 film)

Academy Award Nominations
   Best Song: "Dearly Beloved" (Kern, Johnny Mercer)
   Best Scoring of a Musical Picture: Leigh Haline
   Best Interior Decoration (Color): John Livadary

SELECTED
BIBLIOGRAPHY

Works by or about artists who worked with Jerome Kern are given in the individual's encyclopedic entry.

Alpert, Hollis. *Broadway: 125 Years of Musical Theatre*. New York: Arcade Publishers, 1991.

Altman, Rick. *The American Film Musical*. Bloomington: Indiana University Press, 1987.

Asch, Amy, ed. *The Complete Lyrics of Oscar Hammerstein II*. New York: Alfred Knopf, 2008.

Atkinson, Brooks. *Broadway*. Rev. ed. New York: Macmillan Publishing, 1974.

Aylesworth, Thomas G. *Broadway to Hollywood*. New York: Gallery Books, W. H. Smith Publishers, 1985.

Banfield, Stephen. *Jerome Kern*. New Haven, CT: Yale University Press, 2006.

Banham, Martin, ed. *The Cambridge Guide to Theatre*. New York: Cambridge University Press, 1992.

Benjamin, Ruth, and Arthur Roseblatt. *Movie Song Catalog*. Jefferson, NC: McFarland, 1993.

The Best Plays. 89 editions. Edited by Garrison Sherwood and John Chapman (1894–1919); Burns Mantle (1919–1947); John Chapman (1947–1952); Louis Kronenberger (1952–1961); Henry Hewes (1961–1964); Otis Guernsey, Jr. (1964–2000); Jeffrey Eric Jenkins (2000–2008). New York: Dodd, Mead & Co., 1894–1988; New York: Applause Theatre Book Publishers, 1988–1993; New York: Limelight Editions, 1994–2008.

——. *American Song: The Complete Musical Theatre Companion, 1900–1984*. New York: Facts on File Publications, 1985.

Bloom, Ken. *Broadway: An Encyclopedic Guide to the History, People and Places of Times Square*. New York: Facts on File Publications, 1991.

——. *Hollywood Song: The Complete Film and Musical Companion*. New York: Facts on File, Inc., 1995.

Bloom, Ken, and Frank Vlastnik. *Broadway Musicals: The 101 Greatest Shows of All Time*. New York: Black Dog & Leventhal Publishers, 2004.

Bordman, Gerald. *Jerome Kern: His Life and Music*. New York: Oxford University Press, 1980.

Bordman, Gerald, and Richard Norton. *American Musical Theatre: A Chronicle*. 4th ed. New York: Oxford University Press, 2011.

Bordman, Gerald, and Thomas S. Hischak. *The Oxford Companion to American Theatre*. 3rd ed. New York: Oxford University Press, 2004.

Botto, Louis. *At This Theatre*. New York: Applause Theatre Books, 2002.

Citron, Stephen. *The Wordsmiths: Oscar Hammerstein II and Alan Jay Lerner*. New York: Oxford University Press, 1995.

Contemporary Theatre, Film and Television: Who's Who. Volumes 1–60. Detroit: Gale Research, 1978–2004.

Day, Barry, ed. *The Complete Lyrics of P. G. Wodehouse*. Lanham, MD: Scarecrow Press, 2004.

Decker, Todd. *Show Boat: Performing Race in an American Musical*. New York: Oxford University Press, 2012.

Denkirk, Darcia. *A Fine Romance: Hollywood and Broadway*. New York: Watson-Guptill Publications, 2005.

Druxman, Michael B. *The Musical: From Broadway to Hollywood*. New York: Barnes, 1980.

Engel, Lehman. *Their Words Are Music: The Great Theatre Lyricists and Their Lyrics*. New York: Crown Publishers, 1975.

Ewen, David. *American Popular Songs*. New York: Random House, 1966.

——. *American Songwriters*. New York: H. W. Wilson Co., 1987.

——. *The World of Jerome Kern*. New York: Holt, 1960.

Freedland, Michael. *Jerome Kern: A Biography*. New York: Stein & Day, 1981; revised 1986.

Furia, Philip. *The Poets of Tin Pan Alley: A History of America's Great Lyricists*. New York: Oxford University Press, 1990.

Gammond, Peter. *The Oxford Companion to Popular Music*. New York: Oxford University Press, 2001.

Ganzl, Kurt, and Andrew Lamb. *Ganzl's Encyclopedia of the Musical Theatre*. New York: Schirmer Books, 1993.

Gottfried, Martin. *Broadway Musicals*. New York: Harry N. Abrams, 1980.

——. *More Broadway Musicals*. New York: Harry N. Abrams, 1991.

Grant, Mark N. *The Rise and Fall of the Broadway Musical*. Boston: Northeastern University Press, 2004.

Green, Stanley. *Broadway Musicals of the 1930s*. New York: Da Capo Press, 1982.

——. *Broadway Musicals Show by Show*. 5th ed. Milwaukee: Hal Leonard Publishing Corp., 1996.

——. *Encyclopedia of the Musical Film*. New York: Oxford University Press, 1981.

——. *Encyclopedia of the Musical Theatre*. New York: Dodd, Mead & Co., 1976.

——. *Hollywood Musicals Year by Year*. 2nd ed. Milwaukee: Hal Leonard Publishing Corp., 1999.

——. *The World of Musical Comedy*. New York: A. S. Barnes & Co.,1980.

Halliwell, Leslie. *Halliwell's Film Guide*. New York: Harper & Row, Publishers, 1989.

Hammerstein, Oscar, II. *Lyrics*. Rev. ed. Milwaukee: Hal Leonard Books, 1985.

Herbert, Ian, ed. *Who's Who in the Theatre*. 17 editions. London: Pitman Publishing, 1912–1981.

Hirschhorn, Clive. *The Hollywood Musical*. Rev. 2nd ed. New York: Crown Publishers, 1983.

Hischak, Thomas S. *The American Musical Film Song Encyclopedia*. Westport, CT: Greenwood Press, 1999.

——. *The American Musical Theatre Song Encyclopedia*. Westport, CT: Greenwood Press, 1995.

——. *The Oxford Companion to the American Musical: Theatre, Film, and Television*. New York: Oxford University Press, 2008.

——. *The Rodgers and Hammerstein Encyclopedia*. Westport, CT: Greenwood Press, 2007.

——. *Through the Screen Door: What Happened to the Broadway Musical When It Went to Hollywood*. Lanham, MD: Scarecrow Press, 2004.

Hyland, William G. *The Song Is Ended: Songwriters and American Music, 1900–1950*. New York: Oxford University Press, 1995.

Jackson, Arthur. *The Best Musicals: From Show Boat to A Chorus Line*. New York: Crown Publishers, 1977.

Jacobs, Dick, and Harriet Jacobs. *Who Wrote That Song?* Cincinnati: Writer's Digest Books, 1994.

Kantor, Michael, and Laurence Maslon. *Broadway: The American Musical.* New York: Bullfinch Press, 2004.

Katz, Ephraim. *The Film Encyclopedia.* 3rd ed. New York: Harper-Perennial, 1998.

Kennedy, Michael Patrick, and John Muir. *Musicals.* Glasgow: HarperCollins Publishers, 1997.

Kimball, Robert, Barry Day, Miles Kreuger, and Eric Davis, eds. *The Complete Lyrics of Johnny Mercer.* New York: Alfred A. Knopf, 2009.

Kreuger, Miles. *Show Boat: The Story of a Classic American Musical.* New York: Oxford University Press, 1977.

Lamb, Andrew. *Jerome Kern in Edwardian London.* New York: City University of New York, 1985.

——. *150 Years of Popular Musical Theatre.* New Haven, CT: Yale University Press, 2000.

Laufe, Abe. *Anatomy of a Hit: Long-Run Plays on Broadway from 1900 to the Present Day.* New York: Hawthorn Books, Inc., 1966.

——. *Broadway's Greatest Musicals.* New York: Funk and Wagnalls, 1977.

Lerner, Alan Jay. *The Musical Theatre: A Celebration.* New York: McGraw-Hill, 1986.

Lewis, David H. *Broadway Musicals.* Jefferson, NC: McFarland & Co., Inc., 2002.

Lissauer, Robert. *Lissauer's Encyclopedia of Popular Music, 1888 to the Present.* New York: Paragon House, 1991.

Mast, Gerald. *Can't Help Singin': The American Musical on Stage and Screen.* Woodstock, NY: Overlook Press, 1987.

Matthew-Walker, Robert. *Broadway to Hollywood: The Musical and the Cinema.* London: Sanctuary Publishing, 1996.

Mordden, Ethan. *Beautiful Mornin': The Broadway Musical in the 1940s.* New York: Oxford University Press, 1999.

——. *Broadway Babies: The People Who Made the American Musical.* New York: Oxford University Press, 1983.

——. *Make Believe: The Broadway Musical in the 1920s.* New York: Oxford University Press, 1997.

——. *Sing for Your Supper: The Broadway Musical in the 1930s.* New York: Palgrave Macmillan, 2005.

Morris, James R., J. R. Taylor, and Dwight Blocker Bowers. *American Popular Song.* Washington, DC: Smithsonian Institution Press, 1984.

Norton, Richard C. *A Chronology of American Musical Theatre.* New York: Oxford University Press, 2002.

Parker, Philip M., ed. *Jerome Kern: Webster's Timeline History, 1884–2007.* San Diego, CA: Icon Group International, 2010.

Raymond, Jack. *Show Music on Record: From the 1890s to the 1980s.* New York: Frederick Ungar Publishing Co., 1982.

Sennett, Ted. *Song and Dance: The Musicals of Broadway.* New York: Metro Books, 1998.

Sheward, David. *It's a Hit: The Back Stage Book of Longest-Running Broadway Shows, 1884 to the Present.* New York: Watson-Guptill Publications-BPI Communications, Inc., 1994.

Smith, Cecil, and Glenn Litton. *Musical Comedy in America.* 2nd ed. New York: Theatre Arts Books, 1981.

Suskin, Steven. *The Sound of Broadway Music: A Book of Orchestrators and Orchestrations.* New York: Oxford University Press, 2009.

Swain, Joseph P. *The Broadway Musical: A Critical and Musical Survey.* New York: Oxford University Press, 1990.

Theatre World. 60 editions. Editors: Daniel C. Blum (1946–1964); John Willis (1964–2006); Ben Hodges (2005–2008). New York: Norman McDonald Associates, 1946–1949; New York: Greenberg, 1949–1957; Philadelphia: Chilton, 1957–1964; New York: Crown Publishers, 1964–1991; New York: Applause Theatre Book Publishers, 1991–2006.

Traubner, Richard. *Operetta: A Theatrical History.* Garden City, NY: Doubleday & Co., 1983.

Van Hoogstraten, Nicholas. *Lost Broadway Theatres.* New York: Princeton Architectural Press, 1997.

Wilder, Alec. *American Popular Song: The Great Innovators, 1900–1950.* New York: Oxford University Press, 1972.

Wilmeth, Don B., and Tice Miller, eds. *Cambridge Guide to American Theatre.* New York: Cambridge University Press, 1993.

Wlaschin, Ken. *Opera on Screen.* Los Angeles: Beachwood Press, 1997.

INDEX

Page numbers in **bold** refer to the main entry; page numbers in *italics* refer to photographs.

"All the Things You Are," **2**, 9, 97, 220, 232–33
"All Through the Day," **3**, 37, 157
"All Through the Night," 96
"All You Need Is a Girl," 193
"Allegheny Al," **3**, 82, 158
Allegro, 74
Allen, David, 50
Allen, Gracie, 162
Allen, Louise, 222
Allez-Oop!, 23
Allyn, David, 206
Allyson, June, 42, 110, *149*, 219–20, 221
Aloma of the South Seas, 107
"Alpha Beta Pi," 168
Alton, Robert, 188, 218, 233
Always, 197
Always You, 74
The Amazing Mrs. Holliday, 54
Ambassador, 102
Ambrose and His Orchestra, 32
American Graffiti, 197
An American in Paris, 62, 103
Americana, 23, 76
America's Sweetheart, 240
Ames, Paul V., 20
Anatomy of a Murder, 160
Anchors Aweigh, 103, 189
"And I Am All Alone," **4**, 77
"And Love Was Born," 137
And the Angels Sing, 107
Anderson, George, 143
Andre Charlot's Revue, 16
Andrews, Nancy, 95, 198
Angel Face, 52, 195
Anita, 197
Anja & Viktor, 3
Ankles Aweigh, 19

Anna and the King of Siam, 53
Annie Dear, 224
Annie Get Your Gun, 59, 62, 74, 102, 189, 240
"Another Little Girl," 144–45
Another Woman, 61, 118, 122
Ansell, John, 25
"Any Moment Now," **4**, 30
"Any Old Night," 144
Anya, 19
Anything Else, 237
Anything Goes, 19, 73, 128, 240, 245
Apartment for Peggy, 47
Aphrodite, 44
Applause, 123, 134
Apple Blossoms, 4, 5, 52
"April in Paris," 77
The Arcadians, 62, 178
Arden, Eve, 46, 231
Arlen, Harold, 76, 126, 201
Arms and the Girl, 59
Armstrong, Louis, 60, 197
Arnaud, Leo, 105, 169
Arnheim, Gus, 83
Arnold, Monroe, 109
Around the Bend, 61
Arthur, Daniel V., 142
As Thousands Cheer, 128, 183, 237
Astaire, Adele, **4–5**, 21–22
Astaire, Fred, **5–6**, 7, 11, 14, 16, 17–18, 21–22, 49, 60, 78, 87, 93, 94, 112, 118, 128, 139–40, 158–59, 162, 167–69, 172, *173*, 197, 210–11, 235, 237, 251–53
At Home Abroad, 51
At the Circus, 76, 112
"At the Fair," 186
Audubon Quartet, 50, 86, 93, 95, 118

Gilbert, Billy, 99

Gilda, 78, 234

Gile, Bill, 231

Gillespie, Dizzy, 242

Gilligan's Island, 191

The Girl behind the Gun, 245

Girl Crazy, 67, 68, 172, 180

The Girl from Montmartre, 62

The Girl from Up There, 62, 200

The Girl from Utah, 20, 63, **68–69**, 165, 178, 195, 215

"A Girl Is on Your Mind," 40, **69–70**, 209–10, 223

Girl of the Overland Trail, 30

Girlies, 224

"Girls Are Like a Rainbow," 141

Girls Will Be Girls, 116

Gish, Dorothy, 36, 227

Give a Girl a Break, 38, 39, 68

Give Me a Sailor, 85, 240

Give My Regards to Broadway, 244

Give Us This Night, 74

Go Into Your Dance, 214

Go to It, 161

Go West, Young Lady, 127

Goddard, Charles W., 130

Gods and Monsters, 238

Going All the Way, 243

Going Hollywood, 62

Going Places, 35, 126

Going Up!, 174

Gold Diggers of 1933, 112, 172

Gold Diggers of 1935, 126

Gold Diggers of 1937, 76

Golden, John, 161

The Golden Apple, 240

Golden Boy, 123

Golden Dawn, 75, 179

Goldsmith, Merwin, 20, 225

The Goldwyn Follies, 68, 126

Gomez, Thomas, 29

Gone with the Wind, 125

Good Boy, 23, 75

Good Morning, Dearie, 25, 26, 52, **70**, 71, 101, 174, 180

Good Morning, Vietnam, 197

Good News!, 46, 62

"Good Night Boat," 141

"Goodbye My Lady Love," 157, 186

Goode, Jack, 40, 177

Goodman, Benny, 159, 197

Goodman, Philip, 49

Goodwin, Deidre, 94, 181

Goodwin, Gloria, 117

Gordon, Max, 33–34, **70–71**, 165, 231–32

Gordon, Maude Turner, 176

Gordon, Roy, 77

Gorme, Eydie, 115

Gorney, Jay, 76

Gould, Morton, 59, 98

Gow, James, 90

Gowns by Roberta, 167

Graae, Jason, 20, 193

Graham, Ronald, 66

The Grand Duchess of Gerolstein, 164

Grant, Gogi, 12–13, 29, 136, 143, 243

Grant, Rachel, 22

Grappelli, Stephane, 242, 249

The Grass Harp, 115

The Grass Widow, 125

Grau, Gil, 45, 252

Gray, Alexander, 176, 243

Gray, Glen, 94, 206

Gray, Lawrence, 203

Gray Matters, 93

Grayson, Charles, 154

ABOUT THE AUTHOR

Thomas S. Hischak is professor of theatre at the State University of New York College at Cortland where he has received the Chancellor's Award for Excellence in Creative and Scholarly Activity. He is the author of twenty-three books on theatre, film, and popular music, including *The Oxford Companion to the American Musical: Theatre, Film, and Television*; *Word Crazy: Broadway Lyricists from Cohan to Sondheim*; *Through the Screen Door: What Happened to the Broadway Musical When It Went to Hollywood*; *Theatre as Human Action*; *American Plays and Musicals on Screen*; *Boy Loses Girl: Broadway's Librettists*; *The Tin Pan Alley Song Encyclopedia*; *The Theatregoer's Almanac*; *The American Musical Theatre Song Encyclopedia*; and *The Rodgers and Hammerstein Encyclopedia*. He has also written twenty-six published plays. Hischak is coauthor of *The Oxford Companion to American Theatre* (3rd edition) with Gerald Bordman.